THE GRAND TURK

ALSO BY JOHN FREELY

The Lost Messiah: In Search of Sabbatei Sevi

THE GRAND TURK

SULTAN MEHMET II—
CONQUEROR OF CONSTANTINOPLE
AND MASTER OF AN EMPIRE

JOHN FREELY

THE OVERLOOK PRESS
NEW YORK

This edition first published in the United States in 2009 by

The Overlook Press, Peter Mayer Publishers, Inc.
141 Wooster Street
New York, NY 10012
www.overlookpress.com

Map on p. xviii © Donald Edgar Pilcher, *An Historical Geography
of the Ottoman Empire*, Brill, Leiden, 1972. Map on p. xx © John Freely,
Istanbul: The Imperial City, Penguin, London, 1996

Cataloging-in-Publication Data is available from the Library of Congress

Printed in the United States of America
FIRST EDITION
1 3 5 7 9 8 6 4 2
ISBN 978-1-59020-248-7

To Murat and Nina Köprülü

Contents

Acknowledgements

I would like to acknowledge the generous assistance I have received from the librarians at the American Research Institute in Turkey and Boğaziçi University in Istanbul. I would particularly like to thank Dr Anthony Greenwood, director of the American Research Institute in Turkey, Professor Taha Parla, director of the Boğaziçi University Library, and Hatice Ün, the assistant director. I am very grateful to Professor Heath Lowry of Princeton University and Steven Kinzer for reading my manuscript and making helpful suggestions. I would also like to thank my editor, Tatiana Wilde, who as always has been of great help to me in giving my manuscript its final form.

Turkish Spelling and Pronunciation

Throughout this book, modern Turkish spelling has been used for Turkish proper names and for things that are specifically Turkish, with a few exceptions for Turkish words that have made their way into English. Modern Turkish is rigorously logical and phonetic, and the few letters that are pronounced differently from how they are in English are indicated below. All letters have but a single sound, and none is totally silent. Turkish is very slightly accented, most often on the last syllable, but all syllables should be clearly and almost evenly accented.

Vowels are accentuated as in French or German: i.e. a as in father (the rarely used â sounds rather like ay), e as in met, i as in machine, o as in oh, u as in mute. In addition, there are three other vowels that do not occur in English: these are ı (undotted), pronounced as the u in but; ö, as in German or as the oy in annoy; and ü, as in German or as the ui in suit.

Consonants are pronounced as in English, except for the following:

c as j in jam: e.g. cami (mosque) = jahmy;

ç as ch in chat: e.g. çorba (soup) = chorba;

g as in get, never as in gem;

ğ is almost silent and tends to lengthen the preceding vowel; and

ş as in sugar: e.g. şeker (sugar) = sheker.

Maps and Illustrations

Prologue: Portrait of a Sultan

Half a lifetime ago, at the National Gallery in London, I first saw Gentile Bellini's portrait of the Turkish sultan Mehmet II, the Conqueror. I knew very little about the Conqueror at the time, for I had only recently moved to Istanbul, Greek Constantinople, the city Mehmet had conquered in 1453. Then in the last week of the twentieth century I saw the portrait again at an exhibition in Istanbul, where it had been painted in 1480, a year before the death of the Conqueror, who was known in his time as the Grand Turk, ruler of 'the Glorious Empire of the Turks, the present Terrour of the World'.

When I examined Bellini's painting in Istanbul I knew far more about Mehmet than I did when I first saw the portrait in London, for by then I had read and written much about him and his times and the city he had conquered. Mehmet's capture of Constantinople in 1453 shocked all of Europe, for he had brought to an end the history of the Byzantine Empire, the medieval Christian continuation of the ancient Roman Empire, establishing in its place the Muslim empire of the Ottoman Turks, newly risen out of Asia.

Mehmet, the seventh of his line to rule the Ottoman Turks, was barely twenty-one when he conquered Constantinople, which thenceforth, under the name of Istanbul, became the capital of his empire. At the time the Ottoman Empire comprised north-western Asia Minor, where Osman Gazi, the first Ottoman ruler, had formed a tiny principality at the end of the thirteenth century, extending into the southern Balkans, which his successors in the next five generations took in their march of conquest.

During the thirty years of his reign, 1451–81, Mehmet extended the borders of his empire more than halfway across Asia Minor, while his armies in Europe penetrated as deep as Hungary and even established a foothold in the heel of Italy. Three popes called for crusades against Mehmet, whom Pope Pius II called 'a venomous dragon' whose 'bloodthirsty hordes' threatened Christendom.

The Ottoman Empire expanded even further under Mehmet's immediate successors, particularly Süleyman the Magnificent (r. 1520–66), whose realm encompassed all of south-eastern Europe and stretched through the Middle East, the eastern Mediterranean and north Africa. The Turks continued to occupy a large part of south-eastern Europe for four centuries after Mehmet's death, and his dynasty ruled until 1923, when the Ottoman Empire gave way to the modern Republic of Turkey.

Today only 8 per cent of the land mass of Turkey is in Europe, separated from the Asian part of the country by the famous straits – the Dardanelles, the Sea of Marmara and the Bosphorus – the latter spanned by the urban mass of Istanbul, the only city in the world that stands astride two continents. Turkey's foothold in Europe extends less than a hundred miles inland from the straits, the deepest penetration being at Edirne, where Mehmet was born in 1432. It was there that he began the meteoric career that led to the conquest of the city now known as Istanbul, where pilgrims still come to the tomb of the great hero known to the Turks as Fatih, or the Conqueror.

During the exhibition of Mehmet's portrait in Istanbul a number of friends, both Turks and foreigners, remarked that it was a pity that there was no modern biography of the Conqueror other than that of Franz Babinger, a lengthy scholarly work published in 1953 and now somewhat outdated, and that there was a need for a new book on him and his times written for the general reader. And so that is what I have set out to do in this book, concentrating on the man himself rather than his conquests, though his brilliant military career will be described in detail along with its effect on Europe at the dawn of the Renaissance. As Lord Acton wrote: 'Modern history begins under stress of the Ottoman conquest.'

My biography of Mehmet the Conqueror is focused on the historic conflict between western Europe and the Ottoman Empire, echoed today particularly in the case of Turkey, which is currently facing rejection in its attempt to join the European Union. The interaction between Christian West and Muslim East is usually seen as a clash of civilisations, as it is viewed in the so-called War on Terror. The original conflict that accompanied the rise of Islam brought Graeco-Islamic science to the West, beginning the modern scientific tradition. Mehmet's conquest of Constantinople and his invasion of the Balkans and Italy brought Christian Europe face to face with a new Muslim empire that was actually a rich mixture of peoples, religions and languages, which is still evident today in the lands that were once part of the Ottoman Empire. As Edward Said wrote: 'Partly because of empire, all cultures are involved in one another, none is single and pure, all are hybrid, heterogeneous, extraordinarily differentiated, and unmonolithic.'

Mehmet himself is an enigmatic figure, seen by the West as a cruel tyrant, whom Pope Nicholas V called the 'son of Satan, perdition and death', while being revered by the Turks as a great conqueror. My book will attempt to discover what kind of man posed for Bellini's portrait, which I am looking at as I write these lines, wondering what was going through Mehmet's mind as he sat there in his palace in Istanbul, having conquered an ancient Christian empire and established his own Muslim realm in the marchland between East and West, changing the world for ever.

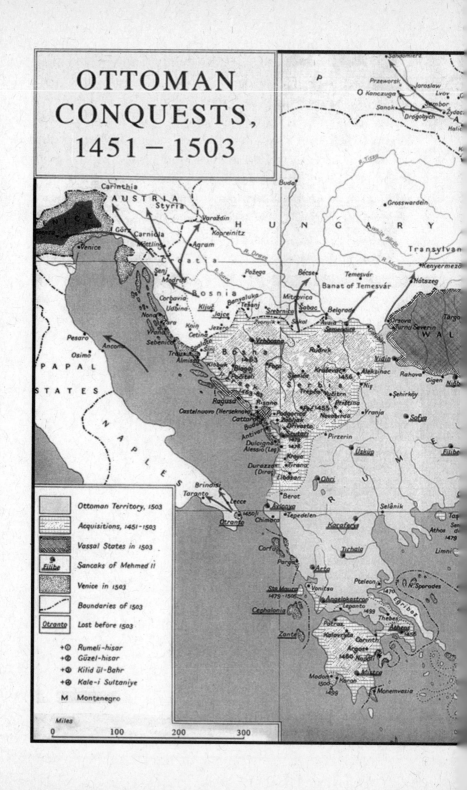

OTTOMAN CONQUESTS, 1451 – 1503

Legend:

- Ottoman Territory, 1503
- Acquisitions, 1451–1503
- Vassal States in 1503
- *Filibe*   Sancaks of Mehmed II
- Venice in 1503
- Boundaries of 1503
- *Otranto*   Lost before 1503

- +① Rumeli-hisar
- +② Güzel-hisar
- +③ Kilid ül-Bahr
- +④ Kale-i Sultaniye
- M   Montenegro

Miles
0   100   200   300

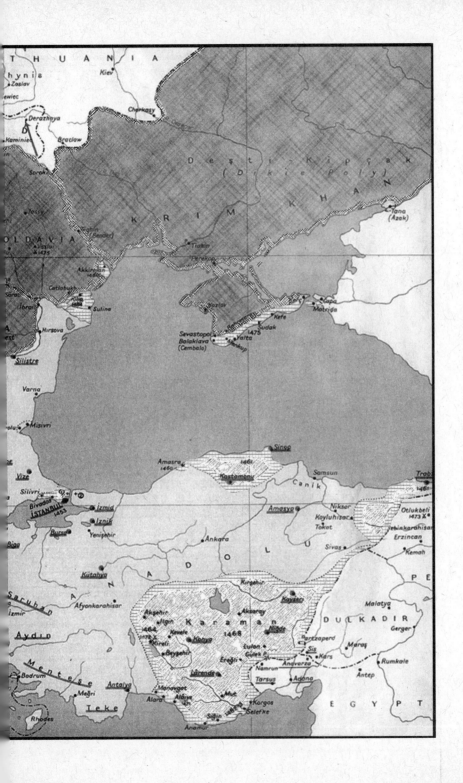

Istanbul and the Bosphorus

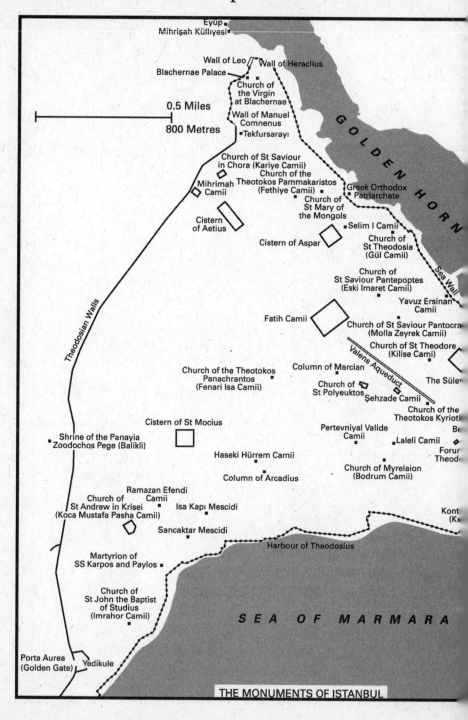

Eyüp
Mihrişah Külliyesi

Wall of Leo
Wall of Heraclius
Blachernae Palace
Church of the Virgin at Blachernae

0.5 Miles

800 Metres

Wall of Manuel Comnenus
Tekfursarayı

GOLDEN HORN

Church of St Saviour in Chora (Kariye Camii)
Church of the Theotokos Pammakaristos (Fethiye Camii)
Mihrimah Camii
Church of St Mary of the Mongols
Greek Orthodox Patriarchate

Cistern of Aetius
Cistern of Aspar
Selim I Camii
Church of St Theodosia (Gül Camii)

Sea Wall

Church of St Saviour Pantepoptes (Eski Imaret Camii)
Yavuz Ersinan Camii

Theodosian Walls

Fatih Camii
Church of St Saviour Pantocra (Molla Zeyrek Camii)
Church of St Theodore (Kilise Cami)

Valens Aqueduct

Church of the Theotokos Panachrantos (Fenari Isa Camii)
Column of Marcian
The Süle

Church of St Polyeuktos
Şehzade Camii

Cistern of St Mocius
Pertevniyal Valide Camii
Church of the Theotokos Kyrioti

Be

Shrine of the Panayia Zoodochos Pege (Balikli)
Laleli Camii

Forur
Theod

Haseki Hürrem Camii

Church of Myrelaion (Bodrum Camii)

Column of Arcadius

Ramazan Efendi Camii
Church of St Andrew in Krisei (Koca Mustafa Pasha Camii)
Isa Kapı Mescidi

Kont
(K

Sancaktar Mescidi

Harbour of Theodosius

Martyrion of SS Karpos and Paylos

Church of St John the Baptist of Studius (Imrahor Camii)

SEA OF MARMARA

Porta Aurea (Golden Gate)
Yedikule

THE MONUMENTS OF ISTANBUL

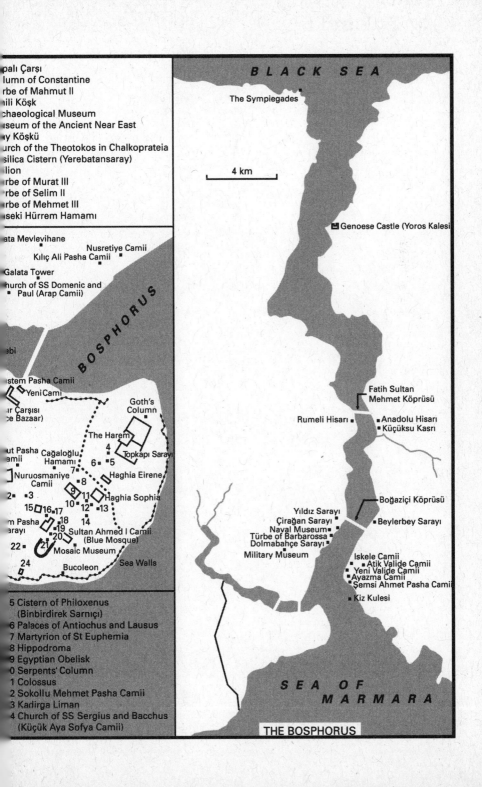

palı Çarşı
lumn of Constantine
rbe of Mahmut II
ili Köşk
chaeological Museum
seum of the Ancient Near East
ay Köşkü
rch of the Theotokos in Chalkoprateia
silica Cistern (Yerebatansaray)
lion
rbe of Murat III
rbe of Selim II
rbe of Mehmet III
seki Hürrem Hamamı

ata Mevlevihane
Nusretiye Camii
Kılıç Ali Pasha Camii
Galata Tower
hurch of SS Domenic and
Paul (Arap Camii)

BOSPHORUS

ebi

stem Pasha Camii
Yeni Cami
r Çarşısı
ce Bazaar)

Goth's Column

The Harem

ut Pasha
amii
Cağaloğlu
Hamamı
4
6 5
Topkapı Sarayı

Nuruosmaniye
Camii
7
8
Haghia Eirene

2 3
9
10 11
12 13
Haghia Sophia

15 16 17
m Pasha
arayı
18
19
14
20 21
Sultan Ahmed I Camii
(Blue Mosque)

22
Mosaic Museum

24
Bucoleon
Sea Walls

5 Cistern of Philoxenus
(Binbirdirek Sarnıçı)
6 Palaces of Antiochus and Lausus
7 Martyrion of St Euphemia
8 Hippodroma
9 Egyptian Obelisk
0 Serpents' Column
1 Colossus
2 Sokollu Mehmet Pasha Camii
3 Kadirga Liman
4 Church of SS Sergius and Bacchus
(Küçük Aya Sofya Camii)

BLACK SEA

The Sympiegades

4 km

Genoese Castle (Yoros Kalesi

Fatih Sultan
Mehmet Köprüsü

Rumeli Hisarı
Anadolu Hisarı
Küçüksu Kasrı

Boğaziçi Köprüsü

Yıldız Sarayı
Çırağan Sarayı
Naval Museum
Türbe of Barbarossa
Dolmabahçe Sarayı
Military Museum
Beylerbey Sarayı

Iskele Camii
Atik Valide Camii
Yeni Valide Camii
Ayazma Camii
Şemsi Ahmet Pasha Camii

Kız Kulesi

SEA OF
MARMARA

THE BOSPHORUS

1   *The Sons of Osman*

Constantine the Great changed the course of history in AD 330, when he shifted his capital from Italy to the Greek city of Byzantium on the Bosphorus, renaming it New Rome, though it came to be called Constantinople.

Constantine's immediate successors established Christianity as the state religion of the empire, and during the next two centuries Greek replaced Latin as the official language. This gave rise to what later historians called the Byzantine Empire, the Hellenised Christian continuation of the Roman Empire, which took its name from the ancient city of Byzantium.

The Byzantine Empire reached its peak under Justinian (r. 527–65), whose realm extended almost entirely around the Mediterranean, including all of Italy, the Balkans, Asia Minor and the Middle East. During the next five centuries the empire was under attack on all sides, but as late as the mid-eleventh century it still controlled all of Asia Minor and the Balkans as well as southern Italy. But then in 1071 the emperor Romanus IV Diogenes was defeated by the Seljuk Turks under Sultan Alp Arslan at a battle near Manzikert in eastern Anatolia, as Asia Minor is now more generally known, while that same year the Normans took the last remaining Byzantine possessions in Italy.

After their victory at Manzikert the Turks overran Anatolia, though the Byzantines, with the help of the army of the First Crusade, reconquered the western part of Asia Minor and the coastal areas along the Black Sea and the Mediterranean. The central and eastern parts of Anatolia became part of the Seljuk Sultanate of Rum, the

Turkish word for Greeks of the Byzantine Empire, whose territory they had conquered.

The Seljuk Sultanate of Rum lasted from the second half of the eleventh century until the beginning of the fourteenth century. At their peak, in the first quarter of the thirteenth century, the Seljuks controlled all of Anatolia except for Bithynia, the north-westernmost part of Asia Minor, which was virtually all that remained of the Byzantine Empire in Asia, while the Greek empire of the Comneni dynasty ruled the eastern Black Sea region from their capital at Trebizond.

The Byzantine Empire was almost destroyed during the Fourth Crusade, when Latin troops and the Venetian navy captured and sacked Constantinople in 1204. Constantinople then became capital of a Latin kingdom called Roumania, which lasted until 1261, when the city was recaptured by the Greeks under Michael VIII Palaeologus, who had survived in exile in the Bithynian city of Nicaea.

But the revived Byzantine Empire was just a small fragment of what it had been in its prime, and by the beginning of the fifteenth century it comprised little more than Bithynia, part of the Peloponnesos, and Thrace, the south-easternmost region of the Balkans up to the Dardanelles, the Sea of Marmara and the Bosphorus, the historic straits that separate Europe and Asia.

The Seljuks declined rapidly after they were defeated by the Mongols in 1246, and at the beginning of the following century their sultanate came to an end, with their former territory divided among a dozen or so Turkish emirates known as *beyliks*. The smallest and least significant of these *beyliks* was that of the Osmanlı, the 'sons of Osman', the Turkish name for the followers of Osman Gazi, whose last name means 'warrior for the Islamic faith'. Osman was known in English as Othman, and his dynasty came to be called the Ottomans. He was the son of Ertuğrul, leader of a tribe of Oğuz Turks who at the end of the thirteenth century settled as vassals of the Seljuk sultan around Söğüt, a small town in the hills of Bithynia, just east of the Byzantine cities of Nicomedia, Nicaea and Prusa. The humble origin of the Osmanlı is described by Richard Knolles in *The Generall Historie of the Turkes* (1609–10), one of the first works in English on the Ottomans:

> Thus is Ertogrul, the Oguzian Turk, with his homely heardsmen, become a petty lord of a countrey village, and in good favour with the Sultan, whose followers, as sturdy heardsmen with their families, lived in Winter with him in Söğüt, but in Summer in tents with their cattle upon

the mountains. Having thus lived certain yeares, and brought great peace with his neighbours, as well the Christians as the Turks... Ertogrul kept himself close in his house in Söğüt, as well contented there as with a kingdom.

The only contemporary Byzantine reference to Osman Gazi is by the chronicler George Pachymeres. According to Pachymeres, the emperor Andronicus II Palaeologus (r. 1282–1328) sent a detachment of 2,000 men under a commander named Muzalon to drive back a force of 5,000 Turkish warriors under Osman (whom he calls Atman), who had encroached upon Byzantine territory. But Osman forced Muzalon to retreat, which attracted other Turkish warriors to join up with him, in the spirit of *gaza*, or holy war against the infidel, attracted also by the prospects of plunder.

With these reinforcements Osman defeated Muzalon in 1302 in a pitched battle at Baphaeus, near Nicomedia. Soon afterwards Osman captured the Byzantine town of Belakoma, Turkish Bilecik, after which he laid siege to Nicaea, whose defence walls were the most formidable fortifications in Bithynia. He then went on to pillage the surrounding countryside, causing a mass exodus of rural Greeks from Bithynia to Constantinople, after which he captured a number of unfortified towns in the region.

Osman Gazi died in 1324 and was succeeded by his son Orhan Gazi, the first Ottoman ruler to use the title of sultan, as he is referred to in an inscription. Two years after his succession Orhan captured Prusa, Turkish Bursa, which became the first Ottoman capital. He then renewed the siege of Nicaea, and in 1329 the emperor Andronicus III Palaeologus (r. 1328–41) personally led an expedition to relieve the city. Orhan routed the Byzantine army at the Battle of Pelekanon, in which the emperor was wounded, leaving his commander John Cantacuzenus to lead the defeated army back to Constantinople.

Nicaea, known to the Turks as Iznik, was finally forced to surrender in 1331, after which Orhan went on to besiege Nicomedia, Turkish Izmit, which finally surrendered six years later. That virtually completed the Ottoman conquest of Bithynia, by which time Orhan had also absorbed the neighbouring Karası *beylik* to the south, so that the Ottomans now controlled all of westernmost Anatolia east of the Bosphorus, the Sea of Marmara and the Dardanelles.

Andronicus III died on 15 June 1341 and was succeeded by his nine-year-old son John V Palaeologus. John Cantacuzenus was appointed regent, and later that year his supporters proclaimed him emperor. This began a civil war that lasted until 8 February 1347, when Cantacuzenus was crowned as John VI, ruling as senior co-emperor with John V.

Meanwhile, Orhan had signed a peace treaty in 1346 with Cantacuzenus. Cantacuzenus sealed the treaty by giving his daughter Theodora in marriage to Orhan, who wed the princess in a festive ceremony at Selymbria, in Thrace on the European shore of the Marmara forty miles west of Constantinople. Shortly after Cantacuzenus was crowned as senior co-emperor in 1347 Orhan came to meet him at Scutari, on the Asian shore of the Bosphorus opposite Constantinople. According to the chronicle that Cantacuzenus later wrote, he and his entourage crossed the Bosphorus in galleys to meet Orhan and his attendants, 'and the two amused themselves for a number of days hunting and feasting'.

Cantacuzenus ruled as co-emperor until 10 December 1354, when he was deposed by the supporters of John V, after which he retired as a monk and wrote his chronicle, the *Historia*, one of the most important sources for the last century of Byzantine history and the rise of the Ottoman Turks.

Throughout his reign Cantacuzenus honoured the alliance he had made with Orhan. During that time Orhan thrice sent his son Süleyman with Turkish troops to aid Cantacuzenus on campaigns in Thrace. On the third of these campaigns, in 1352, Süleyman occupied a fortress on the Dardanelles called Tzympe, which he refused to return until Cantacuzenus promised to pay him 1,000 gold pieces. The emperor paid the money and Süleyman prepared to return the fortress to him, but then, on 2 March 1354, the situation changed when an earthquake destroyed the walls of Gallipoli and other towns on the European shore of the Dardanelles, which were abandoned by their Greek inhabitants. Süleyman took advantage of the disaster to occupy the towns with his troops, restoring the walls of Gallipoli in the process. A Florentine account of the earthquake and its aftermath says that the Turks then 'received a great army of their people and laid siege to Constantinople', but after they were unable to capture it 'they attacked the towns and pillaged the countryside'. Cantacuzenus demanded that Gallipoli and the other towns be returned, but Süleyman insisted that he had not conquered them by force but simply occupied their abandoned ruins. Thus the Ottomans established their first permanent foothold in Europe, which Orhan was able to use as a base to make further conquests in Thrace.

Orhan also extended his territory eastward in Anatolia, as evidenced by a note in the *Historia of Cantacuzenus*, saying that in the summer of 1354 Süleyman captured Ancyra (Ankara), which had belonged to the Eretnid *beylik*, thus adding to the Ottoman realm a city destined to be the capital of the modern Republic of Turkey.

A Turkish source says that Süleyman captured the Thracian towns of Malkara, Ipsala and Vize. This would have been prior to the summer of 1357, when Süleyman was killed when he was thrown from his horse while hunting.

Orhan Gazi died in 1362 and was succeeded by his son Murat, who had been campaigning in Thrace. In 1369 Murat captured the Byzantine city of Adrianople, which as Edirne soon became the Ottoman capital, replacing Bursa. Murat used Edirne as a base to campaign ever deeper into the Balkans, and during the next two decades his raids took him into Greece, Bulgaria, Macedonia, Albania, Serbia, Bosnia and Wallachia. On 26 September 1371 Murat annihilated a Serbian army at the Battle of the Maritza, opening up the Balkans to the advancing Ottomans. By 1376 Bulgaria recognised Ottoman suzerainty, although twelve years later they tried to shed their vassal ties, only provoking a major Turkish attack that cost them more territory.

At the same time, Murat's forces expanded the Ottoman domains eastward and southward into Anatolia, conquering the Germiyan, Hamidid and Teke *beyliks*, the latter conquest including the Mediterranean port of Antalya.

Murat's army occupied Thessalonica in 1387 after a four-year siege, by which time the Ottomans controlled all of southern Macedonia. His capture of Niš in 1385 brought him into conflict with Prince Lazar of Serbia, who organised a Serbian–Kosovan–Bosnian alliance against the Turks. Four years later Murat again invaded Serbia, opposed by Lazar and his allies, who included King Trvtko I of Bosnia.

The two armies clashed on 15 June 1389 near Pristina at Kosovo Polje, the 'Field of Blackbirds', where in a four-hour battle the Turks were victorious over the Christian allies. At the climax of the battle Murat was killed by a Serbian nobleman who had feigned surrender. Lazar was captured and beheaded by Murat's son Beyazit, who then slaughtered all the other Christian captives, including most of the noblemen of Serbia. Serbia never recovered from the catastrophe, and thenceforth it became a vassal of the Ottomans, who were now firmly established in the Balkans.

Soon afterwards Beyazit murdered his own brother Yakup to succeed to the throne, the first instance of fratricide in Ottoman history. Beyazit came to be known as Yıldırım, or Lightning, from the speed with which he moved his army, campaigning both in Europe and Asia, where he extended his domains deep into Anatolia.

Beyazit's army included an elite infantry corps called *yeniçeri*, meaning 'new force', which in the West came to be known as the janissaries. This corps had first been formed by Sultan Murat from prisoners of war taken in his Balkan campaigns. Beyazit institutionalised the janissary corps by a periodic levy of Christian youths called the *devşirme*, first in the Balkans and later in Anatolia as well. Those taken in the *devşirme* were forced to convert to Islam and then trained for service in the military, the most talented rising to the highest ranks in the army and the Ottoman administration, including that of grand vezir, the sultan's first minister. They were trained to be loyal only to the sultan, and since they were not allowed to marry they had no private lives outside the janissary corps. Thus they developed an intense esprit de corps, and were by far the most effective unit in the Ottoman armed forces.

During the winter of 1391–2 Beyazit launched major attacks by his *akinci*, or irregular light cavalry, against Greece, Macedonia and Albania. Early in 1392 Ottoman forces captured Skopje, and most of Serbia accepted Ottoman suzerainty. Then in July 1393 Beyazit captured Turnovo, capital of the Bulgarian Empire, after which Bulgaria became an Ottoman vassal, remaining under Turkish rule for nearly 500 years.

Beyazit laid siege to Constantinople in May 1394, erecting a fortress that came to be known as Anadolu Hisarı on the Asian shore of the Bosphorus at its narrowest stretch. While the siege continued Beyazit led his army into Wallachia, capturing Nicopolis on the Danube in 1395.

King Sigismund of Hungary appealed for a crusade against the Turks, and in July 1396 an army of nearly 100,000 assembled in Buda under his leadership.

The Christian army comprised contingents from Hungary, Wallachia, Germany, Poland, Italy, France, Spain and England, while its fleet had ships contributed by Genoa, Venice and the Knights of St John on Rhodes. Sigismund led his force down the Danube to Nicopolis, where he put the Turkish-occupied fortress under siege. Two days later Beyazit arrived with an army of 200,000, and on 25 September 1396 he defeated the crusaders at Nicopolis and executed most of the Christian captives, though Sigismund managed to escape.

Beyazit then renewed his siege of Constantinople, where the Greeks had been reinforced by 1,200 troops sent by Charles VI of France under Marshal Boucicault, a survivor of the Battle of Nicopolis. The marshal realised that his force was far too small, and so he persuaded the emperor Manuel II to go with him to France so that he could present his case to King Charles. Manuel went on to England, where on 21 December 1400 he was escorted into London by King Henry IV, though he received nothing but pity, returning to Constantinople empty-handed early in 1403.

But by then the situation had completely changed, for the previous spring Beyazit had lifted his siege of the city and rushed his forces back to Anatolia, which had been invaded by a Mongol horde led by Tamerlane. The two armies collided on 28 July 1402 near Ankara, where the Mongols routed the Turks, many of whom deserted at the outset of the battle. Beyazit himself was taken prisoner, and soon afterwards he died in captivity, tradition holding that he had been penned up in a cage by Tamerlane.

Five of Beyazit's sons – Süleyman, Mustafa, Musa, Isa and Mehmet – also fought in the battle. Mustafa and Musa were captured by Tamerlane, while the other three escaped. Musa was eventually freed by Tamerlane, while Mustafa apparently died in captivity, though a pretender known as Düzme (False) Mustafa later appeared to claim the throne. Beyazit's youngest son, Yusuf, escaped to Constantinople, where he converted to Christianity before he died of the plague in 1417.

The Ottoman state was almost destroyed by the catastrophe at Ankara. After his victory Tamerlane reinstated the emirs of the Anatolian *beyliks* that had fallen to the Ottomans, while in the Balkans the Christian rulers who had been Beyazit's vassals regained their independence. The next eleven years were a period of chaos, as Beyazit's surviving sons fought one another in a war of succession, at the same time doing battle with their Turkish and Christian opponents. The struggle was finally won by Mehmet, who on 5 July 1413 defeated and killed his brother Musa at a battle in Bulgaria, their brothers Süleyman and Isa having died earlier in the war of succession.

Mehmet ruled for eight years, virtually all of which he spent in war, striving to re-establish Ottoman rule in Anatolia and the Balkans. His last campaign was a raid across the Danube into Wallachia in 1421, shortly after which he died following a fall from his horse. He was succeeded by his son Murat II, who although only seventeen was already a seasoned warrior, having fought in at least two battles during his father's war of succession.

At the outset of Murat's reign he had to fight two wars of succession, first against the pretender Düzme Mustafa and then against his own younger brother, also named Mustafa, both of whom he defeated and killed. Both of the pretenders had been supported by the emperor Manuel II, and so after Murat put them down he sought to take his revenge on the emperor, putting Constantinople under siege on 20 June 1422. But the Byzantine capital was too strongly fortified for him to conquer, and at the end of the summer he decided to abandon the siege and withdraw.

Manuel suffered a critical stroke during the siege, whereupon his son John was made regent. Manuel died on 21 July 1425, and on that same day his son succeeded him as John VIII.

Murat's two wars of succession had cost him territory in both Anatolia and Europe, and now he set out to recover his losses. In 1423 he launched a campaign against the Isfendiyarid emir of Sinop on the Black Sea, forcing him to return the territory he had taken and to resume his status as an Ottoman vassal.

Immediately afterwards, Murat returned to Europe and marched against the ruler of Wallachia, Vlad II Dracul, and he too was made to give up the land he had seized and to become a vassal of the sultan. Vlad was later forced to give up two of his sons to Murat as hostages. The older of the two, who eventually succeeded his father as Vlad III, came to be known as Tepeş, or the Impaler, the historical prototype of Dracula; his younger brother was Radu cel Frumos, or the Handsome. Both of them remained hostages until after the death of their father, after which they were set up in turn as Ottoman puppets in Wallachia.

The Albanian ruler John Castrioti was also forced to become an Ottoman vassal, and in 1423 he sent his son as a hostage to Edirne, where he nominally converted to Islam, taking the name Iskender. He became one of Murat's favourites, accompanying him on campaigns in both Europe and Asia as a high-ranking Ottoman commander. Later, after he had returned to his native land, he came to be known as Skanderbeg, becoming Albania's greatest national hero in its struggle against Ottoman domination.

Murat then set out to regain Thessalonica, which his uncle Süleyman had ceded in 1403 to the Byzantines, who two decades later gave the city over to the Venetians since they were unable to defend it themselves. When Murat besieged Thessalonica the Venetians made an alliance with the Aydınıd emir Cüneyd, supporting him in his effort to regain the territory his *beylik* had lost to the Ottomans. Murat sent his commander Hamza against Cüneyd, who in April 1425 was defeated and killed, bringing the Aydınıd *beylik* to an end. Hamza went on to invade the Menteşe *beylik*, and that same year it too was conquered and terminated. During the next five years Murat further enlarged his territory in Anatolia, taking the Canik region along the Black Sea coast and annexing the Germiyan *beylik*, as well as putting down a number of rebellious Türkmen tribes.

Murat then turned his attention back to Thessalonica, leading his forces in a final attack that brought about the city's surrender on 29 March 1430, after which 7,000 of its inhabitants were carried off into slavery. The fall of Thessalonica led John VIII to seek help from the West, and he proposed to Pope Martin V that a council be called to reconcile the Greek and Latin Churches, which had been estranged for four centuries. This gave rise to the Council of Ferrara-Florence, in which the Byzantine delegation was headed by John VIII and the Patriarch of Constantinople, Joseph II. The union of the Churches was finally agreed upon on 5 July 1439, uniting the Greek and Latin Churches under the aegis of the Pope, Eugenius IV, who then called for a crusade to save Constantinople from the Turks. But the union was very unpopular among the people and clergy of Constantinople, and so the Byzantine Empire was deeply divided as it faced a showdown with its mortal enemy.

Between campaigns Murat usually returned to his capital at Edirne, though he also spent time in the old capital of Bursa, where in the years 1424–6 he erected an imperial mosque complex called the Muradiye. A decade later he built a mosque of the same name in his new capital as well as a palace called Edirne Sarayı, where he housed his harem. The palace comprised a number of pavilions on an island in the Tunca, one of two rivers that nearly encircle the city.

According to Islamic law, the sultan was allowed four wives in his harem, although he could have as many concubines as he pleased. Murat's first son, Ahmet, was born to one of his concubines in 1420, the year before Murat became sultan. His second son, Alaeddin Ali, was born in 1430 to Murat's favourite wife, Hadice Hatun (Lady), a Türkmen princess. His third son, the future Mehmet II, was born in Edirne Sarayı on 30 March 1432 to a concubine named Hüma Hatun.

Nothing is known of Hüma Hatun's origins, other than the testimony of contemporary sources that she was a slave girl, which means that she would not have been Turkish, for by law Muslims could not be enslaved. The only mention of her is in the fragmentary remains of the deed of a *vakıf*, or pious foundation, where she is identified simply as Hatun bint Abdullah, 'the Lady, daughter of Abdullah'. Abdullah was a name often given as the father of those who had converted to Islam, another indication of her non-Turkish origin.

It is recorded that Mehmet had a *sütanne*, or wet nurse, a Turkish woman named Daye Hatun, to whom he was particularly devoted, as evidenced by the fact that she became very wealthy during his reign and endowed several mosques. She outlived Mehmet by five years, dying in Istanbul on 14 February 1486.

Turkish raids in Serbia forced the despot of that nation, George Branković, to come to terms with the Ottomans in 1428, and then in 1433 he agreed to give his daughter Mara as a bride to Murat. Doukas, the contemporary Greek historian, writes of how Branković 'offered his daughter to Murat in marriage, with the greater part of Serbia, presumably as a dowry, and all he asked for in return was a pact sealed by sacred oaths'. The marriage took place in September 1435, when Mara, who would have been about sixteen, was escorted to Edirne by Murat's vezir Saruca Pasha. Doukas, referring to Hadice Hatun, says Murat 'longed more for this new bride who was beautiful in both mind and soul'. But Mara never bore Murat any children, and there is reason to believe that their marriage, which was arranged primarily for political purposes, was never consummated.

The Turkish raids on Serbia continued nonetheless, and in August 1439 the great fortress city of Smedervo, Branković's capital, fell to the Ottomans after a three-month siege. Branković then fled to Hungary, where he had vast estates, and within two years Serbia was annexed by the Ottomans and disappeared as a state until it gained its freedom from Ottoman rule in the nineteenth century.

During the summer of 1439 Murat's army captured Ioannina in north-western Greece before invading Albania, while his navy raided the Ionian Islands, the Greek archipelago between Greece and Italy. During the next three years Murat conquered much of Albania, and in the following two years he mounted campaigns in Serbia and Bosnia as a prelude to an invasion of Hungary, which he began in 1438. He put Belgrade under siege in April 1440, according to the Turkish chronicler Aşıkpaşazade, who notes that the sultan 'knew that Belgrade was the gateway to Hungary and aimed to open that gate'. But, as Aşıkpaşazade adds, 'many men and lords from the Muslim army were killed', and Murat was forced to lift the siege in October that year.

The following year Murat mounted an expedition into Transylvania under the commander Mezid Bey. But the invasion was stopped by an army led by John Hunyadi, the voyvoda, or prince, of Transylvania, who killed Mezid and routed his forces. Murat sought vengeance and sent another army against Hunyadi, who defeated the Turkish force in Wallachia in September 1442.

Hunyadi's victories encouraged the Christian rulers of Europe to form an anti-Ottoman alliance. On 1 January 1443 Pope Eugenius IV called for a crusade against the Turks, in which the rulers of Burgundy, Poland, Hungary, Wallachia and Venice agreed to join forces with the papacy against Murat, who that winter put down a revolt in central Anatolia by the Karamanid emir Ibrahim Bey.

Meanwhile, Murat's youngest son, Prince Mehmet, saw his father only occasionally. Mehmet's first three years were spent in the harem of Edirne Sarayı with Hüma Hatun and Daye Hatun. He was then sent with his mother to Amasya, near the Black Sea coast of Anatolia, where his half-brother Ahmet was serving as provincial governor. Ahmet died suddenly in 1437 and Mehmet succeeded him as governor, though he was scarcely five years old. At the same time, his half-brother Alaeddin Ali, who was then seven, was appointed provincial governor at Manisa, near the Aegean coast of Anatolia. Mehmet and Alaeddin Ali governed only nominally, for they were under the strict control of advisers appointed by Murat from among his most trusted officers. The two young princes were recalled to Edirne in 1439, when Murat had them circumcised, followed by a festival that lasted for several days. Their assignments were then interchanged, with Alaeddin Ali being sent as governor to Amasya and Mehmet to Manisa.

Murat appointed a number of tutors to educate Mehmet, the first of them being Ilyas Efendi, a Serbian prisoner of war who had converted to Islam and became a *molla*, or teacher of theology. But Mehmet was not interested in his lessons and was so headstrong that he fiercely resisted Ilyas Efendi's attempts to train him. Murat dismissed Ilyas Efendi and appointed a succession of other teachers, but none of them could control the obstreperous young prince. Finally Murat hired Molla Ahmet Gurani, who taught at the *medrese*, or theological school, at the Muradiye in Bursa, giving him a switch with which to punish Mehmet if the prince was not obedient. When Gurani met Mehmet, switch in hand, he said: 'Your father has sent me to instruct you, but also to chastise you in case you should not obey me.' When Mehmet laughed in his face Gurani thrashed him with the switch, and thereafter the prince was overawed by his tutor and payed strict attention during his lessons, or so says the chronicler Taşköprüzade.

Eventually Mehmet studied foreign languages, philosophy and geography as well as Islamic, Latin and Greek history and literature, his foreign tutors supposedly including the renowned Italian humanist Cyriacus of Ancona. Cyriacus was at the Ottoman court in Edirne in the mid- to late 1440s, but although he was in contact with Mehmet there is no evidence that he served as his tutor, or, as also alleged, his secretary. Mehmet was reputed to have known, apart from Turkish, some five languages, and a contemporary, Giacomo da Langusco, credits him with being fluent in Turkish, Greek and Slavic. Julian Raby, in his study of the sultan's scriptorium, writes that 'Mehmet must certainly have had an initial familiarity with Greek because he copied out both the Greek and the Arabic alphabets in one of his schoolbooks, preserved in the Topkapı, but knowledge of foreign languages is a matter of degree...'.

Early in June 1443 Alaeddin Ali was murdered by his adviser Kara Hızır Pasha, who also killed the prince's two infant sons. The murderer was executed without revealing the motive for his crime, which remains a mystery. One might suspect that the murders were committed to clear the way for Mehmet, who thus became Murat's heir presumptive, though no evidence has ever been found to support this suspicion. Murat was heartbroken, for Alaeddin Ali was his favourite son, and after prolonged mourning he buried the prince in the tomb that he had prepared for himself in the Muradiye at Bursa.

Immediately afterwards, Murat recalled Mehmet from Manisa to join him in Edirne. Mehmet arrived at a critical moment, for Murat had just learned that a Christian army had crossed the Danube and was headed south-eastward through Ottoman territory, led by John Hunyadi and Ladislas, King of Poland and Hungary. Murat mobilised his army and in December 1443 he set out to do battle with the crusaders, leaving Mehmet behind with the grand vezir Halil Çandarlı, who was to await the arrival of troops from Anatolia. The crusaders defeated the Ottomans twice in the winter of 1443–4 between Sofia and Niš, with both sides suffering heavy losses, after which Hunyadi and Ladislas led their troops back to Buda and Murat returned to Edirne.

Cyriacus of Ancona, who accompanied a Genoese trade mission to Edirne, reports that on 22 May 1444 he and his associates had an audience with the sultan. Murat received them in Edirne Sarayı, sitting cross-legged on a carpet 'in regal splendor of a barbaric kind', while his son Prince Mehmet stood behind him with his father's vezirs.

Meanwhile, John Castrioti died, some time between 1437 and 1440, after which Murat seized all his lands in Albania, including the great fortress of Kruje, which was taken by the Ottoman governor Hasan Bey. Castrioti's son George, now known as Skanderbeg, continued to serve Sultan Murat, despite pleas from his family that he return to reclaim his father's dominion in Albania. Murat sent Skanderbeg with an army to join the Ottoman forces at Niš, where he deserted along with some 300 Albanian horsemen. Skanderbeg and his followers then rode to Kruje, where he used a forged document from the sultan, supposedly giving him command of the garrison, and tricked Hasan Bey to hand over the fortress to him. He then proclaimed that he had reconverted to Christianity and began a campaign to regain all his family lands that had been taken by the Ottomans. After regaining the Castrioti possessions, in March 1444 he convened a congress at Alessio, a town then held by the Venetians, where all the Albanian chieftains swore allegiance to him in the cause of freeing Albania from the Turks. Murat sent an army to put down the rebellion, but Skanderbeg and his allies defeated them in June 1444.

Murat, faced with a new revolt by the Karamanid emir Ibrahim Bey, decided to negotiate a peace with Ladislas, and on 12 June 1444 a ten-year truce was signed at Edirne by the sultan and envoys of the king, who himself signed the treaty at Szeged in Hungary around 1 August of that same year. That left Murat free to deal with the revolt in Anatolia, and he appointed Prince Mehmet to serve as regent in his absence under the guidance of the grand vezir Çandarlı Halil Pasha. Murat then led his janissaries into Anatolia to deal with Ibrahim Bey, who immediately surrendered and agreed to resume his status as the sultan's vassal.

Meanwhile, Prince Mehmet had to deal with a serious disturbance in Edirne while serving as his father's regent. This involved a Bektaşi dervish from Persia, whose heretical sermons attracted a numerous following in Edirne. Mehmet found the dervish's ideas interesting and protected him and his disciples from the religious authorities. This outraged the Mufti Fahrettin, chief cleric in the Ottoman court, and Mehmet was forced to abandon the dervish, who was burned at the stake by a mob of fundamentalists.

After Ibrahim's surrender Murat did not return directly to Edirne, but instead he rode to Bursa, visiting the royal tomb at the Muradiye where his son Aläeddin Ali was buried. Soon afterwards, around 1 September 1444, Murat stunned his court by announcing that he was abdicating in favour of Prince Mehmet, saying: 'I have given my all – my crown, my throne – to my son, whom you should recognise as sultan.'

Murat's vezirs tried to dissuade him, particularly Halil Pasha, who had seen how immature Mehmet was when the young prince served as his father's regent. But Murat was adamant, and, accompanied by Ishak Pasha and Hamza Bey, he retired to Manisa to spend his time in study and contemplation, leaving Mehmet to govern under the direction of Halil Pasha.

Such was the first accession of Mehmet II, the seventh successive ruler of the House of Osman.

2 *The Boy Sultan*

When Mehmet II succeeded to the throne he was only twelve and one-half years old, the youngest ruler of the House of Osman up to that time. Halil Pasha and the other vezirs were very concerned, for they felt that Mehmet was too young and inexperienced to deal with the threats facing the Ottoman state, particularly the crusade that Pope Eugenius IV had called for the previous year.

When his father Murat abdicated in favour of Mehmet he had assumed that King Ladislas would honour the peace treaty they had agreed upon in the summer of 1444. But it seems that the king had no intention of keeping the peace, for he had already written to Cardinal Cesarini in Rome telling him that he would 'march with a powerful army against the perfidious Turks this very summer'. Then on 4 August 1444, a few days after he had signed the peace treaty at Szeged, Ladislas took a vow before his assembled nobles to make war upon the Turks and drive them from Europe within the year, 'notwithstanding any treaties or negotiations whatsoever...'.

Three weeks after Mehmet came to the throne the crusader army crossed the Danube and began marching eastward along the right bank of the river through Ottoman territory, led by King Ladislas, John Hunyadi and Cardinal Cesarini. The crusader forces also included naval contingents from Burgundy, Venice and the papacy, whose ships patrolled the Danube, the Black Sea and the straits between Europe and Asia.

When news of the invasion reached Edirne Mehmet sent a courier to inform Murat at his place of retirement in Manisa. Murat immediately mustered the troops of the Anatolian army, and in late October he had them ferried across the Bosphorus and led them to Edirne. Leaving Mehmet and Halil Pasha to guard Edirne, Murat then led his army north to Yanbol, where reinforcements under Sihabeddin Pasha joined him, bringing the number of men in his army up to some 60,000, almost three times the size of the Christian force.

Murat caught up with the crusaders on 10 November 1444 near Varna on the Black Sea. During the first stage of the battle the crusaders defeated both wings of the Ottoman army, but Murat led his janissaries in a counter-attack that killed Ladislas. This turned the tide of battle, for when the crusader army learned that the king had died they turned and 'fled like sheep before a wolf', according to an anonymous Turkish chronicler. The chronicler goes on to say that on the following day the crusaders surrendered to the Turks, who 'after making prisoner all their fresh-faced youths, put all the older ones to the sword, so that these proud infidels suffered what they themselves had planned against the community of Muhammed'. John Hunyadi was one of the few crusader leaders to escape, and the following year he was elected regent of Hungary.

After his victory Murat led his army back to Edirne. Soon afterwards he resumed his retirement in Manisa, leaving Mehmet to continue his rule as sultan in Edirne under the tutelage of the grand vezir Halil Pasha.

The Venetians thought to take advantage of Mehmet's youth by negotiating a peace treaty with him, which was signed at Edirne on 23 February 1446. A copy of the treaty is still preserved in the Venetian State Archives, the only extant document from Mehmet's first reign.

Meanwhile, Halil Pasha had been sending a series of messages to Murat, imploring him to resume his rule as sultan, saying that Mehmet was too young and immature to rule. One instance of Mehmet's immaturity cited by Halil Pasha was Mehmet's impetuous plan to attack Constantinople, from which he was dissuaded by the grand vezir. Another concerned the janissaries, who had in April 1446 demanded an increase in pay. When this was refused they rioted and burned down the Edirne *bedesten*, or covered market, whereupon Mehmet gave in to their demands, setting a dangerous precedent that would trouble the Ottoman sultanate for centuries to come.

After the latter incident Halil Pasha persuaded Mehmet to give up the throne and recall his father. Murat reluctantly agreed to return, and at the beginning of September 1446 he came back to Edirne and resumed his rule as sultan, while Mehmet withdrew to Manisa.

Meanwhile, Christian forces had made gains in southern Greece and Albania, and as soon as Murat resumed his reign he launched counter-attacks in both places. His opponent in southern Greece was the Despot of the Morea (Peloponnesos), Constantine Dragases, younger brother of the Byzantine emperor John VIII Palaeologus. During the winter of 1446–7 Murat regained the territory that Constantine had taken. Then the following year he launched a campaign against Skanderbeg, the Albanian leader, who was forced to abandon the Ottoman lands he had retaken and flee into the mountains, where for the next two decades he continued to fight against the Turks.

Pope Nicholas V was elected to the papacy on 6 March 1447, succeeding Eugenius IV, and on 8 March of the following year, spurred on by John Hunyadi, he called for another crusade against the Turks. Hunyadi, this time with only the Vlachs and a few Germans and Czechs as allies, crossed the Danube in September 1448 into Serbia, while Murat set out from Sofia to stop him with a much larger army. The two armies met at Kosovo Polje, the 'Field of Blackbirds', where the Serbs had gone down fighting against the Turks in 1389. The outcome of the second Battle of Kosovo, fought from 17 to 20 October 1448, was the same as that of the first, with the Ottomans routing the Christians. Mehmet had his baptism of fire commanding the right wing of his father's army in the battle, which ended when Hunyadi abandoned his defeated troops and fled the field, living to fight on against the Turks for another eight years.

The Byzantine emperor John VIII Palaeologus died on 31 October 1448. John was survived by his brothers Constantine, Demetrius and Thomas, as well as by his mother, the Empress Helena Dragas. Constantine, the eldest, used the surname Dragases, the Greek form of his mother's maiden name. At the time of John's death Constantine and his brother Thomas were in Mistra, capital of the Despotate of the Morea, while Demetrius was in Selembria, just a day's ride from Constantinople. As soon as he received news of his brother's death Demetrius rushed back to Constantinople to make his claim for the throne. But Helena was determined that Constantine should succeed, and so she stopped Demetrius from taking control and asserted her right to serve as regent in the interim. She then sent a courier to Mistra to inform Constantine that his brother John had died and that he was the rightful successor. When Constantine received the news his supporters acclaimed him as emperor, and they arranged for his coronation to be carried out at once. And so, on 6 January 1449, he was crowned in the church of St Demetrius at Mistra as Constantine XI, fated to be the last Emperor of Byzantium.

After his coronation Constantine divided the Despotate of the Morea between his two brothers, with Demetrius ruling in Mistra and Thomas in Achaia, in the western Peloponnesos. Constantine then left Mistra for Constantinople, where he arrived on 12 March 1449. Shortly afterwards he sent a courier to Sultan Murat to convey his greetings and to ask for a peace agreement.

Mehmet's mother Hüma Hatun died in September 1449, after which she was buried in the garden of the Muradiye mosque in Bursa. The dedicatory inscription on her tomb records that it was built by Mehmet 'for his deceased mother, queen among women – may the earth of her grave be fragrant'.

Meanwhile, Mehmet had become a father for the first time in January 1448, when his concubine Gülbahar gave birth to a son, the future Beyazit II. Little is known of Gülbahar's origins, but she was probably Greek. The concubines in the imperial harem were almost always Christians, although high-born Muslim women were sometimes taken in as wives of the princes or sultans in dynastic marriages. Murat himself had made two such dynastic marriages, the first of them to Princess Mara, daughter of George Brancović, the Despot of Serbia, and the second to Halima Hatun, daughter of Emir Ibrahim II, ruler of the Çandaroğlu Türkmen tribe in central Anatolia, thus seeking to establish cordial relations with powers in both Europe and Asia.

Murat arranged for such a marriage for Mehmet the following year, though without consulting his son beforehand, which made him very resentful. The bride chosen by Murat for Mehmet was Princess Sitti Hatun, daughter of the emir Ibrahim, ruler of the Dulkadırlı Türkmen tribe in central Anatolia. By this dynastic union, together with his own marriage to Halima Hatun, Murat established alliances with two powerful tribes against his most formidable enemy in Anatolia, the Karamanid Türkmen, who blocked the expansion of the Ottomans to the east.

The wedding took place at Edirne Sarayı in September 1450, followed by a celebration that lasted for three months, with music, dancing and competitions in poetry in which Anatolian bards sang verses in praise of the bride and groom. The bride was apparently quite beautiful, as evidenced by her portrait in a Greek codex preserved in Venice, as well as by the testimony of contemporary chroniclers. But Mehmet seems to have had no love for Sitti, who never bore him a child, and he left her behind when he moved from Edirne to Istanbul after the Conquest. Sitti died in Edirne in

1467, alone and forlorn, buried in the garden of a mosque built in her memory by her niece Ayşe.

The following year Mehmet's concubine Gülşah gave birth to his second son, Mustafa, who would always be his favourite. Later that year Murat's wife Halima Hatun gave birth to a son, Ahmet, nicknamed Küçük, or Little, to distinguish him from the late Prince Ahmet, the sultan's first son. Thus Mehmet now had a half-brother, younger than his own sons, who would be a possible rival for the throne.

Meanwhile, Murat had been extending his domains in western Greece, where in 1449 he captured Arta. Then, accompanied by Mehmet, he led a successful expedition against the Albanian leader Skanderbeg, who was forced to give up most of his dominions to the sultan. Skanderbeg managed to hold on to the fortified mountain town of Kruje, which Murat, again accompanied by Mehmet, attacked in mid-May 1450. But Skanderbeg put up such a tenacious defence that Murat was forced to lift the siege at the end of October and withdraw his forces to Edirne. This made Skanderbeg a hero throughout Europe; ambassadors and assistance were sent to Kruje from the Pope, King Alfonso of Aragon and Naples, the regent John Hunyadi of Hungary, and Duke Philip the Good of Burgundy. For Skanderbeg had given Christians hope that they could, as he wrote, defend themselves 'from the oppression and cruel hands of the Turks, our enemies and those of the Catholic faith'.

Early the following year Murat commenced work on several new pavilions in Edirne Sarayı. But the project had barely begun when he died on 8 February 1451, stricken by apoplexy after a drinking bout. He was forty-seven years old and had ruled for three decades, most of which he had spent at war.

Murat's death was kept secret by the grand vezir Halil Pasha so that Mehmet could be summoned from Manisa, where he was serving as provincial governor. The secrecy may have been occasioned by Mehmet's unpopularity with both the army and the populace of Edirne, who might have revolted to prevent his accession. But all went well, and after Mehmet had crossed the Dardanelles to Gallipoli he was met by the Ottoman court and all the people of the surrounding area, who accompanied him to Edirne Sarayı, lamenting the death of Sultan Murat, according to Doukas. 'Proceeding for about half a mile in dead silence, they stopped and, standing together in a body, raised their voices in loud lamentations, shedding tears all the while. Then Mehmet and his subordinates, dismounted and followed suit by rending the air with wailing. The mournful cries heard that day on both sides were a spectacle indeed!'

The following day, 18 February 1451, Mehmet was acclaimed as sultan, one month before his nineteenth birthday. Kritoboulos of Imbros, Mehmet's contemporary Greek biographer, writes: 'When he became heir to a great realm and master of many soldiers and enlisted men, and had under his power already the largest and best parts of both Asia and Europe, he did not believe that these were enough for him nor was he content with what he had: instead he immediately overran the whole world in his calculations and resolved to rule it in emulation of the Alexanders and Pompeys and Caesars and kings and generals of their sort.' Kritoboulous believed that the young sultan was in every way qualified to realise his soaring imperial ambitions. 'His physical powers helped him well. His energies were keen for everything, and the power of his spirit gave him ability to rule and be kingly. To this end also his wisdom aided, as well as his fine knowledge of all the doings of the ancients.'

That same day Mehmet was girded with the sword of his ancestor Osman Gazi – the Ottoman equivalent of coronation – in the presence of the vezirs and other officers of his court. After the ceremony Mehmet appointed Halil as grand vezir, although he loathed his father's old adviser. Mehmet felt that Halil had undermined his first attempt to rule as sultan, and he suspected that the grand vezir had been taking bribes from the Byzantines. Nevertheless, he allowed Halil to continue as grand vezir for the time being, while he waited for the right moment to eliminate him. Halil had just as deep a hatred for Mehmet, whose 'insolence, savagery and violence' he speaks of in a quote by Doukas.

Mehmet also retained another of his father's old vezirs, Ishak Pasha, whom he appointed as *beylerbey*, or governor, of Anatolia. He then ordered Ishak to conduct Murat's remains to Bursa for burial in the Muradiye, the mosque complex that his father had erected early in his reign. There Murat was buried in the *türbe*, or mausoleum, that he had erected for himself beside the mosque, the last sultan to be laid to rest in the first capital of the Osmanlı. Murat's tomb was left open to the elements because of the request he had made in his will: 'Bury me in Bursa near my son Alaeddin. Do not raise a sumptuous mausoleum over my grave…but bury me directly in the ground. May the rain, sign of the benediction of God, fall on me.'

Directly after his coronation Mehmet went to the harem of Edirne Sarayı, where he received the congratulations of all the women there, who also gave him their condolences on the death of his father. The highest-ranking of the deceased sultan's wives at the time of his death was Halima Hatun, who fifteen months before had given birth to Murat's last son, Küçük Ahmet. Succession had often been a matter of contention in the Ottoman dynasty, and had led to two civil wars. So Mehmet decided that in this case he would settle the matter at once by ordering the execution of Küçük Ahmet. While Mehmet was talking with Halima Hatun, one of his men was strangling her baby son in his bath. Mehmet justified the murder of his half-brother as being in accordance with the Ottoman code of fratricide, which on several occasions had been practised by his ancestors to prevent wars of succession. Mehmet later had the code enacted into law, as stated in his imperial edict: 'And to whomsoever of my sons the Sultanate shall pass, it is fitting that for the order of the world that he shall kill his brothers. Most of the Ulema allow it. So let them act on this.'

Mehmet then married off Halima Hatun to Ishak Pasha, the new *beylerbey* of Anatolia. Another of Murat's high-born wives, Mara, the daughter of George Branković, was sent back to her home with rich presents, and afterwards maintained cordial relations with Mehmet. Mehmet took advantage of this to renew a peace treaty with Branković later in 1451.

The treaty with Serbia was one of a number of diplomatic agreements that Mehmet made in the late summer of 1451, as news of his accession spread through Europe and prompted the Christian powers to send embassies to Edirne to see the young sultan.

The first to arrive was an ambassador from Emperor Constantine XI, who negotiated a peace treaty with Mehmet. One of the terms in this treaty concerned Mehmet's cousin Orhan, a grandson of Beyazit I. Orhan was a hostage in Constantinople, having been used by the Byzantines as a possible pretender to destabilise the Ottoman regime. Mehmet agreed to pay for his cousin's upkeep by giving the emperor the revenues of villages in the Struma valley in Greece.

Mehmet also exchanged emissaries with John IV Comnenus, the Byzantine emperor of Trebizond. The Greek chronicler George Sphrantzes, who was serving as ambassador from Constantine XI to Trebizond, tells of how he warned John IV about Mehmet. 'This man, who just became sultan, is young and an enemy of the Christians since childhood, he threatens with proud spirit that he will put into operations certain plans against the Christians. If God should grant that the young sultan be overcome by his youth and evil nature and march against our City, I know not what will happen.'

Sphrantzes also learned that Mehmet had sent Murat's widow Mara back to her father George Branković, the Despot of Serbia. This led him to write to Constantine XI, suggesting that the emperor, who was a widower, marry Princess Mara. Sphrantzes, in discussing possible objections to the marriage, one of which was that Mara had been wed to Sultan Murat, remarked: 'Your potential bride…was the wife of a very powerful monarch, and she, it is generally believed, did not sleep with him.'

Constantine took the suggestion seriously and sent an envoy to Despot George Branković to propose marriage to the princess. According to Sphrantzes, Mara's parents listened to the proposal 'with delight and were ready to settle the final details'. But Mara herself rejected the proposal, for she 'had made a vow to God that if He freed her from the house of her late husband she would not marry for the rest of her life, but would remain in His service, as far as possible. Thus the proposed match failed.'

On 10 September Mehmet received an embassy from Venice and renewed a peace treaty with the Serene Republic that his father had signed five years earlier.

Ten days later representatives of John Hunyadi arrived, and Mehmet signed an agreement for a three-year truce with Hungary. The next embassy to arrive was from the city state of Ragusa, which offered to increase the amount of tribute it paid to the sultan. This was followed by missions from the Grand Master of the Knights of St John at Rhodes, the Prince of Wallachia, and the Genoese lords of Chios and Lesbos, all of whom brought rich gifts for the sultan, receiving from him expressions of goodwill.

Kritoboulos says that, after Mehmet had concluded his meetings with foreign emissaries and signed treaties with them, 'he gave himself over to an examination of his whole realm'. This led him to 'depose some of the governors and substitute others who he deemed to be superior to the former in strategy and justice'. He examined 'the registers and battle order of the troops, cavalry and infantry, which were paid from the royal treasury. He also made the royal palace subject of considerable thought and increased the pay of its troops', particularly that of the janissaries. 'In addition to this, he collected a supply of arms and arrows and other things needful and useful in preparation for war. Then he examined his family treasury, looking especially closely into its overseers. He carefully questioned the officials in charge of the annual taxes and obliged them to render their accounts.'

To Kritoboulos, Mehmet's study of the empire's finances indicated that 'much of the public and royal revenue was being badly spent and wasted to no good purpose, about one-third of the yearly revenues which were recovered for the royal treasury. So he set the keeping of this in good order.' At the conclusion of his account of Mehmet's reorganisation of the government, Kritoboulos writes: 'He greatly increased the annual revenue. He brought many of the tax officials to reason through fear, and for them substituted trustworthy and wise men to collect and safe-keep the funds. His father had dealt with such matters in a much more hit-or-miss manner, but he made short work of them.'

The treaties signed by Mehmet secured his borders in Europe. This left him free to lead an expedition into Anatolia, where his vassal, the Karamanid emir Ibrahim, had rebelled and seized three Ottoman fortresses: Akşehir, Beyşehir and Seydişehir. According to the contemporary Turkish chronicler Tursun Beg, in the spring of 1451 Dayı Karaca Pasha, the *beylerbey* of Rumelia, the European part of the Ottoman realm, was left with his troops at Sofia to guard against the possibility of an attack from Hungary, while Mehmet himself set out against Ibrahim with the standing army and troops from Anatolia. When the Ottoman army reached central Anatolia, Ibrahim fled and sent his vezir Mewlan Weli to negotiate peace terms. According to Tursun Beg, Ibrahim 'agreed to give up Akşehir, Beyşehir and Seydişehir, including the territories around them. In addition, he agreed to send every year a certain number of soldiers to serve in the Ottoman army.'

While Mehmet was on his way back to Europe from this campaign he had to deal with another insurrection by the janissaries, whom he once again appeased by raising their pay, though much against his will. Mehmet vented his rage on the commander of the corps, Kazancı Doğan, having him savagely whipped and then dismissing him from his post. Mehmet then reorganised the janissaries in such a way as to take more direct control of the corps, which he was to use with great effectiveness in his subsequent campaigns.

Around the same time the emperor Constantine sent envoys to renegotiate a point in the peace treaty he had signed with Mehmet, the one concerning the upkeep of the Turkish pretender Orhan. When the embassy reached Mehmet, probably in Bursa, he delegated Halil Pasha to deal with them. The envoys said that the payment for Orhan's upkeep was not sufficient, and he implied that unless it was increased Constantine would allow the pretender to contest the throne with Mehmet. Halil was furious, according to Doukas, and he told the envoys, whom he called 'stupid and foolish Romans', that they were making a fatal mistake in threatening Mehmet, for he was a far more dangerous foe than his father, who had been 'a sincere friend' of the Byzantines.

Mehmet informed the envoys that he would deal with the matter when he returned to Edirne. He then prepared to lead his army back to Europe across the Dardanelles. But when he learned that Italian warships were on patrol there he changed his route and had his troops ferried across the Bosphorus, embarking from Anadolu Hisarı, the fortress that Beyazit I had built in 1394 on the Asian shore at the narrowest stretch of the strait. As soon as Mehmet returned to Edirne he repudiated the treaty he had made with Constantine. His anger at Constantine's threat to support the pretender Orhan was such that he immediately began preparations for a siege of Constantinople, which he had been prevented from doing when he first came to the throne. Kritoboulos writes: Mehmet 'resolved to carry into execution immediately the plan which he had long since studied and elaborated in his mind and toward which he had bent every purpose from the start, and to wait no longer or delay. The plan was to make war against the Romans [Byzantines] and their Emperor Constantine and to besiege the city.'

Thus determined, at the beginning of the second year of his reign Mehmet took the first step in the plan that he had made to attack and conquer Constantinople. According to Kritoboulos, Mehmet decided 'to build a strong fortress on the Bosphorus on the European side, opposite to the Asiatic fortress on the other side, at the point where it is narrowest and swiftest, and so to control the strait'. Kritoboulos goes on to say that in the winter of 1451–2 Mehmet 'ordered all the materials to be prepared for building, namely stone and timbers and iron and whatever else would be of use for this purpose. He set the best and most experienced officers over the work, instructing them to put everything speedily in the best order, so that when spring came he could undertake the task.'

The site that Mehmet chose for the fortress was eight miles north of Constantinople. Originally known in Turkish as Boğaz Kesen, or 'Cut Throat', and later called Rumeli Hisarı, the 'Castle of Europe', it was built directly across the strait from the fortress built in 1394 by Beyazit I, known as Anadolu Hisarı, the 'Castle of Asia'. Constantine sent an embassy to Mehmet complaining that the sultan was violating their treaty by building a fortress on Byzantine territory. Mehmet replied, according to Doukas, 'I take nothing from the City. Beyond the fosse she owns nothing. If I desire to build a fortress...the emperor has no right to stop me.'

Early in the spring of 1452 Mehmet left Edirne for Gallipoli, where the Ottoman fleet was based. There, according to Kritoboulos, 'he filled thirty triremes and armed them fully as for a naval fight... He prepared other ships to carry the equipment, and sent them up from Gallipoli to the Bosphorus.' Mehmet then crossed the Dardanelles with his troops and led them along the Asian side of the strait to the Bosphorus. There he crossed over to the European side from Anadolu Hisarı, to the place that came to be known as Rumeli Hisarı, where he had decided to build his fortress.

Construction of the fortress began on 15 April 1452. Kritoboulos writes of how Mehmet 'marked out with stakes the location where he wished to build, planning the position and the size of the castle, the foundations, the distance between the main towers and the smaller turrets, also the bastions and breastworks and gates, and every other detail as he had carefully worked it out in his mind'.

An army of workmen conveyed building material to the site, including architectural members from ruined Byzantine monuments in the vicinity. Doukas reports that 'as they were removing several columns from the ruins of the Church of the Archangel Michael, some of the inhabitants of the City, angered by what was happening, tried to stop the Turks, but they were all captured and put to death by the sword'.

Mehmet's cavalrymen grazed their horses in the surrounding fields, and when the local Greek farmers tried to drive the animals away a fight broke out in which several men on both sides were killed. The following day Mehmet sent his commander Kaya Bey to punish the locals, forty of whom were killed, according to Doukas, who noted: 'This was the beginning of the conflict that led to the destruction of the Romans.'

When news of the massacre reached Constantine he closed the gates of Constantinople and imprisoned all the Turks who were then in the city. The prisoners included some eunuchs from Edirne Sarayı who happened to be visiting the city. The eunuchs appealed to Constantine, saying that if they did not return to Edirne they would be executed, and so three days later he relented and released them along with the other prisoners. He then sent an embassy in a last attempt to come to terms with Mehmet, who imprisoned the envoys and had them beheaded, thus making a virtual declaration of war.

Mehmet had hired a Hungarian military engineer named Urban, who built for him a large cannon that he claimed could destroy the walls of Babylon. As soon as Rumeli Hisarı was finished, on 31 August 1452, the cannon was placed on one of its main towers. Mehmet then proclaimed that all ships passing on the Bosphorus had to stop for inspection by the commandant of Rumeli Hisarı, otherwise they would be fired upon. Early in November two Venetian ships, sailing from the Black Sea with supplies for Constantinople, took advantage of a favourable north wind to pass the fortress unscathed. But two weeks later another Venetian ship was sunk by the great cannon in Rumeli Hisarı. The captain, Antonio Rizzo, and his crew were captured and brought to Mehmet at Didymoteichon, south of Edirne. Mehmet had Rizzo impaled and his crew beheaded, leaving their bodies beside the road for travellers to see and carry the news to Constantinople.

Meanwhile, Constantine had been making desperate attempts to obtain help from the West. Pope Nicholas V appointed Cardinal Isidore of Kiev as papal legate to Constantinople. Isidore arrived in Constantinople on 26 October 1452, accompanied by the archbishop Leonard of Chios, along with a contingent of 200 Neapolitan archers sent by the pope. Isidore pressed Constantine to agree to a formal declaration of Union, which was read out on 12 December of that year in Haghia Sophia, the Great Church, dedicated to the Divine Wisdom. But most of the populace refused to accept the Union, and thenceforth they stayed away from Haghia Sophia, where only priests who had accepted the delaration were allowed to serve. The Megadux (Grand Duke) Loukas Notaras is supposed to have said: 'I would rather see the Sultan's turban amongst us than the Cardinal's tiara.'

The opposition party was led by George Scholarios, a monk at the Pantocrator monastery in Constantinople. Scholarios retired to his cell after Constantine's acceptance of the Pope's demands, pinning to the door of his room a manifesto condemning the Union, quoted by Doukas: 'Wretched Romans, how you have been deceived! Trusting in the might of the Franks you have removed yourself from the hope of God. Together with the City which will soon be destroyed, you have lost your piety... Woe unto you in the judgment.'

As the year 1452 drew to a close Mehmet spent all his time drawing up his plans for the coming siege of the Byzantine capital. Doukas writes: 'Night and day the ruler's only care and concern, whether he was lying on his bed or standing on his feet, or within his courtyard or without, was what battle plan and stratagem to employ in order to capture Constantinople.' One night he called in Halil Pasha, whom he knew opposed his plan of attacking the city, probably because he was being bribed by the Byzantines. Halil was so terrified by the nocturnal summons that he now readily agreed with Mehmet, who then bade the grand vezir goodnight, telling him: 'Go in peace.'

Late in January 1453 Mehmet assembled his vezirs to hear his plans for the conquest of Constantinople and to obtain their agreement. Kritoboulos records the lengthy speech that Mehmet is supposed to have made on this occasion, in which he gave 'a recital of previous deeds of his forefathers', ending with a stirring call to arms. 'Let us not then delay any longer, but let us attack the City swiftly with all our powers and with this conviction: that we shall either capture it with one blow or shall never withdraw from it, even if we must die, until we become masters of it.'

Kritoboulos writes that 'practically all of those present applauded what was said by the Sultan, praising him for his good will and knowledge, bravery and valor, and agreeing with him, and still further inciting each other to war'. He goes on to say that there were a few vezirs who 'wanted to advise against making war', Halil undoubtedly being one of them. 'However, seeing the insistence and zeal of the Sultan, they were afraid, as it seems to me, and unwillingly yielded and were carried along by the majority. So the war was sanctioned by all.'

And so now, two months before his twenty-first birthday, Mehmet could at last begin to see the fulfilment of his dream of conquering Constantinople.

3

The Conquest of Constantinople

Constantinople was built on a more or less triangular peninsula that forms the south-easternmost extension of Europe. The peninsula is bounded on its south by the Sea of Marmara and on its north by the Golden Horn, a scimitar-shaped body of water that opens into the Bosphorus at the southern end of the strait. The city was protected on its landward side by its mighty defence walls, originally built in AD 447 by the emperor Theodosius II. These walls enclose seven hills, the first of which is the acropolis at the confluence of the Bosphorus and the Golden Horn, where the original Greek colony of Byzantium was founded c. 660 BC. The first six hills are connected by a ridge that rises above the south side of the Golden Horn, while the Seventh Hill rises to two peaks above the Marmara shore of the city. The Seventh Hill is separated from the first six by the deep valley of the Lycus, a stream that flows into the city midway along the land walls and eventually empties into the Marmara. Defence walls protected the city on its seaward sides as well, extending along the shores of the Golden Horn and the Marmara to join the ends of the land walls.

The First Hill is crowned by Haghia Sophia, a magnificent domed basilica erected by the emperor Justinian in the years 532–7. On the Marmara slope of the First Hill was the Great Palace of Byzantine, first built by the emperor Constantine the Great when he established Constantinople as the capital of his empire in 330. Later emperors enlarged and embellished the Great Palace, particularly Justinian, but it was ruined during the Latin occupation of 1204–61. After the Greek recapture of

Constantinople in 1261 the emperors of the Palaeologus dynasty resided in the Palace of Blachernae, built on the slope of the Sixth Hill leading down to the Golden Horn, with an annex known as the Palace of the Porphyrogenitus (Turkish Tekfursaray) standing further up the hill. Both palaces were built into the land walls, which would put the imperial household on the front line during the Ottoman siege of the city.

On the northern side of the lower stretch of the Golden Horn across from Constantinople was the independent city state of Galata, also known as Pera. The Genoese signed a treaty in the spring of 1261 with the emperor Michael VIII Palaeologus, and after his troops recaptured Constantinople that summer Genoa was given control of Galata, governing the city through an official known as the *podesta*. The treaty did not allow the Genoese to fortify Galata, but they disregarded this and soon afterwards they began building fortifications. The bastion of the Genoese fortifications was the Tower of Christ, now known as the Galata Tower, from which defence walls ran down to both the Bosphorus and the Golden Horn, with sea walls along the shore.

Genoa tried to remain neutral, while giving the *podesta* in Galata, Angelo Lomellino, a free hand. The Genoese in Galata were sympathetic to their fellow Christians in Constantinople, a number of them crossing the Horn to join in the defence of the city. Other Genoese came from Genoa to join in the defence, including Maurizio Cattaneo, the two brothers Geronimo and Leonardo di Langasco, and the three Bocchiardo brothers, Paolo, Antonio and Troilo, who brought at their own expense a small company of soldiers. There were also a few volunteers from elsewhere in Europe. These included the Catalan community in Constantinople and their consul, Péré Julia, along with some Catalan sailors; the Castilian nobleman Don Francisco de Toledo, a distant relative of Emperor Constantine; and the military engineer Johannes Grant, usually called a German, but who was probably a Scottish mercenary. Prince Orhan, the Turkish pretender, also volunteered to join in the defence of the city along with the men of his household.

Mehmet's plan to attack Constantinople was already evident in February 1452, when Constantine sent an ambassador to inform the Venetian Senate that the sultan was preparing to besiege the city, which he said would inevitably fall unless the Christian powers of Europe came to the aid of Byzantium.

The Venetians agreed to send supplies to Constantinople, but they held off on promising military assistance, partly because of their own war with

Florence, and also to see what the other Christian powers would do to help Byzantium. The Senate appealed in the name of Byzantium to Pope Nicholas V, the Holy Roman Emperor Frederick III, King Ferrante of Naples and John Hunyadi of Hungary, 'informing them furthermore of the provisions that we have taken on our part, and stating that these are by no means sufficient for so great a crisis'. But all the Christian powers of Europe were too preoccupied with their own problems to send help to Byzantium. Even Constantine's own brothers, Demetrius and Thomas Palaeologus, the Despots of the Morea, were unable to help, for they were threatened by Mehmet's general Ömer Pasha, whose army was stationed on the isthmus of Corinth to block them from sending troops to Constantinople.

Immediately after the meeting with his vezirs, Mehmet ordered Dayı Karaca Pasha, the *beylerbey* of Rumelia, to muster an army and attack the Byzantine coastal towns in Thrace. The towns on the Black Sea coast surrendered at once, but some of those on the Marmara coast attempted to resist, most notably Selembria and Perinthus, which were quickly taken and sacked by Karaca's troops.

At the beginning of March 1453 Mehmet began assembling a fleet at Gallipoli. Kritoboulos writes of how Mehmet 'prepared the fleet, building some new triremes, repairing others that were damaged by time... In addition he built long ships, heavily armed and swift, with thirty to fifty rowers... Furthermore, he chose crews from all his coast-towns, Asiatic and European...for he attached greater importance...to the fleet than to the army.' Kritoboulos says that 'the total number of ships was said to be three hundred and fifty without counting the transports or those engaged in some other necessary services', but modern estimates make it about one-third to one-half that number.

The fleet was commanded by the governor of Gallipoli, Süleyman Baltaoğlu, a Bulgarian convert to Islam. At the end of March the fleet left Gallipoli and made its way into the Sea of Marmara. According to Kritoboulos, 'They set sail with great speed, and with shouts and noise and cheers, and they sang rowing chanties and urged one another to emulation by shouts. When they left the Hellespont, they created the greatest possible astonishment and fear among all who saw them. Nowhere for a very long time had such a large fleet of ships or such great preparations by sea been made.'

Meanwhile, Mehmet had been assembling his army in Thrace, where his armourers and engineers had been at work throughout the winter to prepare weapons, armour, artillery and siege machines. Contemporary Greek estimates of Mehmet's force range as high as 300,000 or 400,000 men, but modern authorities put the number at about 80,000 troops. These included the *sipahis*, or provincial cavalry; the *akinci*, or irregular light cavalry; the janissaries, who fought as infantry, numbering about 12,000; the *azaps*, or irregular light infantry; the *başıbozuks* (literally 'head-breakers'), irregular infantry who were used as shock troops; and a Serbian vassal contingent of 1,500 Christian cavalry, as well as the men of the artillery, engineering and auxiliary units.

Throughout the winter Constantine prepared for the coming siege by stockpiling food supplies, arms and munitions, as well as mobilising manpower to defend the city. He assigned the task of enumerating the able-bodied men of the city to his secretary George Sphrantzes, who informed him, 'in the greatest possible sadness', that there were only 4,983 Greeks and some 200 foreigners, the latter principally local Venetians and Genoese. Other estimates put the number of defenders in Constantinople at about 7,000. The small number of available men was an indication of how much the population of Constantinople had fallen during the first half of the fifteenth century, as the local Greeks fled from the city to take refuge in the West. The population in 1452 is estimated to have been between 40,000 and 50,000, just a tenth of what it had been in the mid-sixth century, during the reign of Justinian. George Scholarios, writing just before the siege, describes Constantinople as 'a city of ruins, poor, and largely uninhabited'.

The Venetian colony in Constantinople offered their complete support to Constantine. The Venetian *bailo*, or governor, Girolamo Minotto, assured the emperor that his people would share fully in the defence of the city, and he would make sure that none of the Venetian ships in the harbour left without his permission. The vessels were armed as warships, and two of their captains, Gabriele Trevisano and Alviso Diedo, agreed to serve as commanders in the defence of the city. Among the Venetians under their command was Niccolo Barbaro, a ship's doctor, whose diary gives the most complete eyewitness account of the siege of Constantinople.

The only other significant reinforcements came on 29 January 1453, when two large ships arrived from Genoa with 700 troops under the command of Giovanni Giustiniani-Longo. Constantine immediately put Giustinani in command of the city's defences, while the local Venetians placed their ships at the emperor's disposal. But then on 26 February six Venetian ships sailed away from Constantinople in defiance of the orders of their local council, taking with them 700 men, so that Constantine had no net gain in manpower. This left the defenders with twenty-six fighting ships in the Golden Horn, ten of them Byzantine, five Venetian, five Genoese, three from Crete, one from Ancona, one from Catalonia, and one from Provence, all together about a fifth the size of the Ottoman fleet.

The troops under Giustiniani's command were hardly enough to man Constantinople's defence walls, which stretched for some twelve miles around the city on both its landward and seaward sides. The original land walls of Theodosius II extended for more than four miles between the Marmara and the Golden Horn. The stretch of walls across the Lycus valley was known as the Mesoteichion, literally the 'Middle of the Walls', which had always been considered the most vulnerable because it could be fired down upon by guns on the ridges to either side.

The main line of defence in the Theodosian fortifications was the inner wall, which was about 5 metres thick at its base and rose to a height of 12 metres above the city. This wall was guarded by ninety-six towers, 18 to 20 metres high, separated by an average interval of 55 metres. Between the inner and outer walls there was a terrace called the *peribolos*, which varied from 15 to 20 metres in breadth, its level about 5 metres above that of the inner city. The outer wall, which was about 2 metres thick and 8.5 metres in height, also had ninety-six towers, alternating in position with those of the inner wall. Outside the walls there was a terrace called the *parateichion*, bounded by a counterscarp nearly 2 metres high that separated it from the fosse, a ditch some 10 metres deep and 20 metres wide. The northernmost stretch of walls, from the Palace of the Porphyrogenitus down to the Golden Horn, was a later construction that replaced the original Theodosian fortifications there. It consisted of a single line of walls, more massive than the original fortifications, and with higher and more closely spaced towers, part of it including the outer walls of the Blachernae Palace.

The Theodosian walls were pierced by 10 gates and a few small posterns, virtually all of which are still in existence. Five of the gates were public entryways and the other five were principally for the use of the military, the two types alternating with one another in position.

The sea walls extended along the shores of both the Golden Horn and the Sea of Marmara. The walls along the Horn were 10 metres high and were protected by 110 defence towers at regular intervals, pierced by sixteen gates. The walls along the Marmara were 12–15 metres high, studded with 188 towers regularly spaced, and with thirteen gates.

Mehmet had by then built up a formidable artillery through the efforts of Urban, who cast a huge cannon twice as large as the one used at Rumeli Hisarı. This cannon, named for its maker, could fire a 1,200 pound stone ball more than two feet in diameter as far as a mile, as Urban demonstrated to the sultan at Edirne in January 1453. A month later Mehmet began moving his artillery forward, with Urban pulled on rollers by a team of sixty oxen. A team of engineers went ahead to improve roads and build bridges, and by March Urban and the other big guns of Mehmet's artillery had reached a point five miles from Constantinople.

Constantine knew that Mehmet's navy would try to penetrate into the Golden Horn, which could be closed by a huge chain floating on wooden buoys attached to a boom. One end of the chain was fixed to a tower in the sea walls below the First Hill of Constantinople, while the other was attached to a fortress known as the Castle of Galata, which stood on the shore at the confluence of the Golden Horn and the Bosphorus. Some of the defending warships were assigned to pull the boom across the entrance to the Golden Horn when the siege began, thus protecting the city from direct assault on that side.

Easter Sunday was celebrated on 1 April, and on the following day an advance guard of Ottoman soldiers came into sight. A small force of defenders went out from the walls and 'killed some of them and wounded a few', according to Kritoboulos. 'But after encountering a larger force in a counter-attack from the [Ottoman] army, they took refuge in the City, closed the gate, and did not sally forth again but simply guarded the City.'

According to the diary of Niccolo Barbaro, the chain was put in place on 2 April, and he reports that on that same day Constantine assigned Venetian commanders to each of the four most strategic gates in the land walls. Three days later sentinels on the Theodosian walls spotted the Turkish army approaching across the downs of Thrace, and Constantine ordered his commanders to take up the positions that had been assigned to them. Constantine himself was in command of the best Greek troops along the Mesoteichion, where he expected Mehmet to concentrate his attack.

Barbaro notes that an hour before sunrise on 5 April Sultan Mehmet 'came before Constantinople with about one-hundred and sixty-five thousand men and encamped about two and a half miles from the walls of the city'. (Modern scholarship puts the number at about half that.) He goes on to write that two days later Mehmet 'moved with a great part of his forces to within about a quarter of a mile from the walls, and they spread in a line along the whole length of the city walls from the Sea of Marmara to the Golden Horn'.

Mehmet set up his red and gold tent outside the Gate of St Romanus, about midway along the Theodosian walls, directly opposite the Mesoteichion. He then reviewed the whole army and assigned his commanders to their various positions. The sultan himself, assisted by Halil Pasha, took command in the Lycus valley, the sector facing the Mesoteichion, with the janissaries and other elite units in front, along with the giant cannon Urban and other heavy guns, while the *azaps* and *başıbozuks* were held in reserve behind. Along the southern stretch of the land walls, from the Lycus valley to the Marmara, were the regular Anatolian troops under Ishak Pasha. Ishak was assisted by Mahmut Pasha, a descendant of an aristocratic Byzantine family living in Serbia, who had been captured by the Ottomans as a youth and converted to Islam when he joined the service of Murat II. Along the northern stretch of walls, from the Lycus valley to the Golden Horn, were the regular European troops under Dayı Karaca Pasha, who had several heavy guns to bombard the single line of walls that protected the Blachernae Palace. Zaganos Pasha was given command of a large contingent of troops on the hills above the northern side of the Golden Horn, around the upper reaches of which a road had been built so that he could communicate with the rest of the army. Meanwhile, the Ottoman fleet under Süleyman Baltaoğlu had anchored off Diplokionion (Beşiktaş), two miles up the European shore from the Golden Horn.

As soon as his forces were in place Mehmet sent emissaries into the city under a flag of truce, offering terms of surrender to the defenders. According to Kritoboulos, Mehmet said 'that if they were willing to deliver over the City and themselves to him with agreements and solemn oaths they might live with their wives and children and all their belongings in safety, suffering no evils and carrying on their business in peace'. But the offer was rejected, and the answer given to Mehmet's emissaries was that the Greeks 'were willing to make another sort of treaty, but they would not surrender the City to him'.

The following day, 6 April, Mehmet's artillery began bombarding the city, concentrating their fire on the stretch of walls between the Sixth and Seventh Hills, where the river Lycus flows into the city in a deep valley. By sunset that day the bombardment had damaged a section of the fortifications by the Gate of Charisius, on the Sixth Hill, and the following day a section of wall collapsed in ruins, but the defenders managed to repair it during the night. Mehmet decided to defer further bombardment until his entire artillery park was in place and ready, particularly the huge Urban, and in the interim he ordered his sappers to begin undermining the weaker section of walls in the Lycus valley, while his labour battalions began filling in the great fosse in front of the walls.

All Mehmet's artillery was in place by 11 April, when he ordered the bombardment of the city to resume, a barrage that was to continue without interruption for the remainder of the siege. The heaviest damage was done by Urban, which could be fired only seven times a day, but each one of its giant cannon balls smashed the curtain walls and towers that it struck, killing the defenders who manned them. Each night the defenders worked ceaselessly to repair the damage to the fortifications, joined by the townspeople, including women and children.

On 12 April Baltaoğlu led the largest ships in his fleet in an attack on the chain closing the Golden Horn, which was guarded by the Byzantine and Italian galleons, aided by a reserve force commanded by Grand Duke Notaras. Notaras and his men fought off the attackers in a furious battle at the mouth of the Golden Horn, and at the end of the day Baltaoğlu was forced to break off the assault and lead his fleet back to Diplokionion.

Early in the evening of 18 April Mehmet launched an infantry attack on the Mesoteichion. Giustiniani led the defence, which drove back the attackers after a hard-fought battle of four hours in which some 200 of Mehmet's soldiers were killed, without any Christian fatalities, according to Barbaro.

Two days later a flotilla of four Christian ships appeared in the Sea of Marmara, and Mehmet ordered Baltaoğlu to sail out with the Turkish fleet to intercept them. After an inconclusive battle the Christian ships eluded the Turkish force, and under the cover of night the Byzantine defenders opened the chain to let them into the Golden Horn. One of the ships was a Byzantine freighter loaded with grain, while the other three were Genoese vessels carrying soldiers, arms, ammunition and food supplies. Mehmet was furious, and ordered his executioner to behead Baltaoğlu. But the admiral's officers persuaded Mehmet to spare Baltaoğlu, who was stripped of his rank and possessions and, after being bastinadoed, left to spend the rest of his days as a pauper. He was replaced as admiral by Hamza Bey, one of Mehmet's inner circle.

Mehmet then set in motion an ingenious stratagem that he had devised to get his fleet into the Golden Horn. At the beginning of his siege he had ordered his engineers to build a road that led over the hills from the Bosphorus to the Golden Horn, passing behind the town of Galata. On 22 April Mehmet's engineers used teams of oxen to drag seventy-two ships on greased rollers up this road and then down to the shore of the Golden Horn at the Valley of the Springs (Kasımpaşa), where they were mounted with guns that had been stored there.

The defenders in Constantinople were shocked by the entry of the Turkish warships into the Golden Horn, which now exposed the northern side of the city to attack. Kritoboulos writes that the Greeks, seeing the Turkish fleet in the Golden Horn, 'were astounded at the impossibility of the spectacle, and were overcome by the greatest consternation and perplexity. They did not know what to do now, but were in despair.'

The Venetian leaders in Constantinople decided that they would try to set fire to the Turkish fleet in the Golden Horn in a night attack. Early in the morning of 28 April a small flotilla of Venetian ships under Giacomo Coco sailed out of the Neorion harbour, inside the chain on the Constantinople side of the Golden Horn, and headed upstream towards the anchorage of the Turkish fleet on the northern shore. Just as Coco was about to launch his attack the Turkish fleet opened fire and sank his ship, which went to the bottom with all hands aboard.

Another Venetian ship was also sunk, and when some of its crew swam ashore they were captured, after which they were beheaded on Mehmet's orders. The defenders in Constantinople retaliated by beheading 260 Turkish prisoners of war, both mass executions being carried out in full view of the enemy on opposite sides of the Golden Horn.

Mehmet had now drawn the net tighter, placing cannons on the hills above Galata to fire on the northern side of the city from across the Golden Horn, so that the city was besieged from two sides. Supplies were now dwindling in Constantinople, and in Barbaro's diary entry for 1–2 May he writes: 'The city was in great distress because of a growing lack of provisions, particularly of bread, wine and other things necessary to sustain life.'

Girolamo Minotto, the Venetian *bailo*, had written to the Senate in January 1453 urging them to send supplies to Constantinople immediately. The Senate voted on 19 February to send supplies, but two months elapsed before a relief flotilla left from Venice under the command of Admiral Alviso Longo. Longo's orders were to sail to the isle of Tenedos, just outside the

Dardanelles, and to remain there until 20 May, when he would be joined by another Venetian flotilla commanded by Giacomo Loredan, Captain-General of the Sea, after which they would proceed through the straits to Constantinople. Loredan did not leave Venice until 7 May, and in the end neither his flotilla nor that of Longo reached Constantinople; nor did another relief convoy sent by Pope Nicholas.

The Venetians in Constantinople, concerned about the delay, sent off a fast brigantine from the Golden Horn under the cover of night on 3 May, with orders to find the relief convoy from Venice and urge its commander to make haste.

Meanwhile, Mehmet launched a series of infantry assaults against the Theodosian walls. The first of them began on 7 May, 'at the fourth hour of the night', according to Barbaro, when a force that he estimated at 30,000 troops with battering rams attacked the stretch of walls by the Blachernae Palace, on the slope of the Sixth Hill leading down to the Golden Horn, only to be driven away by the defenders after a three-hour battle.

Five days later there was another night attack in the Blachernae area, this time by 50,000 troops, according to Barbaro, and once again the Turkish force was repelled. Mehmet then moved the cannons that he had placed on the hill above the northern shore of the Golden Horn and positioned them with the rest of his artillery park outside the Gate of St Romanus. The Turkish artillery then began a virtually continuous bombardment of the Mesoteichion, large sections of which were destroyed, with the townspeople working through the night to repair the damage.

On 16 May the main Turkish fleet in the Bosphorus sailed down to the Golden Horn, where they made a show of attacking but were stopped by the great chain. They made a similar demonstration the following day, and again on 21 May, each time with drums pounding and trumpets blaring as if to herald an attack, but each time they retired without firing a shot.

At the same time, Mehmet's sappers had been digging tunnels in an attempt to make their way under the defence walls. After one of these mines was discovered by the defenders on 16 May outside the Gate of the Caligari in the Blachernae area, Constantine put Grand Duke Notaras in change of countermeasures.

One of Giustiniani's officers, Johannes Grant, who had experience in mining, was assigned to work with Notaras, and during the next week they discovered four more mines outside the Gate of the Caligari, all of which they destroyed.

On 18 May Mehmet's engineers began constructing a huge siege tower outside the walls of the Mesoteichion, along with a roadway over the fosse. During the night the defenders crept out and blew up the tower, and at the same time they destroyed the roadway and half cleared the fosse. Other attempts by the Turks to erect siege towers elsewhere along the walls were thwarted in much the same way.

On 19 May Mehmet's engineers began building a pontoon bridge across the Golden Horn just outside the city. Floating gun platforms were attached to the pontoons, and Mehmet put cannons on them to bombard both the land and sea walls in the Blachernae area.

On 23 May a Venetian brigantine was spotted on the Sea of Marmara, and as it approached the city a squadron of Turkish warships went out to intercept it. The Venetian ship eluded them and made its way to the Golden Horn, where under the cover of night the defenders opened the chain to let it into the port. At first the defenders thought that it was the forerunner of a Christian fleet, but then they realised that it was the brigantine that had left Constantinople twenty days before to contact the Venetian flotilla bringing troops and supplies to the city. The captain reported to Constantine that he had searched in vain through the Greek archipelago, seeing no sign of the Venetian convoy nor hearing any word of its impending arrival. Constantine despaired when he heard the news, according to Barbaro, who writes that the emperor wept as he thanked the captain and his crew for their courage and devotion in returning to the doomed city, which he said could now only put its faith in Christ, the Virgin, and St Constantine the Great, founder of Constantinople.

The following day, according to Barbaro, 'the Turks made frenzied assaults with cannon-fire and gun-fire and countless arrows'. That night there was an eclipse of the moon, and many took this as an omen of doom. The clergy led the townspeople in making a last appeal to the Mother of God, and they walked in procession behind the sacred icon of the Virgin Hodegitria, the legendary protectress of the city. But the procession had to be abandoned when a thunderstorm was followed by hail and a torrential rain, and it seemed as if even the elements had turned against the 'God-guarded city' that had been a bastion of Christianity for more than 1,000 years.

Doukas reports that about this time Mehmet offered terms to Constantine. He promised to lift the siege if the emperor paid an annual tribute of 100,000 gold coins, another possible option being that the Greeks could have safe conduct to abandon the city and take with them all their movable possessions. In any event, nothing came of the negotiations, and Mehmet met with his council to decide on their next move. The grand vezir Halil Pasha demanded that the siege be abandoned, since they had made no headway despite seven weeks of constant effort, and he advised Mehmet to offer Constantine suitable terms so that they could withdraw before the Christian powers came to the aid of Byzantium.

Zaganos Pasha repudiated the grand vezir's arguments, and in the strongest terms he advised Mehmet to make an immediate attack on the city. This was exactly what Mehmet wanted to hear, and on 27 May he sent heralds around the Turkish camp to announce that a general assault on the city would be made in a few days' time. According to Archbishop Leonard of Chios, Halil Pasha, who was probably in the pay of the Byzantines, sent a message to Constantine telling him of Mehmet's decision, urging him to hold out for two or three days longer and 'not to be frightened by the follies of an intoxicated youth'. At dawn on 28 May Mehmet ordered his troops to take their assigned positions for the assault the following day, and some 2,000 ladders were brought up before the walls. Mehmet then rode to Diplokionion to give orders to the new admiral, Hamza Bey. He instructed him to sail his fleet down to the Golden Horn and station some of his ships outside the chain, while the rest would form a cordon around the Marmara shore of the city, thus diverting some of the defenders to guard the sea walls there.

As Mehmet rode back to the Golden Horn he stopped outside the upper gate of Galata, where he was met by the *podesta* and other officials of what the Genoese called the Magnificent Community of Pera. Mehmet said that they should maintain their neutrality, and he warned them that if they attempted to aid the Greeks in Constantinople the following day they would pay with their lives.

Later that day Mehmet rode along the whole line of the Theodosian walls, checking the positions of his troops and talking to his officers. He then summoned his generals to his tent and reviewed their assignments, saying, according to Kritoboulos, that he himself would be directing the main attack and would see what each of them did. The Greek chronicler Melissourgos, who wrote a continuation of the work of George Sphrantzes, says that Mehmet promised his officers and men that when they conquered Constantinople they would be free to sack the city for three days, which was in any event established Muslim practice.

Following the meeting with his commanders, according to Kritoboulos, Mehmet consulted with his gunners and the cavalry and infantry units of the royal guard, after which he rode round the camp to rally all his troops before retiring.

Meanwhile, the clergy and townspeople again formed a procession, holding aloft the icon of the Virgin Hodegitria and holy relics from all their churches, singing hymns as they walked through the city and out to the Theodosian walls. Doukas writes of the repeated cries of supplication that were heard throughout the city, as the townspeople implored Christ and the Virgin to save them from the Turks: 'Spare us, O Lord, from Thy just wrath and deliver us from the hands of the enemy!'

When the procession ended Constantine addressed his officers and the notables of the city, as well as the leaders of his Genoese and Venetian allies. Archbishop Leonard of Chios quotes Constantine's exhortation to those who were defending the city in its most desperate hour: 'Finally, my fellow soldiers, show obedience to your superiors in all things, and know that this is the day of your glory. If but a drop of your blood is shed, you will earn for yourselves the crown of martyrdom and everlasting renown.'

That evening everyone who was not on duty along the walls began congregating in Haghia Sophia, praying for the city's salvation. Melissourgos, writing as if he were George Sphrantzes, describes how Constantine prayed in Haghia Sophia and then stopped at the Palace of Blachernae, where he 'asked to be forgiven by all. Who can describe the wailing and tears that arose in the palace at that hour? No man, even if he were made of wood and stone, could have held back his tears.'

After leaving the palace, Constantine and Sphrantzes rode to the nearby Gate of the Caligaria. They dismounted there and Sphrantzes waited while Constantine ascended a tower beside the gateway, listening to the ominous sounds of the Turkish army preparing for the final assault. When Constantine returned he mounted his horse and said goodbye to Sphrantzes, who watched as the emperor rode off towards his command post on the Murus Bacchatureus, the section of the Mesoteichion by the Gate of St Romanus.

The Turkish engineering battalions had been working throughout the night filling in the fosse in front of the Theodosian walls along the Mesoteichion, where the main attack would be made. About two o'clock in the morning of Tuesday 29 May, Mehmet gave orders to begin the attack. The first assault was made by the *başıbozuks*, who charged with wild battle

41

cries to the din of drums and the skirl of bagpipes. The watchmen on the towers of the Theodosian walls heard the noise and sounded the alarm, and soon all the church bells within the city were rung to alert the populace. Meanwhile, the *başıbozuks* had made their way across the fosse and set up scaling ladders against the outer walls, some of them ascending to the battlements before they were cut down by the defenders. After two hours of intense fighting the *başıbozuks* were withdrawn, having worn down the defenders with their unrelenting attack.

Mehmet then launched the second wave, the regular Anatolian infantry under the command of Ishak Pasha and Mahmut Pasha, their charge accompanied by a heavy bombardment from the Turkish artillery. An hour before dawn a huge cannon ball fired by Urban made a direct hit on the outer wall of the Mesoteichion, creating a breach through which some of the Turkish infantry tried to make their way into the city. But they were quickly surrounded and slaughtered by the defenders, led by the emperor himself. This broke the brunt of the assault, forcing Ishak Pasha to withdraw his infantry.

Mehmet then brought on the janissaries, leading them himself as far as the fosse. There, according to Kritoboulos, he stood aside to urge them forward, shouting: 'Friends, we have the City! We have it! They are already fleeing from us! The wall is bare of defenders! It needs just a little more effort and the City is taken! Don't weaken, but on with the work with all your might, and be men and I am with you!'

The defenders fought with desperation, holding back the janissaries for an hour. But then, at daybreak, about 300 janissaries forced their way through the breach that Urban had made in the outer wall near the Gate of St Romanus, where both Constantine and Giustiniani had their command posts.

The janissaries had still not penetrated the inner wall, but then the tide of battle turned when Giustiniani suffered a severe wound and, despite Constantine's pleas that he remain at his post, he allowed himself to be carried to a Genoese ship in the harbour. Constantine tried to stem the tide as the janissaries now penetrated the inner wall, and when last seen he was at his command post on the Murus Bacchatureus, fighting valiantly alongside his faithful comrade John Dalmata and his kinsmen Theophilus Palaeologus and Don Francisco of Toledo.

The Turkish star and crescent was soon waving from the towers of the Theodosian walls and the Palace of Blachernae, as the Turkish troops now made their way through the inner wall, killing or capturing the defenders on the Theodosian walls and then fanning out through the city. The last pockets of resistance were mopped up before the morning was over, with many of the surviving Italians escaping aboard Venetian ships, leaving the Greeks to face their fate. Mehmet then turned loose his troops to sack the city for three days, as he had promised them. The Greek and Italian chroniclers write of how the Turkish soldiers killed those they did not enslave, and stripped Haghia Sophia and the other churches of their sacred relics and treasures, plundering the imperial palace and the houses of the rich. Kritoboulos says that nearly 4,000 were slain in the siege and its aftermath, and that more than 50,000 were enslaved, virtually the entire population of the city, which was stripped bare of everything that could be carried away by the looters.

Mehmet had given his soldiers permission to sack the city on condition that they did not destroy its public buildings, which now belonged to him. But from contemporary accounts it would appear that the Turkish forces did considerable damage to the city during their orgy of looting, enslavement, rape and massacre. Kritoboulos writes of Mehmet's reaction to the death and destruction he saw when he first entered the city he had conquered.

> After this the Sultan entered the City and looked about to see its great size, its situation, its grandeur and beauty, its teeming population, its loveliness, and the costliness of its churches and public buildings. When he saw what a large number had been killed, and the wreckage of the buildings, and the wholesale ruin and desolation of the City, he was filled with compassion and repented not a little at the destruction and plundering. Tears fell from his eyes as he groaned deeply and passionately: 'What a city have we given over to plunder and destruction.'

4 *Istanbul, Capital of the Ottoman Empire*

Sultan Mehmet II made his triumphal entry into the city late in the afternoon of the day he captured it, Tuesday 29 May 1453, passing through the Adrianople Gate, now known as Edirne Kapı. As he passed through the gate he was acclaimed by his troops as Fatih, or the Conqueror, the name by which he would thenceforth be known to the Turks. The city that he had conquered had been known to the Turks as Kostantiniye, but after the Conquest its name in common Turkish usage became Istanbul, a corruption of the Greek '*eis tin polin*', meaning 'in the city' or 'to the city'.

A plaque on the Edirne Gate records Fatih's triumphal entry, a scene described by the seventeenth-century Turkish traveller Evliya Çelebi in his *Seyahatname*, or *Narrative of Travels*: 'The sultan then having a pontifical turban on his head and sky-blue boots on his feet, mounted on a mule and bearing the sword of Muhammed in his hand, marched in at the head of seventy or eighty thousand Muslim heroes, crying out, "Halt not conquerors! God be praised! Ye are the conquerors of Constantinople!"'

Mehmet rode into the city along the Roman thoroughfare known as the Mese, or Middle Way, which took him from the Sixth Hill to the First Hill, the ancient acropolis of Byzantium. This brought him to Haghia Sophia, the Great Church of the Divine Wisdom. The townspeople of Constantinople had filled the church the night before, praying for divine deliverance that never came, and when the Turkish soldiers broke in that morning they enslaved those of the congregation they did not slaughter.

Before Mehmet entered the building he dismounted and fell to his knees, pouring a handful of earth over his turban in a gesture of humility, since Haghia Sophia was as revered in Islam as it was in Christianity. He then surveyed the church and ordered that it be immediately converted to Islamic worship under the name of Aya Sofya Camii Kabir, the Great Mosque of Haghia Sophia. This required the erection of a wooden minaret for the *müezzin* to give the call to prayer, and also some internal constructions, including the *mimber*, or pulpit for the *imam* who directed the Muslim prayers, and the *mihrab*, the niche that indicates the *kıble*, the direction of Mecca. This done, Mehmet attended the first noon prayer in the mosque that Friday, 1 June 1453, accompanied by his two chief clerics, Akşemsettin and Karaşemsettin. Evliya Çelebi describes the scene:

> On the following Friday the faithful were summoned to prayer by the *müezzins*, who proclaimed with a loud voice this text of the Koran: 'Verily God and his angels bless the Prophet.' Akşemsettin and Karaşemsettin then arose, and placing themselves on each side of the sultan, supported him under his arms; the former placed his own turban on the head of the Conqueror, fixing in it the black and white feather of a crane, and putting into his hand a naked sword. Thus conducted to the *mimber* he ascended it, and cried out with a voice as loud as David's, 'Praise be to God, the Lord of all the world,' on which the victorious Muslims lifted up their hands and uttered a shout of joy.

After Mehmet's first visit to Haghia Sophia he also inspected the remains of the Great Palace of Byzantium on the Marmara slope of the First Hill. Mehmet was deeply saddened by the noble ruins, and those who were with him heard him recite a melancholy distich by the Persian poet Saadi: 'The spider is the curtain-holder in the Palace of the Caesars/The owl hoots its night-call on the Towers of Afrasiab.'

Mehmet tried to find out what had happened to Constantine, but the emperor's body was never found, and there were conflicting reports about the circumstances of his death. There are two variant Greek traditions about the place of Constantine's burial, but both of these date from long after the Conquest and may be apocryphal. One is that he was laid to rest in a Greek church in the district of Vefa, on the slope of the Third Hill leading down to the Golden Horn. This church is still in the hands of the Greeks, and there are those who continue to believe that Constantine is buried there in an unmarked grave. The other tradition is that he is buried in the former church of St Theodosia, now known as Gül Camii, the Mosque of the Rose, near the shore of the Golden Horn below the Fifth Hill. The name of the mosque stems from a tradition dating back to the Conquest. The feast of St Theodosia falls on 29 May, the day that the city fell to the Turks, and the church was decorated with bouquets of roses. When the Turkish soldiers burst into the church the sight of these bouquets led them to call it the Mosque of the Rose when it was subsequently converted to a house of Islamic worship. There is an ancient tomb in the pier to the right of the nave, and it is there that some believe Constantine to be buried.

Immediately after seeing Haghia Sophia and the Great Palace Mehmet returned to his headquarters outside the Gate of St Romanus. There he divided up the booty and captives taken in the conquest of the city, first taking his own share, which included Grand Duke Notaras and his family. According to Kritoboulos, 'Among these was Notaras himself, a man among the most able and notable in knowledge, wealth, virtue and political power. The Sultan honoured him with a personal interview, spoke soothing words to him, and filled him with hope, and not only him but the rest who were with him.'

Mehmet showed no such mercy to his Latin captives, executing those for whom sufficient ransom was not paid. According to Barbaro, who himself escaped, 'Twenty-nine nobles of Venice who were taken prisoner by the Turks returned to Venice within the space of a year, after having paid ransoms of two thousand, or one thousand, or eight hundred ducats.' Among those executed was the Venetian *bailo* Girolamo Minotto, who was beheaded along with one of his sons and seven of his compatriots. The Catalan consul, Péré Julia, was executed along with half a dozen of his companions. Archbishop Leonard of Chios was captured but not recognised, and was soon ransomed by a Genoese merchant from Galata. Cardinal Isidore of Kiev abandoned his robes and gave them to a beggar in exchange for his rags. The beggar was captured and executed, his head displayed as the cardinal's, while Isidore was ransomed for a pittance by a Genoese merchant from Galata. The Turkish pretender, Prince Orhan, tried to escape by disguising himself as a Greek monk, but he was betrayed by another prisoner and beheaded.

According to Kritoboulos, Mehmet originally 'contemplated making Notaras the commandant of the city, and putting him in charge of its repopulation'. But some of his vezirs warned him not to trust the grand duke or any of the other Greek notables whose lives he had spared. Five days after the conquest, as a test of the grand duke's loyalty, Mehmet demanded that Notaras give up his twelve-year-old son Isaac to serve in the imperial household. Notaras refused, whereupon Mehmet had him and his son beheaded, and the following day nine other prominent Greeks were also executed.

George Sphrantzes survived the fall of the city, and after being held prisoner for eighteen months he and his wife were ransomed and made their way to Mistra, but their young son and daughter were taken into Mehmet's household. Sphrantzes writes that his son John was executed by Mehmet in December 1453, 'on the grounds that the child had conspired to murder him', and that in September 1455 'my beautiful daughter Thamar died of an infectious disease in the sultan's seraglio'.

Some of the younger males of the Byzantine aristocracy survived the siege and were taken by Mehmet into his household. Kritoboulos writes that Mehmet 'appointed some of the youths of high family, whom he had chosen according to their merits, to be in his bodyguard and to be constantly near him, and others to other service as his pages'. These captives included two sons of Thomas Palaeologus, brother of the late emperor Constantine XI, who came to be known as Hass Murat Pasha and Mesih Pasha. Hass Murat was a particular favourite of Mehmet, probably his lover, and eventually was appointed *beylerbey* of Rumelia. Mesih also rose to high rank in Mehmet's service, and during the reign of the Conqueror's son and successor Beyazit II he thrice served as grand vezir. Other Christian converts who rose to high rank in Mehmet's service include four who served him as grand vezir: Zaganos Pasha, Mahmut Pasha, Rum (Greek) Mehmet Pasha and Gedik Ahmet Pasha.

Kritoboulos of Imbros, Mehmet's Greek biographer, became acquainted with the sultan soon after the Conquest. He played an important part in the peaceful surrender of his native island to Mehmet, who appointed him governor of Imbros, in the Aegean just north of the Dardanelles. Kritoboulos also arranged for the surrender of the nearby islands of Thasos and Lemnos.

George Scholarios, the leader of the anti-unionist party, was in his cell at the Pantocrator monastery on the Fourth Hill when the city fell. He was taken prisoner along with the other monks and was bought by a Turkish notable in Edirne, who treated him with due courtesy when he realised that his slave was a renowned churchman. Mehmet learned of the capture of Scholarios and had him escorted back to Istanbul, where he was treated with great honour.

The Genoese in Galata had opened their gates to the Turkish forces on the same day that Constantinople fell, and since they had surrendered without a struggle the town was not sacked. Mehmet granted a *firman*, or imperial decree, to the Genoese *podesta*, Angelo Lomellino, giving the Magnificent Community of Pera the rights to regulate their own internal affairs and to keep their homes and businesses, allowing them to retain their churches but not to build new ones, and exempting them from the *devşirme*, the levy of youths for the sultan's service, so long as they obeyed the sultan's laws and paid the *haraç*, or poll tax imposed on all non-Muslims. The *firman* also noted 'that no *doghandji* or *kul*, Sultan's men, will come and stay as guests in their houses; that the inhabitants of the fortress as well as the merchants be free of all kinds of forced labor', Mehmet forced the Genoese to tear down some of their fortifications, as well as the Byzantine castle on the Golden Horn to which one end of the chain had been attached. The main bastion of the Genoese fortifications, the huge Tower of Galata on the hill above the town, remained standing, but Mehmet garrisoned it with janissaries and made it the headquarters of the *subaşı* and *kadı*, the Ottoman officials who had responsibility for the security of Galata and the administration of the sultan's laws.

Lomellino wrote to his brother on 23 June 1453 describing the fall of Constantinople, and in conclusion warning of the imperial ambitions of Sultan Mehmet. Writing of Mehmet, he says, 'In sum, he has become so insolent after the capture of Constantinople that he sees himself soon becoming master of the whole world, and swears publicly that before two years have passed he intends to reach Rome; and... unless the Christians take action quickly, he is likely to do things that will fill them with amazement.'

News of the fall of Constantinople first reached the West on 9 June 1453, when a Cretan ship that had escaped from the city docked at Candia (Herakleion), the Venetian capital of Crete. A monk from the mountains of central Crete brought the sad news back to his brethren at the monastery of Angarathos, where one of them recorded it in their archives. 'Nothing worse than this has happened, nor will happen' he noted, writing that he was praying to God to deliver his island from the Turks.

The news reached Venice on 29 June on a ship from Corfu, and on the following day the Senate wrote to inform Pope Nicholas V 'of the horrible and most deplorable fall of the cities of Constantinople and Pera'. The pope, who received the news on 8 July, referred to the fall of Constantinople as the 'shame of Christendom'. The news reached England in a papal letter, which Thomas Gascoigne, chancellor of Oxford University, recorded in his *Chronicles of London*, writing: 'Also in this yere...was the Cite of Constantyn the noble lost by Cristen men, and wonne by the Prynce of Turkes named Mahumet.' A Georgian chronicle recorded: 'On the day when the Turks took Constantinople the sun was darkened.'

Three weeks after the Conquest Mehmet left Istanbul for Edirne. According to Tursun Beg, before leaving for Edirne, Mehmet announced 'to his vezirs and his commanders and his officers that henceforth his capital was to be Istanbul'. At the same time Mehmet appointed Karıştıran Süleyman Bey as prefect of Istanbul.

Kritoboulos describes Süleyman Bey as 'a most intelligent and useful man, possessed of the finest manners', and he writes that Mehmet 'put him in charge of everything, but in particular over the repopulating of the City, and instructed him to be very zealous about this matter'.

Mehmet then spent the summer in Edirne Sarayı, which he had expanded and embellished the year before the Conquest. One of Mehmet's first orders of business at Edirne Sarayı was to deal with the grand vezir Çandarlı Halil Pasha, who had been undermining him since he first came to the throne, and whom he had suspected of being in the pay of the Byzantines. According to Archbishop Leonard of Chios, before Grand Duke Notaras was executed he told Mehmet that Halil 'had often sent letters to the Emperor, had dissuaded him from making peace, and had persuaded him to stand firm'. This enraged Mehmet, and 'he ordered that Halil should be bound and imprisoned and stripped of all his wealth and property; and after this he gave orders that he should be removed to Edirne and deprived of his life'. Mehmet then appointed Zaganos Pasha as grand vezir, ending the virtual monopoly that the powerful Çandarlı family had held on that office.

During the summer of 1453 a succession of foreign ambassadors came to call on Mehmet at Edirne Sarayı, including envoys from the Venetians, Genoese, Serbs, Albanians, Greeks, Egyptians, Persians, Karamanid Türkmen, and the Knights of St John from Rhodes, all of them seeking friendly relations with the young conqueror, who imposed tribute on those who recognised his suzerainty. George Branković, Despot of Serbia, was to pay him 12,000 ducats annually; Demetrius and Thomas Palaeologus, Despots of the Morea, were levied 10,000; the Genoese administration of Chios 6,000; Dorino Gattilusio, the Genoese lord of Lesbos and other northern Aegean isles, 3,000; and John IV Comnenus, the Byzantine emperor of Trebizond, 2,000. The Knights of St John refused to pay tribute, saying that they could only do so with permission from the pope. Mehmet did not press the point, for his naval forces were not strong enough for him to impose his will on Rhodes, whose capital was the most heavily fortified on the Aegean isles.

When Mehmet returned from Edirne to Istanbul, his first concern was to repopulate the city. According to Kritoboulos, 'He sent an order in the form of an imperial command to every part of his realm, that as many inhabitants as possible be transferred to the City, not only Christians but also his own people and many of the Hebrews... He gathered them there from all parts of Asia and Europe, and he transferred them with all possible care and speed, people of all nations, but more especially Christians.'

Mehmet also resettled in the city all the Greek prisoners who had been part of his share of the spoils. Kritoboulos writes that he gave them land and houses 'along the shores of the city harbor', and 'freed them from taxes for a specified time'. He notes further that Mehmet 'commanded also that the Roman prisoners should work, and should receive a daily wage of six aspers or more', which was about the same as the enlisted men of the janissaries were paid. He goes on to say: 'This was in a way a piece of wise foresight on the part of the Sultan, for it fed the prisoners and enabled them to provide for their own ransom by earning enough to pay their masters thus. Also, when they should become free, they might dwell in the City.'

The non-Muslims among the new settlers were grouped into *millets*, or 'nations', according to their religion. Thus the Greek *millet* was headed by the Orthodox patriarch, the Armenian by the Gregorian patriarch and the Jewish by the chief rabbi. The authority granted to the head of each *millet* extended not only to religious matters but also to most legal questions other than criminal cases, which were always tried before the sultan's judges. The *millet* system instituted by Mehmet was continued by his successors right down to the end of the Ottoman Empire, forming the core of its multi-ethnic character.

The first Armenian patriarch after the Conquest was Havakim, whose patriarchate was at the church of the Virgin Peribleptos on the Seventh Hill. The first chief rabbi was Moses Kapsali, whose headquarters were in Balat, on the shore of the Golden Horn below the Fifth Hill, an area that had been the principal Jewish quarter since late Byzantine times.

There was no Greek Orthodox patriarch of Constantinople at the time of the Conquest, for the last to hold that position before the siege, Gregory

III Mammas, abandoned the city in August 1451 and fled to Rome, never to return.

Thus it was that Mehmet decided to choose a new patriarch to head the Greek *millet*, as Melissourgos writes: 'He issued orders for the election of a patriarch, according to custom and protocol... The high clerics who happened to be present, and the very few members of the church and the lay population designated the scholar George Scholarios, and elected him patriarch under the name Gennadios.'

Gennadios took office on 6 January 1454, when he was consecrated by the metropolitan of Heracleia on the Black Sea. Before the ceremony Mehmet received Gennadios and invited him to share his meal, after which he presented him with a silver sceptre and a palfrey from the royal stables. Mehmet then personally escorted Gennadios in the first stage of his procession to the church of the Holy Apostles on the Fourth Hill, which had been assigned to the new patriarch as his headquarters. The sultan later issued a *firman* that guaranteed to Gennadios 'that no one should vex or disturb him; that unmolested, untaxed, and unoppressed by an adversary, he should, with all the bishops under him, be exempted from taxes for all time'.

Gennadios found that the church of the Holy Apostles was not a suitable location for the patriarchate, and so he received permission from Mehmet to move to the church of the Virgin Pammakaristos on the Fifth Hill. Mehmet made three visits to the Pammakaristos to call on Gennadios, and in their conversations, through an interpreter, they ranged widely over questions of Christian theology. Gennadios wrote a summary of his theological beliefs and had it translated into Turkish for Mehmet's private study.

The sultan's contacts with Gennadios give rise to rumours that he was inclined towards Christian beliefs. Mehmet had always been interested in Christianity, perhaps because of his mother, who may have been Greek, but would have converted to Islam when she entered the harem of Murat II. Mehmet's favourite wife, Gülbahar, mother of the future Beyazit II, was probably also Greek, and tradition has it that she never converted to Islam.

Teodoro Spandugnino, an Italian who lived in Galata, claims that Mehmet took to worshipping Christian relics and always kept candles burning in front of them. Another story about Mehmet's attraction towards Christianity is reported by Brother George of Mühlenbach, who spent the years 1438–58 as a Turkish prisoner. As he writes in his *Treatise on the customs, conditions and inequity of the Turks*: 'The Franciscan brothers living in Pera have assured me that he [Mehmet] came to their church and sat down in the choir to attend the ceremonies and the sacrifice of the Mass. To satisfy his curiosity, they ordered him an unconsecrated wafer at the elevation of the host, for pearls must not be cast before swine.'

Mehmet's interest in Christianity appears to have been superficial, for he seems to have been basically irreligious, and in his observance of Islam he merely observed the forms of the Muslim faith, as was necessary for him as head of state. Giovanni-Maria Angiolello, an Italian captive in the Ottoman service, writes that Prince Beyazit was heard to say that 'his father was domineering and did not believe in the Prophet Mohammed'.

The Ottomans were orthodox Muslims, as opposed to what they condemned as the heterodox doctrine of the Persian Shiites. Mehmet had shown a leaning towards Shiite beliefs since his first brief sultanate in Edirne, when the Persian dervish he tried to protect was burned at the stake. Mehmet was also very interested in Persian literature, particularly the poetry of the Sufi mystics. This was taken as further evidence of his heterodoxy, since an old Ottoman proverb says: 'A man who reads Persian loses half his religion.'

The Ottoman court in Mehmet's time was still simple in its customs, free of the ostentation and elaborate ceremonies surrounding the sultan that would develop in later times, as Brother George of Mühlenbach observes.

I saw the ruler, followed only by two young men, on his way to the mosque far away from his palace. I saw him going to the baths in the same way. When he returned from the mosque to his palace, no one would have dared to join his followers, no one would have made bold to approach him and to cheer him as is done in our country, to burst into the cry 'Long live the king,' or other such applause as is customary with us. I have seen the sultan at prayer in the mosque. He sat neither in a chair or on a throne, but like the others had taken his place on a carpet spread out on the floor. Around him no decoration had been placed, hung, or spread out. On his clothing or on his horse the sultan had no special mark to distinguish him. I watched him at his mother's funeral, and if he had not been pointed out to me, I would not have recognized him. It is strictly forbidden to accompany him or to approach him without having received express permission. I pass over many particulars that have been related to me about his affability in conversation. In his judgments he shows maturity and indulgence. He is generous in giving alms and benevolent in all his actions.

Mehmet began the reconstruction of his new capital in the summer of 1453, when he issued orders for the repair of the Theodosian walls and the other fortifications damaged in the siege. Since both the Great Palace of Byzantium and the Blachernae Palace were in ruins, Mehmet began construction of a new imperial residence on the Third Hill, on a site described by Kritoboulos as 'the finest and best location in the centre of the City'. This came to be known as Eski Saray, the Old Palace, because a few years later Mehmet decided to build a new palace on the First Hill, the famous Topkapı Sarayı.

Kritoboulos, in writing of Eski Saray, also notes that Mehmet at the same time 'ordered the construction of a strong fortress near the Golden Gate' in the south-western corner of the city, a monument that came to be called Yedikule, the Castle of the Seven Towers. Then, at the beginning of his chronicle for the year 1456, Kritoboulos reports the sultan's satisfaction at the completion of Eski Saray and Yedikule, as well as his initiation of new construction projects, most notably the great marketplace known as Kapalı Çarşı, or the Covered Bazaar.

Five years after the Conquest, Mehmet built a large mosque complex outside the city walls on the upper reaches of the Golden Horn. The mosque was dedicated to Eba Eyüp Ensari, friend and standard-bearer of the Prophet Mohammed. Eyüp is said to have been among the leaders of the first Arab siege of Constantinople in 674–8, during which, according to Islamic tradition, he was killed and buried outside the walls of Constantinople. During the siege of the city in 1453 Mehmet launched a search for Eyüp's grave, which was miraculously discovered by Akşemsettin, his *seyhülislam*, or chief cleric, a fabulous story told by Evliya Çelebi.

Mehmet II having laid siege to Constantinople was, with seventy saintly companions, seven whole days searching for Eyüp's tomb. At last Akşemsettin exclaimed, 'Good news, my prince, of Eyüp's tomb'; thus saying he began to pray and then fell asleep. Some interpreted this sleep as a veil cast by shame over his ignorance of the tomb, but after some time he raised his head, his eyes became bloodshot, the sweat ran from his forehead, and he said to the Sultan, 'Eyüp's tomb is on the very spot where I spread the carpet for prayer.' Upon this three of his attendants together with the Şeyh and the Sultan began to dig up the ground, when at a depth of three yards they found a square stone of verd antique on which was written in Cufic letters: 'This is the tomb of Eba Eyüp.' They lifted the stone and found below it the body of Eyüp wrapt up in a saffron-coloured shroud, with a brazen play-ball in his hand, fresh and well preserved. They replaced the stone, formed a little mound of the earth they had dug up, and laid the foundation of the mausoleum amidst the prayers of the whole army. The tomb, the mosque, the *medrese*, the caravansarai, the public bath, the refectory, and the market were built by Mehmet II, and his successors added some improvements to its splendour, so that Eyüp's funeral monument now resembles a kiosk of Paradise.

That following year, according to Kritoboulos, Sultan Mehmet issued a 'command...to all able persons to build splendid and costly buildings inside the City', Kritoboulos goes on to say that Mehmet 'also commanded them to build baths and inns and marketplaces, and very many and beautiful workshops, to erect places of worship, and to adorn and embellish the City with many other such buildings, sparing no expense, as each man had the means and ability'.

Mehmet himself led the way by selecting a site on the Fourth Hill, where a decade after the Conquest he began building an enormous complex known as Fatih Camii, the Mosque of the Conqueror. The ancient church of the Holy Apostles occupied a large part of the site, and so Mehmet had it demolished to make way for his new mosque complex. Kritoboulos also notes Mehmet's orders to build a new palace on the First Hill, the pleasure dome that would come to be known as Topkapı Sarayı.

Kritoboulos goes on to write that Mehmet also ordered his notables 'to construct many very fine arsenals to shelter the ships and their furnishings, and to build very strong, large buildings for the storing of arms, cannon, and other such supplies'. The naval arsenal, known as the Tersane, was on the Golden Horn, while the armoury, called Tophane, was on the Bosphorus, both of them just outside the walls of Galata on those sides.

A number of Mehmet's vezirs also erected mosque complexes in Istanbul. The earliest of these is Mahmut Pasha Camii. This mosque complex was built on the Second Hill in 1462 by Mahmut Pasha, who succeeded Zaganos Pasha as grand vezir three years after the Conquest. Kritoboulos writes in praise of Mahmut Pasha, who by all accounts was the greatest of all of the Conqueror's grand vezirs and one of the best who ever held that post in the Ottoman Empire. 'This man had so fine a nature that he outshone not only all his contemporaries but also his predecessors in wisdom, bravery, virtue, and other good qualities. He was...a man of better character than them all, as shown by his accomplishments.'

The mosques and other structures built by Mehmet and his vezirs marked the first phase of the transition in which Greek Constantinople, capital of the Byzantine Empire, became Turkish Istanbul, capital of the Ottoman Empire. One can see this transition in the famous Buondelmonti maps, the earliest of which is dated 1420 and the latest 1480. The city looks essentially the same in these two maps, but in the later one we can see the castles of Rumeli Hisarı and Yedikule, the Mosques of the Conqueror and Mahmut Pasha, the palaces of Eski Saray and Topkapı Sarayı, the Covered Bazaar, the naval arsenal on the Golden Horn, the cannon foundry on the Bosphorus, and even the minaret on what was now the Great Mosque of Haghia Sophia, which in itself symbolises the transition from Byzantine Constantinople to Ottoman Istanbul.

5   *Europe in Terror*

When news of the fall of Constantinople reached western Europe there was general consternation, and it was reported that Mehmet was assembling a huge army and fleet to attack Sicily and Italy. Cardinal Bessarion's letter to the Doge of Venice after the fall of Constantinople catches the sense of terror in Europe caused by the Turkish onslaught: 'A city which was so flourishing...the splendour and glory of the East...the refuge of all good things, has been captured, despoiled, ravaged and completely sacked by the most inhuman barbarians...by the fiercest of wild beasts... Much danger threatens Italy, not to mention other lands, if the violent assaults of the most ferocious barbarians are not checked.'

Frederick III, the Holy Roman Emperor, broke down in tears when he heard the news and shut himself away in his quarters to pray and meditate. His adviser, Bishop Aeneas Silvio Piccolomini, the future Pope Pius II, convinced him that he should take direct action and lead a holy war against the Turks. Aeneas wrote to Pope Nicholas V with this same proposal on 12 July 1453, pointing out the terrible threat posed by the Grand Turk, and urging him to call for a crusade:

> Here we have horrible news of the fall of Constantinople – if only it were false... Now we see one of the two lights of Christendom extinguished. We behold the seat of eastern empire overthrown, all the Glory that was Greece blotted out ... Now Mohammed reigns among us. Now the Turk hangs over our very head. The Black Sea is closed to us, the Don has become inaccessible. Now the Vlachs must obey the Turk. Next his sword

will reach the Hungarians and then the Germans. In the meantime we are beset by internecine strife... Let them make a peace or a truce with their fellow Christians, and with joined forces take up arms against the enemies of salvations.

The Pope issued a bull calling for a crusade, condemning Mehmet as the 'son of Satan, perdition and death'. But disunity among the Christian rulers kept them from taking action, and when Pope Nicholas died on 24 March 1455 the crusade was abandoned, at least for the time being.

Nicholas was succeeded by the Catalan Alfonso Borgia, who on 20 April 1455 became Pope Calixtus III. On the eve of his coronation Calixtus wrote to the young King Ladislas Posthumus of Bohemia and Hungary, declaring his dedication to a crusade against the Turks, 'even to the shedding of his own blood', so 'that those most hideous enemies of the Christian name should be entirely expelled not only from the city of Constantinople, which they have recently occupied, but also from the confines of Europe'. The Hungarian leaders wrote back to Calixtus from Buda on 21 July, saying: 'How very much indeed the pitiable condition of Christians now has need of your Holiness's protection.'

The Venetian Republic was the Christian state most directly involved with the Ottomans, for its maritime empire included commercial concessions in Istanbul as well as possessions in Greece, Albania and the Aegean that were threatened by the Turks. In July 1453 the Senate decided to fortify Negroponte, Greek Chalkis, the town that they controlled on the narrow strait between the Greek mainland and the Aegean island of Euboea. The Venetian fleet under Giacomo Loredan, who had failed to come to the aid of Constantinople, remained on duty in the Aegean, and late in July he captured seventeen Turkish light galleys. The Senate congratulated Loredan on his action, and the following month they voted funds for the construction of fifty new galleys for his fleet.

On 17 July 1453 the Senate sent Bartolomeo Marcello as an envoy to Istanbul, instructing him to negotiate with Mehmet a renewal of the treaty that Venice had signed with Murat II on 10 September 1451. While the negotiations were under way the Peace of Lodi on 9 April 1454 ended war between Venice and Milan. Freed from the enormous expense of the Italian war, the Senate was better able to negotiate with Mehmet, and on 18 April Marcello concluded a treaty with the sultan. This treaty, which reaffirmed the terms of the 1451 pact, gave the Venetians protection for their property and commerce in the Ottoman Empire and free access to Istanbul and other Turkish ports, Mehmet promising that 'they shall be safe on the sea and on the land as was customary before, in the time of my father'. Another term of the treaty gave the Venetians the right to have a commercial colony in Istanbul headed by a *bailo*, and Marcello was appointed to the post.

One of the Venetian emissaries, Giacomo de' Languschi, gives a detailed description of Mehmet, adding four years to his age.

> The sovereign, the Grand Turk Mehmed Bey, is a young man of twenty-six years of age, well formed and of a stature rather above the average. He is skilled in the use of weapons. His appearance inspires fear rather than respect. He laughs rarely, is cautious in his judgements, and is endowed with great generosity. He shows great tenacity in all his undertakings, and bravery under all conditions. He aspires to equal the glory of Alexander the Great, and every day has histories of Rome and other nations read to him... There is nothing which he studies with greater pleasure and eagerness than the geography of the world, and the art of warfare; he burns with the desire to rule, while being prudent in his investigation of what he undertakes. Such is the man, and so made, with whom we Christians have to deal.

Languschi goes on to write of Mehmet's desire to put the entire world under his rule, reversing the eastward march of conquest of Western rulers such as Alexander the Great, an imperial ambition for which he seemed perfectly suited by nature.

> He is a man continually watchful, able to endure weariness, heat and cold, thirst and hunger, inexorably set upon the destruction of Christians, and would admit to fearing no man. He...says the Caesar and Hannibal were of no account compared with himself, and that Alexander...entered Asia with a far smaller force than his. Now he says, times have changed, and he will march from the East to the West, as the West once marched against the East; now there must be only one empire in the world, one faith for all, and one kingdom. There is no place anywhere for such a union than Constantinople, and with the help of this city, he can make the Christians his subjects. He is not a man given to lustful desires, and of sober habits, not wishing to hear of any drunkenness at the time of Rhamadan. He is not enslaved by any pleasures or delights, but only by the love of glory.

After establishing his capital in Istanbul, Mehmet launched a campaign into Serbia in the spring of 1454, his objective being to reclaim the territory his father had returned to the despot George Brancović by the Treaty of Edirne in 1444.

Mehmet and Ishak Pasha captured two Serbian fortresses, but they were forced to abandon their conquests when John Hunyadi appeared with a Hungarian army. Mehmet launched another campaign into Serbia the following year, when he captured the town of Novo Brdo, noted for its gold and silver mines. Among those captured by the Turks was a young Serb named Constantine Mihailović, who was enrolled in the janissaries and later wrote a memoir of his experiences, including his capture at Novo Brdo.

All those among the men who were the most important and distinguished he [Mehmet] ordered decapitated. The remainder he ordered released to the city. As for their possessions, nothing of theirs was harmed. The boys were 320 in number and the females 74. The females he distributed among the heathens [Turks], but he took the boys for himself into the Janissaries, and sent them beyond the sea to Anatolia, where their preserve is. I was also taken in that city with my two brothers...

The sixteenth-century chronicler Mustafa Ali notes that, on the sultan's return from campaign in 1454, 'Mehmet spent many nights in debauchery with lovely-eyed, fairylike slave girls, and his days drinking with pages who looked like angels. But he was only seemingly engaged in debauchery and wantonness, in reality he was working, guided by the love of justice, to relieve the oppression of his subjects in the land.'

During the years 1454–5 Mehmet also sent his navy into the Aegean under the command of Hamza Bey, who attacked the islands of Nisyros, Kalymnos, Kos and Chios. One of the Turkish galleys was sunk at Chios, which led Mehmet to dismiss Hamza Bey and replace him with Yunus Bey. At the beginning of November 1455 Yunus captured the Genoese colony of Nea Phokaia on the Aegean coast of Asia Minor north of Izmir. Six weeks later another Turkish force seized the Genoese colony at Palaeo Phokaia, a short way to the south of Nea Phokaia. This gave Mehmet control of the lucrative alum mines that the Genoese had developed through the two Phokaias, their principal commercial colonies on the Aegean coast Asia Minor, now permanently lost to them.

The two ports and the mines had been the property of Dorino II Gattilusio, the Genoese lord of Lesbos and the islands of Samothrace and Imbros as well as the port of Enez (Aenos) north of the Gallipoli peninsula. Early in 1456 Mehmet himself led a force of janissaries against Enez, which surrendered without a struggle, while at the same time Yunus Bey captured the islands of Imbros and Samothrace, where he took Dorino Gattilusio prisoner. Gattilusio was forced to give up all his possessions to Mehmet, who in compensation gave him a small fief in Macedonia. Mehmet then appointed Kritoboulos, his biographer, to be the Ottoman governor of his native Imbros.

Mehmet spent the winter of 1455–6 preparing a major campaign against Serbia and Hungary, which he regarded as his major enemies in Europe now that he had made peace with Venice. His major objective in this campaign was Belgrade, the great fortress city at the confluence of the Danube and the Sava, for its capture would open the way to Buda, the capital of Hungary. Mehmet's plan was to send his fleet up the Danube to meet his army when he began the siege of Belgrade.

Meanwhile, Pope Calixtus had renewed his predecessor's call for a crusade against the Turks, setting 1 March 1456 as the date for the departure of 'all the Christian princes and peoples' for the holy war. A great diet convened at Buda on 6 February 1456, when the Franciscan monk Fra Giovanni da Capistrano presented the Pope's appeal for a crusade, with King Ladislas in attendance. On 6 April the assembly finally decided that they would march against the Turks, but on the following day a messenger arrived with word that Mehmet's army was already marching north towards the Danube.

John Hunyadi, who had served as regent of King Ladislas Posthumus in 1452, though still considered by the Hungarians as their true leader, commanded the defence of Belgrade, which began on 14 July 1456 with a terrific bombardment by the Turkish artillery. A week later Mehmet ordered in his janissaries, who penetrated the defences and made their way into the city, only to be virtually annihilated there by the defenders. Fra Capistrano then led a force of some 2,000 defenders out of the city to charge the surrounding Turks, whom they routed after a furious five-hour battle in which Mehmet himself was wounded in his left thigh by a javelin. The following day Mehmet lifted the siege, abandoning his artillery as he hurriedly withdrew his forces and began the long march back to Edirne.

News of the Christian victory at Belgrade reached Rome on 6 August, sparking a celebration that echoed throughout western Europe as word spread through the Christian world that the Grand Turk had at last met his match. The two heroes of the siege died not long afterwards, Hunyadi succumbing to the plague on 11 August and Fra Capistrano dying on 23 October, supposedly of exhaustion.

Meanwhile, a new pretender to the Ottoman throne appeared in Rome early in 1456, when an eight-year-old boy named Beyazit Osman was brought to the Vatican by an Italian from Istanbul, Giovanni Torcello. Torcello claimed that the boy, who had been born in 1448, was the son of Sultan Murat II, and thus a half-brother of Mehmet. When Mehmet became sultan the boy was smuggled out of Edirne Sarayı so that he would not be killed like Küçük Ahmet, after which he was taken to Istanbul and raised by Torcello – or so he said. After the capture of Constantinople Torcello and the boy were sold as slaves, and eventually they were redeemed by Pope Calixtus, who had been convinced that 'Beyazit Osman' was in fact a son of Murat II. The boy was baptised in Rome on 8 March 1456, taking the name Calixtus Ottomanus, becoming a ward of the Pope, who thought to use him as a pretender to the Ottoman throne in a crusade against the Turks.

After his retreat from Belgrade, Mehmet spent a year at Edirne Sarayı, recovering from his wound and rebuilding his shattered army. The following spring he sent messengers throughout his empire and abroad to announce the coming circumcision of his two sons Beyazit and Mustafa, the invited guests including the Doge of Venice, Francesco Foscari, who sent his regrets.

The circumcision feast is described by the Turkish chronicler Aşıkpaşazade, who writes that for four days there were continuous festivities at Edirne Sarayı, on its island in the river Tunca. The island was covered with the tents of the notables who had come from all over the empire and beyond at the sultan's bidding. Mehmet sat enthroned in his imperial tent at the centre of the assemblage, flanked by four distinguished clerics. On the first day there were readings from the Kuran that were commented upon by the scholars present, followed by the recitation of poems composed for the occasion by the court poets. The scholars and poets were rewarded with gifts of money and robes of honour, after which everyone sat down to an abundant feast. The next day the poor of Edirne were lavishly entertained, and on the following day there was a feast for the nobles of the empire and honoured guests, with a display of martial exercises, horse races and an archery contest. Then on the final day the dignitaries presented gifts to the sultan, after which he cast handfuls of coins among the poor of the city. Throughout the festivities Mehmet remained in the highest humour, showing no sign that he had endured the worst defeat of his life thus far less than a year before.

Meanwhile, Pope Calixtus had launched a fleet of sixteen galleys under the command of Cardinal Ludovico Trevisan, who set sail from Naples on

6 August 1456, bound for the Aegean. The Pope, in a letter to Ludovico, expressed the extravagant hope that this would be the first step in a campaign that would lead to the recapture of Constantinople, the recovery of the Holy Land, and even the extermination of Islam. Ludovico captured the northern Aegean islands of Lemnos, Samothrace and Thasos, garrisoning them with papal troops, and in August 1457 he defeated an Ottoman fleet off Lesbos, capturing twenty-five Turkish vessels. That would be the extent of his victories, which did little more than provoke the wrath of Sultan Mehmet, who soon set out to reconquer the islands that Ludovico had taken.

Despite their humiliating defeat at Belgrade, Mehmet's forces continued their march of conquest, and in the summer of 1456 an Ottoman army under Ömer Bey, son of Turahan Bey, besieged Athens, which since 1385 had been held by the Florentine dynasty of the Acciajuoli. Ömer Bey's forces occupied the lower city while the defenders retreated to the Acropolis, where they held out until they finally surrendered in June 1458.

Mehmet himself led a major expedition into the Peloponnesos in the spring of 1458, his pretext being that the two surviving brothers of the deceased Emperor Constantine, Demetrius and Thomas Palaeologus, the Despots of the Morea, were three years in arrears with the tribute that had been levied upon them. Thomas paid part of the tribute he owed in an attempt to appease Mehmet, who took the money and went on with his invasion, crossing the isthmus of Corinth on 15 May 1458. He left a force to besiege the citadel of Corinth while he went on into the interior of the Peloponnesos. According to Sphrantzes, 'The Sultan invaded the central regions of the Peloponnesos, and all places suffered. Some were enslaved and razed, especially Akova, Aitos and Pentachoria.'

Mehmet then returned to Corinth, where the defenders in the citadel surrendered to him on 2 August. Shortly afterwards he concluded a treaty with Thomas Palaeologus, who surrendered to him Patras and other places in the northern Peloponnesos, which were put under the governorship of Ömer Bey. On his homeward march Mehmet took the opportunity to see Athens, whose defenders had finally surrendered to Ömer Bey just two months beforehand. Kritoboulos describes Mehmet's enthusiasm on seeing the famous city he had read about in his Greek studies.

> He saw it and was amazed, and he praised it, and especially the Acropolis as he went up into it. And from the ruins and the remains, he reconstructed mentally the ancient buildings, being a wise man and a

Philhellene and as a great king, and he conjectured how they must have been originally. He noted with pleasure the respect of the city for their ancestors, and he rewarded them in many ways. They received from him whatever they asked for.

When Mehmet entered Athens he was given the keys to the city by the abbot of the Kaiseriani Monastery. Mehmet responded by exempting the abbot and his monks from the head tax imposed on all non-Muslims, and the monastery itself was taxed at the rate of only one gold coin a year. The people of Athens, which by that time was a small town huddled around the ruins of the ancient city, were allowed to run their internal affairs through a *gerousia*, or council of elders, while Ömer Bey and his successors as governor resided in the palace that the Acciajuoli had abandoned in the Propylaea, the monumental entryway to the Acropolis. Mehmet also endowed a small mosque – Fatih Camii – in the Roman agora, where it can still be seen.

On Mehmet's return journey he stopped off to visit Negroponte (Chalkis), having informed the Venetian *bailo* Paolo Barbarigo in advance. The fortified town of Negroponte stood at the tip of the peninsula on Euboea that projects to within 40 metres of the mainland, from which the island is separated by the Euripos strait, famed for the tidal current that changes direction a dozen times each day. The defence wall formed a triangular circuit around the town, two sides along the coast and the third on the landward side, which was protected by a ditch 6 metres deep and 30 metres wide. The main gate was at the tip of the peninsula, where a bridge spanned the strait, with a huge tower at the end near the mainland, to which it was connected by a drawbridge.

According to Kritoboulos, when Mehmet came within sight of Chalkis he paused to survey the fortress of Negroponte across the narrow strait in the island of Euboea: 'Proceeding according to plan, he arrived opposite Chalkis, in Euboea. There he saw the frequent currents and changes of the Euripos, the peculiar situation of the island, its condition and its excellence, and the way in which it was related to the mainland, with only a very narrow strait between.'

Then, accompanied by 1,000 horsemen, Mehmet rode down to the bridge, where the *bailo* Barbarigo was waiting to greet him at the gateway of the Venetian fortress, along with all the terrified townspeople of Negroponte, who were carrying palm branches to welcome the sultan. Mehmet then rode through the town, closely examining the fortress, the most powerful Venetian stronghold on the eastern coast of

Greece, which he would have to deal with in expanding his empire in the Aegean.

Meanwhile, Mehmet was paying close attention to his dominions in the Balkans, where dynastic changes in Hungary and Serbia had destabilised the whole region.

Ladislas Posthumus died in November 1457, shortly before his eighteenth birthday, to be succeeded as King of Bohemia by George of Podebrady and as King of Hungary by Matthias Corvinus, son of John Hunyadi, the former regent.

The old Despot of Serbia, George Branković, died on 2 May 1457, whereupon his daughter Mara, widow of Murat II, fled to take refuge with Mehmet for fear of her brother Lazar, who succeeded his father. Then on 20 January 1458 Lazar himself died, and a regency was formed by his widow Helena, his blind brother Stephen and Michael Angelović, who had been the Grand Voyvoda, or chief minister, of the late despot. The regents were divided in their political aims, for Helena and Stephen favoured Hungary, while Michael, a brother of Mehmet's grand vezir Mahmut Pasha, was pro-Ottoman. Michael and his followers began a revolt in Smederova, the Serbian capital, but he was defeated and captured by Helena, who gave him over as a prisoner to the Hungarians.

All this led Mehmet to launch an expedition into Serbia under Mahmut Pasha in the spring of 1458, while he himself was campaigning in the Peloponnesos. Mahmut took the lower town of Smederova but he was unable to capture the citadel, so he lifted his siege to attack other places in Serbia as well as the Hungarian fortress of Trnav. He then proceeded to Skopje to meet Mehmet, who had arrived there with his troops after his campaign in the Peloponnesos. Mehmet had planned to demobilise his army in Skopje, but Mahmut Pasha advised him to keep his men under arms because he had learned that the Hungarians were preparing to attack them. News then arrived that a Hungarian force had attacked an Ottoman fortress at Tahtalu, where they were routed by the Turkish defenders. Only then did Mehmet demobilise his army, after which he returned to Edirne to spend the winter at Edirne Sarayı.

The following spring Mehmet led a campaign into Serbia, his objective being the capture of Smederova, which surrendered to him without a struggle on 20 June 1459. The fall of Smederova led all the smaller fortresses of northern Serbia to surrender as well. By the end of 1459 all of Serbia was under Mehmet's control, with some 200,000 Serbs enslaved, beginning an Ottoman occupation that would last for more than four centuries.

At the beginning of January 1459 civil war erupted in the Peloponnesos between Thomas and Demetrius Palaeologus, a struggle in which the Turkish forces, papal troops and Albanian marauders also became involved. Mehmet at first left the war to his local commanders, but then in May 1460 he mustered his forces in Edirne and led them into the Peloponnesos. According to Sphrantzes, Mehmet 'marched straight into Mistra, where the despot Lord Demetrius was... Demetrius had no alternative but to surrender to the sultan, who took possession of Mistra and imprisoned Demetrius'. Mehmet then went on to conquer the rest of the Peloponnesos, apart from Monemvasia and the Venetian fortresses at Koroni, Methoni and Nauplion.

When he captured the Byzantine stronghold at Gardiki, according to Sphrantzes, Mehmet slaughtered all 6,000 or so inhabitants, including women and children – a savage example that led Greeks in other places to surrender to him without a struggle.

The despot Thomas Palaeologus fled to Corfu, which was held by the Venetians. Thomas then made his way to Rome, carrying with him the head of St Andrew, which had been preserved in the metropolitan cathedral of Patras. On 12 April 1462 he presented the Apostle's head to Pope Pius, who had it enshrined in the basilica of St Peter. Thomas then spent the rest of his days as a guest of the Pope in Rome, where he died on 12 May 1465, his wife having passed away three years earlier. One of their two sons, Andreas, died a pauper in Rome in 1502, while the other, Manuel, moved to Istanbul, where he may have converted to Islam. One of their two daughters, Helena, married the Serbian despot Lazar, while the other, Zoë, wed Grand Duke Ivan III Vasilievich of Russia, changing her name to Sophia. Through her the Russian imperial line claimed a link with the Byzantine emperors, so that in 1492 the metropolitan Zosimus called the prince of Moscow 'sovereign and autocrat of all Russia, the new Tsar Constantine of the new city of Constantine, Moscow'. And when Sophia's son succeeded as Tsar Basil III the monk Philotheus hailed him as the only true emperor: 'The Christian Empires have fallen, in their stead only stands our ruler... Two Romes have fallen but the third stands and a fourth there shall not be. Thou art the only Christian sovereign in the world, the lord of all faithful Christians.'

After his conquest of the Peloponnesos, Mehmet took Demetrius Palaeologus and his wife and daughter back with him to Edirne. Mehmet then gave Demetrius an endowed estate at Aenos, where he and his family lived comfortably for the next decade. Demetrius then retired to a monastery in Edirne, where he died in 1470, his wife and daughter passing away in the same year.

When Mehmet was not on campaign he divided his time between Edirne Sarayı and the palace he had been building on the Third Hill of Istanbul. The new palace in Istanbul, which later came to be known as Eski Saray, was completed in 1458, and thenceforth it supplanted Edirne Sarayı as the principal imperial residence. One of Mehmet's concubines, a girl known as Çiçek, or Flower, gave birth to his son Jem in Eski Saray on 2 December 1959, the first male of the imperial Ottoman line to be born in Istanbul. By that time Mehmet's two older sons had been sent off to serve as provincial governors, with Beyazit residing in Amasya and Mustafa in Manisa, from where he would later be transferred to Konya.

Meanwhile, Pope Calixtus III had died in Rome early in August 1458. He was succeeded by Cardinal Aeneas Sylvius Piccolomini, who on 3 September was consecrated as Pope Pius II. Soon after his coronation he announced that on 1 June 1459 he would convene at Mantua a congress of the Christian powers to organise a crusade against the Turks. After the congress the emperor Frederick III and other German princes agreed to contribute to the crusade 32,000 infantry and 10,000 cavalry. On 14 January 1460 Pius declared a three-year crusade against the Turks, promising a plenary indulgence for all those who fought in the Christian army or who supported those who did, and he promised that he himself would serve if his health permitted.

The Ottomans in the meanwhile had been advancing in Anatolia as well as in Europe. Before his final conquest of the Peloponnesos, Mehmet sent his grand vezir Mahmut Pasha on an expedition against the port town of Amasra, Genoa's principal commercial colony on the Black Sea coast of Anatolia. The Genoese surrendered without a struggle in the autumn of 1459, after which two-thirds of the populace were carried off to Istanbul as slaves.

Then in the spring of 1461 Mehmet launched an expedition against the Byzantine Empire of Trebizond, sending a fleet of 300 vessels along the Black Sea coast of Anatolia under Kasım Pasha, while he and Mahmut Pasha led an army overland, a force estimated as 80,000 infantry and 60,000 cavalry in addition to the artillery and supply train. The fleet and army converged at the port town of Sinop, then held by the Isfendiyarid emir Ismail, who surrendered to Mehmet without a struggle.

Meanwhile, David Comnenus, who succeeded his brother John IV as Emperor of Trebizond in 1458, had established an anti-Ottoman alliance with Uzun Hasan, chieftain of the Akkoyunlu, or White Sheep, a powerful Türkmen tribe that controlled much of eastern Anatolia. Uzun Hasan's mother, Sara Hatun, was born a Syrian Christian; his paternal grandmother was a Byzantine princess from Trebizond, as was his wife Theodora, a daughter of John IV Comnenus, of whom a Venetian traveller had written that 'it was common knowledge that no woman of greater beauty was living at that time'.

Uzun Hasan sent Sara Hatun as an emissary to Mehmet, whom she met when he paused in his march at Erzincan. She negotiated a peace treaty between Uzun Hasan and Mehmet, and then she tried to persuade the sultan to give up his campaign by pointing out the great difficulty of marching through the Pontic Alps, saying: 'Why tire yourself, my son, for nothing better than Trebizond?'

But Mehmet was adamant and continued his march towards Trebizond, the difficulties of which are described by Constantine Mihailović:

> And we marched in great force and with great effort to Trebizond, not just the army, but the Sultan himself; first because of the distance; second because of the harassment of the people; third, hunger; fourth, because of the high and great mountains and, besides, wet and marshy places. And also rains fell every day so that the road was churned up as high as the horses' bellies everywhere.

While crossing the mountains above Trebizond the sultan's supply train of 100 horse-drawn wagons bogged down in the mud. Mehmet had the supplies loaded on to 800 camels he had brought along for just such an emergency. But one of the camels, which were carrying chests with 60,000 gold pieces, slipped and fell down the mountainside, scattering the coins along the slope. The convoy was halted until the coins had been recovered, according to Mihailović, who writes: 'The Emperor stayed there that day resting and gave the janissaries 50,000 pieces to divide among themselves.'

By the time that Mehmet's army reached Trebizond the fleet under Kasım Pasha had begun to besiege the city, which was held by the emperor David Comnenus, the last Byzantine ruler still holding out against Mehmet. Mahmut Pasha sent a message from Mehmet to David offering him terms of surrender. According to Doukas, Mehmet warned David that 'if you do not give ear to these proposals, know that annihilation awaits your city. For I will not leave this spot until I have leveled the walls and ignominiously killed all the inhabitants.'

David agreed to the terms and Mehmet took possession of Trebizond on 15 August 1461, exactly 200 years to the day after Michael VIII Palaeologus had recaptured Constantinople from the Latins. David Comnenus was allowed to move with his family and all his portable possessions to Edirne, where Mehmet gave him an estate in Thrace. David lived comfortably there for nearly two years, but then on 26 March 1463 Mehmet had him and the male members of his family arrested and brought to the Castle of the Seven Towers in Istanbul. There, on 1 November 1463, David was executed along with six of his seven sons and a nephew. Mehmet spared David's wife, Helena, their youngest son George, and their daughter, Anna. The empress Helena buried her six sons and died soon afterwards. George, who was only three, was given to a Turkish family and raised as a Muslim; when he came of age he fled to Georgia and reverted to Christianity, after which he disappeared from history, the male imperial line of the Comneni vanishing with him. Anna was married successively to two Ottoman pashas, becoming a Muslim, and after the death of her second husband she ended her days in Mehmet's harem in Istanbul.

Thus Mehmet, who had now added nearly the whole Black Sea coast of Anatolia to his realm, extinguished the last embers of Byzantium in Trebizond, having previously dispossessed the branch of the imperial line that had ruled in the Peloponnesos. Byzantium had passed away and its former dominions in Europe and Asia from the Mediterranean to the Black Sea were now ruled by Mehmet the Conqueror, who could thus style himself 'Sultan of the two Continents and Emperor of the two Seas'.

6　　*War with Venice*

News of the fall of Trebizond reached Rome early in the fall of 1461, stirring Pope Pius II to reflect on what could be done to stop the Turks. He himself had achieved nothing in this regard since his declaration of a crusade at the Congress of Mantua, as he remarked in a meeting with a small group of cardinals early in March 1462. 'We have done nothing against the enemies of the Cross; that is evident. But the reason for our silence was not indifference but a kind of despair. Power, not will, was lacking...'

During the interim Pius had been writing an extraordinary document entitled *Epistola ad Mahumetan*, or *Letter to Mehmet*, the original text of which has only recently been rediscovered, though the contents have been known for centuries.

This letter, which almost certainly was never sent to Istanbul, assures Mehmet that Pius does not hate him, since the teachings of Christ made the Pope love his enemy. Pius goes on to tell Mehmet that continued warfare with the Christian world would lead the Turks only to disaster, and that if the sultan wanted to extend his domains into western Europe he need only allow himself to be baptised and convert to Christianity.

> Once you have done this there will be no prince on earth to outdo you in fame or equal you in power. We shall appoint you emperor of the Greeks and the Orient, and what you have now obtained by violence, and hold unjustly, will be your possession by right. All Christians will honor you and make you arbiter of their quarrels. All the oppressed will take refuge in you as in their common protector; men will turn to you from

71

nearly all the countries on earth. Men will submit to you voluntarily, appear before your judgment seat, and pay taxes to you. It will be given to you to quell tyrants, to support the good and combat the wicked. And the Roman Church will not oppose you if you walk in the right path...

After his conquest of Trebizond Mehmet returned to Istanbul on 6 October 1461, and then soon afterwards he went to Edirne, where he spent the ensuing winter at Edirne Sarayı. Then in the spring of 1462 Mehmet prepared to set off on another campaign, this one brought on by a revolt in the trans-Danubian principality of Wallachia.

Wallachia had been a vassal of the Ottomans under the reign of the voyvoda Vlad II Dracul, whose last name means the 'Dragon' or 'Devil'. The voyvoda had two sons, Vlad and Radu, who were kept in the Ottoman court as hostages. When the voyvoda died in 1456 Mehmet sent Vlad, the eldest, to Wallachia, where he ruled as Vlad III, while Radu remained a hostage in Istanbul. Vlad paid tribute to the Ottomans until 1459, and then the following year he formed an alliance with King Matthias Corvinus of Hungary. Mehmet sent an embassy to deal with Vlad led by his chief falconer Hamza Bey, who was then governing the Danubian provinces. Vlad had Hamza Bey and his party impaled and then led his army across the frozen Danube in mid-winter to attack Ottoman territory south of Nicopolis. Vlad thenceforth was known to the Turks as Tepeş, or the Impaler, whose bloodthirstiness made him the historical prototype for Count Dracula, the fictional vampire lord of Bram Stoker's novel.

Mehmet was enraged by this and decided to invade Wallachia. The sultan mustered his forces at Edirne and sent Mahmut Pasha on ahead with the advance guard, while he himself followed with the rest of the army. Tursun Beg says that the entire army numbered 300,000, but modern estimates put it at about 80,000. Mahmut was accompanied by Vlad's younger brother Radu, whom Mehmet intended to set up as his puppet after Tepeş was overthrown.

Mehmet defeated Vlad in a hard-fought battle immediately after the Turkish forces crossed the Danube. Vlad was then forced to flee and take refuge with King Matthias Corvinus, who imprisoned him. Corvinus eventually released Vlad, whom he hoped to restore as a Hungarian puppet in Wallachia, giving him his young cousin as a bride. Meanwhile, Mehmet appointed Vlad's younger brother Radu as voyvoda of Wallachia, which was now totally under Ottoman control. Mehmet then returned to

Edirne in mid-July 1462, having now conquered lands on both the north and south of the Black Sea.

That same summer Mehmet accompanied Mahmut Pasha on a campaign against Niccolo Gattilusio of Lesbos, who surrendered his fortress at Mytilene after a siege of fifteen days. After the surrender of Mytilene, Mahmut Pasha, on Mehmet's orders, divided the populace into three parts, one of which he allowed to remain in the city as the sultan's subjects, the second group to be resettled in Istanbul, and the third to be given as slaves to the janissaries who had captured the fortress. The Italian mercenaries who had defended the fortress were executed. Niccolo Gattilusio was taken as a prisoner to Istanbul, where he tried to save himself by converting to Islam, but soon afterwards he too was executed.

At the beginning of the Mytilene campaign Mehmet had visited the site of ancient Troy, on the Asian shore of the Dardenelles where the strait enters the Aegean. Kritoboulos says the Mehmet 'inquired about the tombs of the heroes – Achilles and Ajax and the rest. And he praised and congratulated them, their memory and their deeds, and on having a person like the poet Homer to extol them.' He said proudly that he had settled the score with the ancient Greeks for their victory over the 'Asiatics' at Troy, where he was referring to the Mysian people who inhabited the Troad in antiquity.

He is reported to have said, shaking his head a little, 'God has reserved for me, through so long a period of years, the right to avenge this city and its inhabitants. For I have subdued their enemies and have plundered their city and made them the spoils of the Mysians. It was the Greeks and Macedonians and Thessalians and Peloponnesians who ravaged this place in the past, and whose descendants have now through my efforts paid the just penalty, after a long period of years, for their injustice to us Asiatics at that time and so often in subsequent times.

Mehmet's campaign in Mytilene seems to have convinced him, as Kritoboulos writes, that he had to 'build a great navy and have control of the sea'.

Then he gave orders that, in addition to the existing ships, a large number of others should speedily be built and many sailors selected from all his domains for this purpose and set aside for this work alone. He did this because he saw that sea-power was a great thing, that the navy of the Italians was large and that they dominated the sea and ruled all the islands in the Aegean, and that to no small extent they injured his own coastlands, both Asiatic and European – especially the navy of the

Venetians... For this purpose he got together as quickly as possible a great fleet, and began to gain control of the sea.

Kritoboulos goes on to say that Mehmet also decided he should build a pair of fortresses on the European and Asian shores of the Dardanelles, which would control the maritime approach to Istanbul from the Aegean, just as Rumeli Hisarı and Anadolu Hisarı controlled the approach to the city from the Black Sea through the Bosphorus. That same summer Mehmet began construction of a pair of fortresses on either side of the Dardanelles near its Aegean end. The project was directed by Yakup Pasha, admiral and governor of Gelibolu, who completed the two fortresses in the spring of 1463. The fortress on the European side was called Kılıt ül-Bahriye (Key of the Sea) and the one on the Asian shore Kalei Sultaniye (Sultan's Castle). A new and larger harbour for galleys was also completed at Gelibolu, while an intensive programme of shipbuilding went on at the Tershane, or naval arsenal, in Istanbul on the Golden Horn.

The following year Mehmet led a campaign into Bosnia together with Mahmut Pasha. The pretext for the campaign was that the Bosnian king, Stephen VII Tomasević, had refused to pay tribute to the sultan as had his father, feeling secure that his alliance with Hungary would protect him from the Ottomans. The Hungarian alliance had been facilitated by Pope Pius II, who had persuaded King Matthias Corvinus to end his quarrel with Stephen. The Pope had been led to intervene after receiving a letter from Stephen explaining his perilous situation and the threat that Mehmet posed to Christendom.

> If Mehmet only demanded my kingdom and would go no further, it would be possible to leave Bosnia to its fate and there would be no need for you to disturb the rest of Christendom in my defence. But his insatiable lust for power knows no bounds. After me he will attack Hungary and the Venetian province of Dalmatia. By way of Krain and Istria he will go to Italy, which he wishes to subjugate. He often speaks of Rome and longs to go there. If he conquers my kingdom thanks to the indifference of the Christians, he will find here the right country to fulfill his desires. I shall be the first victim. But after me the Hungarians and the Venetians and other peoples will suffer the same fate.

Once again Mahmut Pasha led the advance guard and Mehmet followed with the rest of the army. The first place in Bosnia that they attacked was Bobovac, a day's march north-west of Sarajevo, which they took after a three-day siege. Mehmet then ordered Mahmut Pasha to march the Rumelian troops westward to Jajce, the capital of Bosnia, hoping to capture King Stephen. When Mahmut reached Jajce he found that Stephen had fled to Ključ, a day's march to the north-west. Mahmut put Ključ under siege and then sent a messenger to negotiate with Stephen, who agreed to surrender on a written promise that he would be given safe conduct. Mehmet was angered when he learned of the safe conduct that Mahmut Pasha had given Stephen. When Mehmet reached Jajce he had Stephen brought before him in the presence of Şeyh Ali Bistami, the chief Ottoman cleric. When Stephen produced his safe conduct the Bistami declared that the document was invalid, since it had been issued by one of the sultan's servants without Mehmet's permission, adding that 'The killing of such infidels is holy war.' Mehmet then ordered that Stephen be executed, and most Turkish sources say that Şeyh Ali Bistami beheaded the king with his own hands in front of the sultan.

Stephen's death marked the end of the Kingdom of Bosnia. Mahmut Pasha went on to conquer most of Hercegovina, which was ruled by Duke Stephen Vukčić, who fled to Hungary.

Mehmet's conquest of Bosnia exposed Venetian-held Dalmatia, the independent city of Ragusa (Dubrovnik) and ports in southern Italy to Turkish attacks. Cristoforo Moro, the Doge of Venice, wrote to the government in Florence on 14 June 1463, appealing for their help against the Grand Turk.

> Impelled by his lusts and his inexorable hatred of the Catholic faith, the bitterest and fiercest enemy of the Christian name, the prince of the Turks has carried his audacity so far that among the princes of Christendom there is virtually none willing to oppose his designs... Not content with such a triumph [in Bosnia], he, as one demanding more and hoping for still greater conquests, has not hesitated to advance, arrogantly and with arms in readiness, to the coast of Segno [Senj, in Croatia], that is almost to the gate and entrance of Italy.

Ömer Bey, the Ottoman commander in Athens, launched an attack in November 1462 on the Venetian fortress at Naupactos, on the northern shore of the Gulf of Corinth, and nearly captured it. Then the following spring Isa Bey, the Turkish commander in the Peloponnesos, besieged the Venetian fortress at Argos, which he captured on 3 April 1463.

After the fall of Argos the Venetian Senate began preparing for war against the Turks, and on 17 May 1463 they reached an agreement to support King Matthias Corvinus, who had sent a plea 'setting forth the power and greatness of the Turk and the dangers threatening the kingdom of Hungary and Christianity'. Then on 28 July 1463, after an impassioned speech by Vettore Capello, who said that the republic would be lost if it did not fight back against the Turks, the Senate formally declared war against the Ottoman government.

The Venetians, whatever their attitude might have been earlier, now saw the benefit of supporting the Pope's crusade as part of their own war effort, in which they hoped to reconquer the whole of the Morea. Pius looked upon the Turco-Venetian war as part of the crusade that he had preached at Mantua. At a public consistory in Rome on 22 October 1463 Pius declared war on the Turks in the bull entitled *Ezechielis prophetae*, vowing: 'We shall do battle with the power of speech, not the sword. We shall aid warriors with our prayers. We shall take our stand on the tall deck of a ship or on some nearby height of land, bless our soldiers, and render the enemy accursed...this we can do and this we shall do in the fullness of our strength. The Lord will not despise the contrite and humble heart!' Then he urged the princes of western Europe to put aside their differences, reminding them of what had had happened to their fellow Christian rulers in the Balkans and Asia Minor at the hands of Mehmet.

> You Germans who do not help the Hungarians, do not hope for the help of the French! And you Frenchmen, do not hope for the assistance of the Spaniards unless you help the Germans. With what measures ye mete, it shall be measured to you. What is to be gained by looking on and waiting has been learned by the emperors of Constantinople and Trebizond, the kings of Bosnia and Serbia, and other princes, who have all, one after another, been overpowered and have perished. Now that Mehmet has conquered the Orient, he wishes to conquer the West.

The first action of the war began on 12 August 1463, when Alvise Loredan, the Venetian Admiral of the Sea, sent a force that captured the fortress at Argos. On 3 September another Venetian force attacked the citadel at Corinth under the command of Bertoldo d'Este, who was killed in action while trying to breach the walls. A Turkish relief force under Mahmut Pasha forced the Venetians to lift the siege and flee aboard Loredan's ships.

This was the only defeat suffered by the Venetians during the first month of the war, and by September they had taken all of the Turkish-held fortresses in the Morea except for Mistra, Patras and Corinth. When news of these victories reached Rome, Pope Pius praised the Venetians 'who alone keep watch, who alone labour, who alone come to the aid of the Christians'.

But before the year was over a Turkish force under Mahmut Pasha broke through the Hexamilion, the ancient defence wall across the Isthmus of Corinth, and went on to recapture Argos, penetrating into the heart of the Morea before winter set in.

On 12 September 1463 Venice entered into an anti-Turkish alliance with King Matthias Corvinus of Hungary. At the end of September Corvinus led an army of 4,000 troops into Bosnia and attacked Jajce, which surrendered after a siege of three months. By the end of the year more than sixty places in Bosnia surrendered to the Hungarians without a struggle, and in Hercegovina Duke Stephen Vukčić regained possession of his duchy when the Ottoman forces withdrew.

Mehmet was infuriated by the Hungarian invasion, but during the winter of 1463–4 he was incapacitated in Istanbul with a painful attack of gout, which was to plague him for the rest of his days. His Jewish physician Maestro Iacopo eventually managed to alleviate his condition, so that by the spring he was able to lead an expedition into Bosnia to regain the places captured by the Hungarians.

The first place that Mehmet attacked was Jajce, which he put under siege on 10 July 1464. But the Hungarian garrison resisted fiercely, withstanding more than six weeks of constant bombardment and repeated attacks by the Turkish infantry. After learning that King Matthias Corvinus was encamped north of the Savas with a large army, Mehmet finally lifted the siege on 24 August and withdrew to Sofia. Corvinus chose not to risk coming up against Mehmet's army, and, instead of proceeding to Jajce, he marched his troops to the Turkish-held town of Zvornik (Izvornik) on the river Drina, which he put under siege.

Meanwhile, in the late spring of 1464 the Venetians sent a fleet into the northern Aegean under the command of Orsato Giustinian and occupied the island of Lemnos. The fleet then sailed to the harbour of Mytilene on Lesbos, putting the Turkish-held fortress under siege. When news of the Venetian attack reached Mehmet he sent a fleet to Lesbos under the command of Mahmut Pasha, and when Giustinian learned of this he lifted the siege and sailed away. Mahmut Pasha refrained from pursuing the Venetians and returned with the fleet to Istanbul, after which he went on to Sofia to join Mehmet.

Mehmet then sent an army of 40,000 men under Mahmut Pasha to relieve the Turkish garrison at Zvornik, while he himself returned to Edirne. When the Hungarians learned of the approach of the Ottoman army they lifted the siege of Zvornik and fled, many of them being cut down by the advance guard of the pursuing Turks.

Mahmut Pasha then returned to Edirne with the Ottoman army in December 1464, leaving the Hungarians in control of Jajce and a few other strongholds in the north. The rest of Bosnia remained in the hands of the Ottomans, and when Stephen Vukčić died in 1466 Mehmet annexed Hercegovina. Stephen's son Sigismund was taken into the Ottoman service and became a Muslim, reaching high rank as Hersekzade Ahmet Pasha and marrying a granddaughter of Mehmet.

After his conquest of Hercegovina, Mehmet garrisoned the fortresses he had conquered, after which he returned with his army to Edirne. One of these fortresses was at Zvečaj, where Constantine Mihailović was given command of fifty janissaries. Mihailović describes how he was finally liberated from the Turks when Matthias Corvinus recaptured Zvečaj and Jajce. 'And King Matyas, having taken Jajce with a treaty, immediately marched back with the Hungarians at Zvečaj, and we also had to surrender... And I thanked the Lord God that I had thus got back among the Christians with honor. And thus did King Matyas take Jajce and also Zvečaj.'

Meanwhile, preparations were being made for the crusade organised by Pope Pius II, who apparently thought of enrolling the exiled despot Thomas Palaeologus as a crusader and restoring him to his despotate in the Morea. The Venetian Senate was totally opposed to this, since one of the main reasons they were going to war was to make the Morea part of the republic's maritime empire. Thus Doge Cristoforo Moro wrote to Lodovico Foscarini, the Venetian ambassador in Rome, instructing him to do whatever he could to dissuade the Pope from sending Thomas Palaeologus to the Morea in his crusade.

Pius himself took the cross in the basilica of St Peter in Rome on 18 June 1464. That same day, although he was very ill, Pius left for Ancona on the Adriatic, where he was to meet the Venetian fleet with Doge Cristoforo Moro, as well as contingents of Catalan, Spanish, French and Saxon crusaders. Pius and his party, which included six cardinals, was joined at Spoleto by the Ottoman pretender Calixtus Ottomano, whom the Pope may have wanted to send off on the crusade. The papal party finally arrived in Ancona on 19 July, where they were put up at the episcopal palace to await the arrival of the doge and his fleet. But the doge was reluctant to leave Venice, giving his age and poor health as an excuse, and only after being pressured by the Senate did he finally set sail in a flotilla of a dozen

Venetian galleys, arriving in Ancona on 12 August. By then Pius had contracted pneumonia, as the Milanese ambassador wrote in a letter to Sforza on 1 August, noting that the Pope's physicians 'indicate that, if he puts to sea, he will not live two days'. Pius finally passed away on 15 August, and three days later the doge left with the Venetian fleet and returned to Venice, for the crusade was now over.

The cardinals who had been with Pius in Ancona rushed back to Rome, where a conclave was held on 29 August to elect a new Pope. On the first vote the conclave elected the Venetian Pietro Barbo, who the following day was consecrated as Pope Paul II.

Although the new Pope was a Venetian, he had not been on good terms with the government of his native city. Nevertheless, he tried to avoid a break with the Serenissima for fear that the republic should make peace with the Turks, which would end all possibilities for Paul to carry on with his predecessor's crusading policy The Venetian *bailo* in Istanbul, Paolo Barbarigo, had an interview with Mahmut Pasha in February 1465, in which the grand vezir expressed surprise that Venice was still persisting in war with the Ottomans, implying that peace terms might be a possibility. The Venetians were interested in peace, but they knew that Mehmet would propose only terms that the republic could never accept, such as the loss of the Morea and other possessions of its maritime empire.

On 16 May 1465 the Pope appealed to the Signoria, the Venetian government, to contribute to the war effort being made by the Hungarians against Sultan Mehmet, the 'common enemy and calamity of Christians'. The Signoria responded on 1 June, acknowledging the need to support the Hungarians against the Turks, but asking to be excused from contributing to the war effort, for 'many and grave difficulties are arising which make it so hard for us that we cannot see how action can be taken on your wish and our own desire, which is always attendant upon a pontiff's wish'.

Although the Italian rulers and other Christian princes were reluctant to support another crusade, the Pope did manage to give significant financial support to the Hungarians, and a contemporary observer notes that in 1465 alone Paul sent King Matthias Corvinus some 80,000 ducats. But this was a paltry sum compared to what Venice was spending, as the Senate informed Paul on 26 September 1465, noting that the annual expense to the republic of maintaining her army and navy in her war against the Turks, which she fought almost alone, was 700,000 ducats, which exceeded her entire income from maritime trade.

Then in the early spring of 1465 Venice was suddenly faced with the threat of war with another powerful Muslim ruler, the Mamluk *soldan* (sultan) of Egypt, az-Zahir Saif-ad-Din Khushkadam. This came about when Venetian galleys carrying Egyptian merchants from Alexandria to Rhodes were attacked and captured by the Knights of St John. The Mamluk sultan threatened Venice with war unless the merchants were released and compensated, and several years of negotiations were necessary before the matter was finally resolved peacefully.

Venice continued to fight on against Mehmet on several fronts, as the Senate noted in their response to an appeal for aid from an envoy of the Albanian leader Skanderbeg, who was still holding out against the Turks in his mountain fortress at Kruje. Expressing their gratitude for Skanderbeg's valorous defence of Kruje, the Senate went on to say 'and as to the money he asks for, we certainly wish that we could satisfy [him] to the fullest extent of his desire, but we must inform him that we have been incurring huge and intolerable expenses both on land and at sea, and not only in Albania and Dalmatia, but in the Morea, Negroponte, and other points in the east'.

Then Venice had an unexpected respite, when Mehmet decided to rest himself and his army before going on with his march of conquest. Kritoboulos writes of this hiatus in his chronicle of the events of the year 1465, when Mehmet first moved in to his new palace of Topkapı Sarayı on the First Hill of Istanbul.

> The Sultan himself was greatly exhausted and worn out in body and mind by his continuous and unremitting planning and care and indefatigable labors and dangers and trials, and he needed a time of respite and recuperation. For this reason he knew he ought to remain at home and rest himself and his army during the approaching summer, so that he could have his troops fresher and more enthusiastic for the other undertakings which were ahead.

7

The House of Felicity

The new imperial residence that Mehmet moved into during the winter of 1464–5 came to be known as Topkapı Sarayı, the Palace of the Cannon Gate, from the row of cannons that guarded its marine entrance at the confluence of the Bosphorus and the Golden Horn, where their waters meet and flow together into the Sea of Marmara. Thenceforth the earlier residence Mehmet had built on the Third Hill came to be called Eski Saray, the Old Palace, which continued to be used by the imperial household, though the sultan now clearly preferred the new pleasure dome he had erected on the First Hill, described by Kritoboulos in his first entry for the year 1465.

> Both as to view and as to enjoyment as well as in its construction and its charm, it was in no respect lacking as compared with the famous and magnificent old buildings and sites. In it he had towers built of unusual height and beauty and grandeur, and apartments for men and others for women, and bedrooms and lounging-rooms and sleeping-quarters, and very many other fine rooms. There were also various out-buildings and vestibules and halls and porticoes and gateways and porches, and bakeshops and baths of notable design.

Aside from Kritoboulos, there are a number of chroniclers who describe the organisation of Topkapı Sarayı and life in the palace during the first century of its existence, written by men who were intimately acquainted with the Saray through being attached to its service. All of them were foreigners, slaves of the sultan who later retired or escaped from the imperial service.

The earliest of these chroniclers are Iacopo de Camois Promontario, a Genoese merchant who served the Ottoman court in the years 1430–75, and Giovanni-Maria Angiolello of Vicenza, who was captured in 1470 and remained in the Ottoman court until 1483, serving both Mehmet II and his son and successor Beyazit II. Chroniclers from the sixteenth century include Giovanni Antonio Menavino, a Genoese who served as a page in the reign of Beyazit II (r. 1481–1512); Teodoro Spandugino, who came to Pera in the first decade of the sixteenth century; Luigi Bassano da Zara, who lived in Istanbul in the 1530s, and Bernardo Navagero, the Venetian *bailo*, who visited the palace in 1550. Their chronicles give a picture of life in Topkapı Sarayı during the century after the palace was built by Mehmet. Angiolello also describes the Conqueror as he would have appeared in the last decade of his life.

> The Emperor Mehmet, who, as I said, was known as the Grand Turk, was of medium height, fat and fleshy; he had a wide forehead, large eyes with thick lashes, an aquiline nose, a small mouth with a round copious reddish-tinged beard, a short, thick neck, a sallow complexion, rather high shoulders, and a loud voice. He suffered from gout in the legs.

Angiolello says that the palace comprised 'three courts each enclosed by walls', each one entered through a double gate, the entire complex surrounded by an outer wall ten feet high, underestimating its height by a factor of about three. The outer wall encloses the palace on its landward side, extending from the Golden Horn to the Sea of Marmara, where it connected with the sea walls that extended around the tip of the Constantinopolitan peninsula. The wall built by Sultan Mehmet is still perfectly preserved, looking much the same as it is shown in the Nuremberg woodcut of 1493 by Hartman Schedel, studded with a series of mighty defence towers. The enclosed area coincided with the site of the ancient Greek city of Byzantium, which originally comprised only the First Hill. The main buildings of Topkapı Sarayı were erected on what had been the Byzantine acropolis, or upper city, while the palace gardens were laid out on the slopes leading down to the Golden Horn and the Marmara.

According to Angiolello, the gardens also included fruit orchards, vineyards, game parks and an aviary, as well as a zoological park and botanical gardens.

> And here in this garden there are many kinds of fruit tree planted in order, and similarly pergolas with grapevines of many kinds, roses, lilacs,

saffron, flowers of every sort, and everywhere there is an abundance of most gentle waters, that is fountains and pools. Also in this garden are some separate places in which are kept many kinds of animals, such as deer, does, roe deer, foxes, hares, sheep, goats and Indian cows, which are much larger than ours, and many other sorts of animals. This garden is inhabited by many sorts of birds, and when it is spring it is pleasant to listen to them sing, and likewise there is a marshy lake which is planted with reeds, where a large number of wild geese and ducks dwell, and in that place the Grand Turk derives pleasure in shooting with his gun.

Bassano also says that the palace built by Sultan Mehmet had three courts, which were aligned one after the other in the form of a great rectangle. The fourth court of the present palace is really a large garden with isolated pavilions mostly added in the late Ottoman period. The Harem, or women's quarters, in its present state belongs largely to the time of Murat III (r. 1574–95), with fairly extensive reconstructions and additions chiefly under Mehmet IV (r. 1648–87) and Osman III (1754–7). Three serious fires – in 1574, 1665 and 1856 – devastated large sections of the palace, so that, while the three main courts have preserved essentially the arrangements given them by Mehmet the Conqueror, many of the buildings have either disappeared (as most of those in the First Court) or have been reconstructed and redecorated in later periods.

Topkapı Sarayı was not merely the private residence of the sultan and his court, for Mehmet also made it the centre of his government. It was the seat of the so-called Divan, the supreme executive and judicial council of the empire, and it housed the famous Palace School, the largest and most select of the training schools for the imperial civil service. The separate divisions of the Saray corresponded closely with these various functions, all of which took their original form under Mehmet the Conqueror.

The First Court, which was open to the public, was the service area, containing a hospital, a bakery, an arsenal, the mint and outer treasury, and a large number of storage places and dormitories for guards and domestics of the Outer Service, those who would not normally come into contact with the sultan and his household. The Second Court was the seat of the Divan, devoted to the public administration of the empire; it could be entered by anyone who had business to contract with the council; beyond this court to left and right were other service areas, most notably the kitchens and the privy stables. The Third Court, strictly reserved for officials of the court and government, was largely given over to various divisions of the Palace School, but also contained some of the chambers of the Selamlık, the reception rooms of the sultan. The Harem, specifically the women's quarter of the palace, had further rooms of the Selamlık and the sultan's own bedroom, as well as quarters for the Black Eunuchs who guarded the women's quarters. The White Eunuchs, who looked after the pages and the students in the Palace School, were housed in the Third Court. The Fourth Court was an extension of the Selamlık added in later times, the only structure remaining from the Conqueror's time being Hekimbaşı Odası, the Chamber of the Chief Physician.

The main entrance to Topkapı Sarayı has always been Bab-ı Hümayun, the Imperial Gate, opposite the north-east corner of Haghia Sophia. The great gatehouse is basically the work of Mehmet the Conqueror, though its appearance has changed rather radically in the course of time. Originally there was a second storey with two rows of windows, but this was removed in subsequent remodellings. The seventeenth-century Turkish historian Hezarfen Hüseyin notes that this upper storey was added by Mehmet to create a vantage point from which he could look out over the city.

The rooms on the ground floor of the gatehouse were for the Kapıcıs, or corps of guards, of whom fifty were on duty at all times. The side niches in the gateway were in Ottoman times used for the display of the severed heads of executed offenders of importance, each labelled with his crime.

The Imperial Gate opens into the First Court, which no longer looks like a courtyard because most of the buildings that formed its periphery have disappeared through fire and earthquake. This was once called the Court of the janissaries, for those members of the elite corps of the Ottoman army who were on duty in the palace assembled here.

The most prominent building in the court is off to the left as one enters; this is the former church of Haghia Eirene, built by Justinian in the years 532–7 at the same time that he erected Haghia Sophia. This was one of the few Byzantine churches in the city that was not converted into a mosque after the Conquest, since it was within the bounds of Topkapı Sarayı. Sultan Mehmet used it to store captured weapons and other trophies of his conquests, and in the late Ottoman era it became an archaeological museum.

On the west or left-hand side of the First Court, between the outer wall of the Saray and Haghia Eirene, there once stood a great quadrangle that housed the Straw Weavers and Carriers of Silver Pitchers. The large courtyard of this building served as a storage place for the firewood of the palace and the buffalo carts used to transport it.

North of Haghia Eirene on the left side of the court is the Darphane, the buildings formerly used for the Imperial Mint and the Privy Treasury. Beyond these buildings a road leads downhill through a gateway called Kız Bekçiler Kapısı, the Gate of the Guardians of the Girls, referring to the Black Eunuchs who guarded the Harem. This road led to the outer gardens of the palace on the slope of the First Hill leading down to the Golden Horn, now the site of Gülhane Park.

A short way down the road a gateway leads to a terrace below the north side of the First Court, an enclosure containing the Archaeological Museum, the Museum of the Ancient Orient, both of them founded in the late nineteenth century, and the Çinili Köşk, or Tiled Pavilion, one of the very few original buildings of Sultan Mehmet's palace that has not been significantly altered. Sultan Mehmet seems to have built the kiosk in 1472 as a review pavilion, which he is known to have used to watch the palace pages playing *jirit*, a form of polo.

Between Kız Bekçiler Kapısı and the wall of the Second Court to the north there once stood a number of buildings, including a large storehouse, two barracks for domestics of the Outer Service, and a small mosque for their use; all of these, which were probably largely constructed of wood, have disappeared except for some undistinguished foundations.

On the east or right-hand side of the First Court is the site of the famous infirmary for the pages of the Palace School. This was a large building with a courtyard and a number of wards allotted to the various divisions of the school. Beyond the site of the infirmary a road led to the outer gardens of the palace on the slope leading down to the Marmara. This area is still covered with Byzantine substructures, including remains of the Great Palace of Byzantium, the sight of whose ruins had so saddened Mehmet when he first saw them on the day he conquered Constantinople.

The rest of the east side of the First Court beyond the road consists of a blank stone wall with a gate and a water tower halfway along. Behind this wall stood the bakery of the palace, famous for the superfine quality of the white bread baked for the sultan and those favourites on whom he chose to bestow it. Beyond the bakery are the waterworks of the palace, built by Mehmet and subsequently reconstructed.

Just before the gate to the Second Court, against the wall on the right, is a famous and sinister fountain. This is Cellâl Çeşmesi, the Executioner's

Fountain, in which the chief executioner washed his hands and sword after a decapitation, which took place just outside the gate. If the culprit was of sufficient importance the severed head was placed on one of the two Ibret Taşları, or Example Stones, on either side of the gate, as a warning of what happened to those who broke the sultan's laws.

The entryway to the Second Court is called Bab-es Selam, or the Gate of Salutations, also known as Orta Kapı, the Middle Gate. The gateway is shown in Schedel's woodcut of 1493 and is essentially a construction of Mehmet II, with repairs and alterations by later sultans, as evidenced by inscriptions. The chief executioner had a small apartment in the gatehouse, one room of which served as a cell where the condemned man was held before his execution. Other chambers within the gatehouse were used as waiting rooms for ambassadors and other officials attending an audience with the sultan or the grand vezir.

Here one enters the palace proper, which now houses the Topkapı Sarayı Museum. At this point the vezirs and other high functionaries and the ambassadors of foreign powers, who were permitted to ride through the First Court, had to dismount from their horses, for only the sultan himself and his three favourite pages when in his company could ride through this gate.

The Second Court, also known as the Court of the Divan, is still very much as it was when Sultan Mehmet laid it out, as evidenced by the descriptions of earlier chroniclers. The courtyard is a tranquil cloister of imposing proportions, planted with venerable cypress trees; several fountains once adorned it and mild-eyed gazelles pastured on the glebe. Except for the chambers of the Divan and the Inner Treasury to the northwest there are no buildings in this court, which consists simply of blank walls with colonnaded porticoes in front of them. Beyond the colonnade the whole of the eastern side is occupied by the palace kitchens, while beyond the western colonnade are the Privy Stables and the quarters of the guards known as the Halberdiers-with-Tresses. These guards took their peculiar name from the fact that false locks of hair hung down on either side of their face, supposedly to prevent them from taking sidelong glances at the concubines they might see when on duty in the Inner Palace.

The Court of the Divan seems to have been designed essentially for the pageantry connected with the public business of the empire. Here four times a week the Divan, or Imperial Council, met to deliberate on administrative affairs or to discharge its official functions. On such occasions the whole courtyard was filled with a vast throng of magnificently dressed officials and the corps of palace guards and janissaries, at least 5,000 on ordinary days, but up to 10,000 when ambassadors were received or other extraordinary business was transacted. Even at such times an almost absolute silence prevailed throughout the courtyard, as commented upon in the accounts of foreign travellers, the earliest being that of the Venetian ambassador Andrea Gritti in 1503. He writes: 'I entered into the court, where I found on one side all of the Janissaries on foot, and on the other side all of the persons of high esteem, and the salaried officials of His Majesty, who stood with such great silence and with such a beautiful order, that it was a marvelous thing not believable to one who has not seen it with his own eyes.'

The Divan, together with the Inner Treasury, projects from the north-west corner of the court, thus breaking the symmetry of the rectangle. This group of rooms is dominated by the square tower with a conical roof that is such a conspicuous feature of the Saray from many points of view. The complex dates in essentials to the time of Mehmet II, though it was rebuilt by Süleyman the Magnificent and subsequently remodelled by later sultans. The Divan tower is already clearly visible in Schedel's panorama of 1493, indicating that it too is a work of Mehmet II, although it was lower then and had a pyramidal roof, having taken on its present appearance through a remodelling by Mahmut II in 1820.

In front of the tower stand the three rooms of the Divan, all of them domed chambers of square cross-section; the Council Chamber itself, the Public Records Office and the Office of the Grand Vezir. The first two open widely into each other by a great arch, being divided only by a screen reaching to the springing of the arch, while the Grand Vezir's office was originally entered by a door from the Public Records Office.

The Divan chamber took its name from the low couches that extend from wall to wall around three sides of the room. During meetings of the Divan the members of the Imperial Council sat here in strict order of rank: the grand vezir in the centre opposite the door; on his right the Lord Chancellor (*Nişancı*), the *beylerbeys* of Rumelia and Anatolia, and the Lord High Admiral (*Kaptan Pasha*); on his left were the two Lords Chief Justice (*Kadıaskers*), and beyond them the two Lords of the Treasury (*Defterdars*) and the ağa of the janissaries. Other high officials attended as required, most notably the first vezirs, the chief black eunuch (*kızlar ağası*), the chief white eunuch (*kapı ağası*) and the two captains of the Imperial Gate (*Kapıcıbaşı*).

Over the seat of the grand vezir is a grilled window – known as 'the Eye of the Sultan' – giving into a small room below the Divan Tower. This takes its name from the fact that the sultan, when he was not in attendance in the Divan, could look out from this window to observe what was going on in the Imperial Council.

Mehmet II originally attended all meetings of the council, until one day an incident occurred that convinced him that he would thenceforth observe its proceedings unseen. This was when a peasant who wanted to present his case before the council entered the Divan, looked impatiently at all the assembled dignitaries, and shouted: 'Which of you worthies is the sultan?', which led Mehmet to have the man thrown out and bastinadoed, after which he left the chamber in disgust, never to return.

The building to the north of the three Divan chambers, without a portico, is the Public Treasury. It is a long room with eight domes in four pairs supported by three massive piers, in structure and plan very like the *bedesten* that Mehmet II erected in the centre of Istanbul's Covered Bazaar, indicating that it was a construction of the Conqueror, thought it too was rebuilt by Süleyman. Here and in the vaults below were stored the treasure of the empire as it arrived from the provinces. Here it was kept until the quarterly pay days for the use of the council and for the payment of the officials, the janissaries and other corps of guards and servants; at the end of each quarter what remained unspent was transferred to the Imperial Treasury in the Third Court. The Public Treasury was also used to store financial records as well as precious fabrics, furs and robes worn by the sultan and his vezirs.

At the north-west corner of the Second Court, beneath the Tower of the Divan, there is a doorway called Araba Kapısı, or the Carriage Gate. This is one of the two main entrances to the Harem, the other being in the Third Court. The gate takes its name from the fact that the women in the Harem passed through it on the rare occasions when they were allowed to go for drives in the city or to the surrounding countryside, accompanied by a guard of black eunuchs.

The Harem is a labyrinth of several hundred rooms, few of them very large, on half a dozen levels, of passages, staircases, courtyards and gardens. The site is at the western edge of the acropolis of ancient Byzantium and the hill falls steeply down to the plain below; thus almost the whole of the Harem had to be built on tall substructures to bring it to the level of the rest of the palace. The complex of buildings that for brevity is commonly referred to as the Harem includes also the Selamlık – that is to say, the private rooms for the sultan himself and the semi-public ones where he occasionally entertained the high officials of the court and government; there is no clear dividing line between the two.

According to Promontorio, writing in 1475, Mehmet had 400 women in his harem, of whom 150 lived with him in Topkapı Sarayı, while the rest remained in Eski Saray, which he calls the 'second seraglio for damsels'. He says that the women in the harem of Topkapı Sarayı slept on individual beds three or four to a room. Twenty servants were assigned to each room, and the harem was guarded by twenty-five black eunuchs, headed by the chief black eunuch, whose title was *kızlar ağası*, or ağa of the girls. Few of the women in Mehmet's harem were his concubines and bore him children, the rest being attendants and servants.

The earliest extant buildings of the Topkapı Sarayı Harem date from a century after the reign of Mehmet II. Mehmet reserved an apartment for himself in both palaces, an arrangement that was continued by his successors up to the time of Süleyman, who early in his reign, under the influence of his favourite wife Roxelana, moved his harem from the Old Palace to Topkapı Sarayı. Süleyman's harem was very modest, as was that of his son and successor Selim II (r. 1566–74), and it seems certain that no extensive building projects in the Inner Palace were undertaken by either of those sultans, and any structures they might have erected were destroyed by a great fire in 1574. At all events, the fact is that the oldest rooms still extant in the Harem that can be dated with certainty belong to the reign of Murat III (r. 1574–95), son and successor of Selim II, and were built by the great Ottoman architect Sinan.

At the south end of the west wall of the Second Court is another door called Meyyit Kapısı, the Gate of the Dead, because the bodies of those who died in the Saray were taken out by it for burial. The gateway leads down to the area of the Has Ahır, or Privy Stables, which are on the lower slope of the hill. These stables, which were built by Mehmet II, were used only for the twenty to thirty of the choicest horses for the personal use of the sultan and his favourite pages. There was a much larger palace stable for several hundred horses just outside the walls of the Saray on the Marmara shore, the name of which is still preserved in that of one of the gates in the Byzantine sea walls, Ahır Kapısı, the Stable Gate.

The entire east side of the Second Court is taken up by the palace kitchens, whose long line of ten pairs of domes and chimneys is one of the most distinctive features of the skyline of the Saray as seen from the Marmara. A long, narrow courtyard or open passageway runs the entire length of the area. On the east or outer side of this open the kitchens, while across from them on the west side of the corridor are the storerooms for food and utensils, rooms for the various categories of cooks, and two small mosques.

The kitchens consist of a long series of ten spacious rooms with lofty domes on the Marmara side, and equally lofty conical chimneys on the side of the courtyard. The original kitchens were built here by Mehmet II, of which there remain from his time the two southernmost ones, while the other eight were built by Beyazit II. The huge chimneys were built in 1575 for Murat III by Sinan, who restored the whole complex, which had been badly damaged by the fire of 1574.

The entryway to the Third Court is called Bab-üs Saadet, the Gate of Felicity. The name comes from the fact that it gave entrance to Enderun, the Inner Palace, also known as Dar-üs Saadet, the House of Felicity. The gateway is described by an anonymous European traveller: 'When you go to the Seraglio you have to enter by a gate which is very richly gilded, and is called the Gate of Felicity. Sometimes you see over it, stuck upon the point of a pike, the head of a grand vezir, or some other personage, who has been decapitated in the morning, at the caprice of the Grand Signior.'

The Third Gate itself dates back to the time of Mehmet II, though it was rebuilt in later times. The gate is preceded by a great canopy supported on four columns with a small dome above. Promontorio refers to it as a 'magnificent and excellent portico roofed with lead', and he says that under it Mehmet sat on a 'dazzling and high throne'. Under this canopy the sultans upon their accession and at *bayrams* received the homage of their officials, seated upon a golden throne studded with emeralds. A miniature in the Topkapı Sarayı museum shows Sultan Mehmet enthroned in front of the Third Gate in the company of the grand vezir Mahmut Pasha and the Crimean scholar Mevlana Seyyid Ahmet, with his sword-bearer standing in front of them.

Just beyond the inner threshold of the Bab-üs Saadet stands the Arz Odası, or Chamber of Petitions. The Throne Room occupies a small building with a very heavy and widely overhanging roof supported on a colonnade of antique marble columns. The foundations of the building date from the time of the Conqueror, though most of the superstructure is due to a rebuilding by his great-grandson Süleyman. The earliest mention of the chamber is by Angiolello, who describes its situation as it would have been in the time of Mehmet II: 'At the other end of [the second] court is another double portal, and as one enters it there is a loggia covered with lead, and here sits the Grand Turk when he gives audience; next comes the third court, which is as long and large as the other two.'

Although in the Third Court, the Chamber of Petitions belongs by function and use rather to the Second, for it was here that the last act of the ceremonies connected with the meetings of the Divan was played out. Here, at the end of each session of the council, the grand vezir and the other high functionaries waited on the sultan and reported to him upon the business transacted and the decisions taken, which could not be considered final until they had received the royal assent. Here also the ambassadors of foreign powers were presented at their arrival and leave-taking, but even among all the pomp and panoply on such an occasion an all but complete silence reigned. This is quaintly described by a nobleman named Marc'Antonio Piga-Ferrata, in the suite of an Italian embassy in 1567: 'From both sides of the loggia [outside the Throne Room], all being quiet and in the most profound silence, alone are heard certain little birds sweetly singing and playfully flying about in that verdure which gives shade thereabouts, so that it seems indeed they alone have sole licence to make a noise there.'

The Third Court was largely given over to the Palace School, which was founded by Mehmet II. The purpose of the school was to train the most promising of the sultan's slaves, most of whom were Christian youths who had been converted to Islam, some of them captives and others taken up in the *devşirme*, or levy of young men for the janissaries. Many of the grand vezirs and other pashas in the Ottoman Empire from the time of Mehmet II and his successors up to the early seventeenth century were former Christians who were graduates of the Palace School.

The six halls (*oda*) of the Palace School were arrayed around the periphery of the Third Court along with other buildings. Unfortunately, this court has undergone far greater changes than the Second Court, chiefly as a result of fires, so that, although four of the six halls still exist in something like their old outlines, the details have been so greatly altered that it takes some imagination to picture them as they once were. Two of the halls were introductory schools. The other four were vocational schools: the Hall of the Expeditionary Force, the Hall of the Treasury, the Hall of the Commissariat and the Hall of the Royal Bedchamber. The latter was the highest-ranking of the six halls, and is described in the *Kanunname*, the *Code of Laws of Mehmet II*:

> There has been formed a Hall of the Royal Bedchamber which has thirty-two pages and four officers. The first of these is the Sword-Bearer, the Second is Master of the Horse, the third is Master of the Wardrobe, and the fourth is Master of the Turban The Sword-Bearer has charge of the Discipline of the Novices, and he has also been appointed Head Gate-Keeper of the Palace... The First Officer of the Royal Bedchamber has been given charge of all the royal pages.

The *Kanunname* also mentions the Hass Oda, or Privy Chamber, a complex of domed chambers in the north-west corner of the Third Court. The complex dates from the reign of Mehmet II, with remodelling by his grandson Selim I. This was Sultan Mehmet's private apartment, commanding a view of the Golden Horn and Galata from its porticoes and gardens. The earliest description of this complex, known today as the Pavilion of the Holy Mantle, is by Angiolello:

> On the left side of the [third] court is the palace where the Grand Turk resides; most of that palace is vaulted in construction and has many chambers and summer and winter rooms. The part that looks toward Pera has a portico which is above the large garden, from which rise many cypresses that reach [the height of] the balconies of this portico, and that portico is built on two columns and is completely vaulted, and in the middle is a fountain that flows into a beautiful basin worked in marble with profiles and colonettes of porphyry and serpentine; and in this basin are many sorts of fish, and the Grand Turk takes great pleasure from watching them.

The chambers that form the east side of the Third Court are part of the so-called treasury-bath complex, dating from the original palace erected by Mehmet II. The southernmost of these chambers is the Privy Bath, which later was rebuilt as the Hall of the Expeditionary Force. The Privy Bath is described in detail by Menavino:

> This bath is always kept ready, so that if the Grand Turk or one of his gentlemen wants to bathe himself, he can as soon as he wants. Ten salaried men stand there ready to serve everyone... In this bath there is also a pool paved with marble, large as a room, that is filled with tepid water and so deep that the water comes up to one's neck. In it the youngsters swimming, now on, now under the water, entertain themselves, and when tired they can run to the cool-water pool and

[then] having bathed in their fashion, they dress and give something to the servants as a courtesy, and leave.

The rest of the complex extends around the north-east corner of the Third Court, with three domed chambers opening onto an Ionic portico on the east side, another on the north side, and an open marble loggia at the corner. The three chambers on the east side, which have underground vaults, formed the Inner Treasury mentioned by Angiolello and several other sources in the time of the Conqueror and his immediate successors. According to the nineteenth-century Turkish historian Tayyarzade Ata, this complex was originally known as Fatih Köşkü, or the Conqueror's Pavilion, and it served as Sultan Mehmet's apartment until the completion of the Privy Chamber on the other side of the court a few years later. When Mehmet moved into the Privy Chamber he converted the Fatih Köşkü into a treasury for his gold and silver coins and other precious belongings.

The marble loggia, with its charming fountain and its great arched openings facing north-east and south-east, commands a stunning view of the Bosphorus and the Sea of Marmara, with the Princes Islands floating in the sea off the Asian coast of the Marmara, the peak of Mount Olympus of Bithynia (Uludağ) rising in the distance on a clear day. As Evliya Çelebi wrote of Topkapı Sarayı, which he called the Abode of Felicity: 'Never hath a more delightful edifice been erected by the art of man; for...it is rather a town situated on the border of two seas than a palace.'

8 A Renaissance Court in Istanbul

After describing the new palace of Topkapı Sarayı, Kritoboulos goes on to tell of how Sultan Mehmet spent his time there in the summer and autumn of 1465, embellishing his new capital and gathering around himself a circle of scholars who would make Istanbul a cultural centre, just as Constantinople had been in Byzantine times.

> He himself spent the summer in Byzantium; but, as his custom was, he did not neglect his efforts for the City, that is, for its populace, giving diligent care to buildings and improvements. He also occupied himself with philosophy, such as that of the Arabs and Persians and Greeks, especially that translated into Arabic. He associated daily with the leaders and teachers among these, and had not a few of them around him and conversed with them. He held philosophical discussions with them about the principles of philosophy, particularly those of the Peripatetics and Stoics...

During the summer of 1465 Sultan Mehmet devoted himself to the study of geography. This interest had been stimulated by his discovery of a manuscript of the *Geographia* of the Greek scientist Claudius Ptolemaios of Alexandria, better known as Ptolemy, written in the mid-second century AD. According to Kritoboulos, Mehmet was particularly interested in the maps in this manuscript, which described the whole of the Greek *oecumenos*, or inhabited world, extending from the Pillars of Hercules (the straits of Gibraltar) to India and China.

He [Mehmet] also ran across, somewhere, the charts of Ptolemy, in which he set forth scientifically and philosophically the entire description and outline of the earth. But he wanted to have these, scattered as they were in the various parts of the work, and for that reason hard to understand, brought together into one united whole as a single picture or representation, and thus made clearer or more comprehensible, so as to be more easily understood by the mind, and grasped and well apprehended, for this lesson seemed to him very necessary and most important.

During the summer of 1465 Mehmet enlisted the aid of the Greek scholar George Amiroutzes of Trebizond, a cousin of the grand vezir Mahmut Pasha whom the sultan had brought to Istanbul along with the emperor David Comnenus and his family. Kritoboulos, who calls him Amiroukis, writes of 'how the Sultan received him and honored him':

Among the companions of the ruler of Trebizond was a man named George Amiroukis, a great philosopher, learned in the studies of physics and dogmatics and mathematics and geometry and the analogy of numbers, and also in the philosophy of the Peripatetics and Stoics. He was also full of encyclopedic knowledge, and was an orator and poet as well. The Sultan learned about this man and sent for him. On getting acquainted with his training and wisdom, through contact and conversation, he admired him more than anyone else. He gave him a suitable position in his court and honored him with frequent audiences and conversations, questioning him on the teachings of the ancients and philosophical problems and their discussion and solution. For the Sultan himself was one of the most acute philosophers.

Kritoboulus tells of how Amiroutzes created a huge wall map for Mehmet that combined all the individual maps in Ptolemy's *Geographia*, so that the sultan could see at a glance how his empire was expanding through the *oecumenos*.

So he called for the philosopher George [Amiroutzes], and put before him the burden of this plan, with the promise of royal reward and honor. And this man gladly agreed to do the work, and carried out with enthusiasm the proposals and command of the Sultan. He took the book in hand with joy, and read it and studied it all summer. By considerable investigation and by analyzing its wisdom, he wrote out most satisfactorily and skillfully the whole story of the inhabited earth in one representation as a connected whole – of the land and sea, the rivers, harbors, islands, mountains, cities and all, in plain language, giving in this the rules as to measurements of distance and all other essential things. He instructed the Sultan in the method most necessary and suitable for students and those fond of investigation and what is useful. He also put down on the chart the names of the countries and places and cities, writing them in Arabic, using as an interpreter his son who was expert in the languages of the Arabs and the Greeks. The Sultan was much delighted with this work, and admired the wisdom and ingenuity of Ptolemy, and still more that of the man who had so well exhibited this to him. He rewarded him in many ways and with many honors. He also ordered him to issue the entire book in Arabic, and promised him large pay and gifts for this work.

The son of George Amiroutzes referred to by Kritoboulos is Mehmet Bey, who, along with his brother Skender Bey, had converted to Islam. Mehmet Bey was proficient in Turkish and Arabic, and the Conqueror is known to have commissioned him to do translations of other Greek manuscripts, both religious and secular, including the Bible, but no copy remains of the latter work, if in fact it was translated.

Sultan Mehmet was also interested in Ptolemy's *Almagest*, the great work in astronomy that served as the basis for the further development of this science in the Muslim world, after its translation into Arabic, and in western Europe in Latin translation. Here Mehmet was assisted by another Greek scholar, George Trapezuntios, a Cretan whose family had come from Trebizond. Trapezuntios had been working in Rome under the patronage of Cardinal Bessarion, who had commissioned him to translate Ptolemy's *Almagest* from Greek into Latin. Trapezuntios came from Crete to Istanbul in November 1465, and apparently remained there until he returned to Rome on 18 March 1466.

When Trapezuntios returned to Rome he was arrested and imprisoned for four months in Castel Sant'Angelo, until he was finally released by Pope Paul II, his former pupil in grammar and the humanities. He had been arrested on suspicion of having informed the sultan on 'developments in the West and the dissatisfaction of its people', and of having 'encouraged the Grand Turk to hasten his invasion of Italy'. The evidence for this accusation came from two letters written by Trapezuntios to Mehmet, in which he praised the sultan as being a far greater ruler than King Cyrus of Persia, Alexander the Great or Julius Caesar. At the end of the first letter, dated from Galata on 25 February 1466, he says that he has completed a Latin translation of the *Almagest* and dedicated it to the sultan. In the second letter, which he seems to have sent soon after his return to Rome, he

speaks of his good fortune in having met Sultan Mehmet, whom he said
he had praised to the Pope and the College of Cardinals as a just and
intelligent ruler who was highly knowledgable in Aristotelian philosophy
and all the sciences. He went on to say that Mehmet was the one man who,
with God's help, could lead all the people on earth into one faith and create
a unified empire of all humanity. He had already written about this unified
religion in a treatise entitled *On the Truth of the Christian Faith*, in which he
tried to show that there was no fundamental difference between Christianity
and Islam. He hoped to have this treatise translated into Turkish and
submitted to Muslim scholars; he thought that Sultan Mehmet could easily
reconcile the two religions and could thus rule over all the nations that
professed either faith. As he wrote to Sultan Mehmet:

> Let no one doubt you are by right the emperor of the Romans. For he is
> the emperor who by right possesses the seat of the empire, but the seat of
> the Roman Empire is in Constantinople: thus he who by right possesses
> this city is the emperor. But it is not from men but from God that you,
> thanks to your sword, have received this throne. Consequently, you are
> the legitimate emperor of the Romans... And he who is and remains
> emperor of the Romans is also emperor of the entire earth.

Mehmet's interest in astronomy led him to contact the greatest Muslim
astronomer of the age, Ali Kuşci, who had been chief astronomer at the
observatory that had been founded in Samarkand by the Timurid khan Ulu
Beg, grandson of Tamerlane. Ali was born in Samarkand, taking the name
Kuşci, or the Birdman, since in his youth he had been Ulu Beg's falconer. He
subsequently became Ulu Beg's ambassador to China. After becoming chief
astronomer he completed Ulu Beg's astronomical tables, the famous *Zij-i
Sultaniye*, which were first published in 1438. These tables were probably first
written in Persian and soon afterwards translated into Arabic and Turkish,
remaining in use in the Muslim world up until the nineteenth century.

Ali left Samarkand soon after Ulu Beg was assassinated in 1449. He
then went to Tabriz and was welcomed to the court of Uzun Hasan, who
appointed him chief astrologer. Uzun Hasan sent him on an embassy to
Mehmet II, who offered him the post of chief astronomer at his court. Ali
accepted the offer and said that he would return to Istanbul after competing
his mission in Tabriz.

Ali left Tabriz for Istanbul early in 1472, accompanied by an entourage
said to number 200, some of them courtiers from Topkapı Sarayı sent to
escort him by Sultan Mehmet, who had provided generous funds for his

journey. When Ali arrived in Istanbul he presented the sultan with a book of 194 pages entitled *Muhammadiye*, a work on mathematics that he had written on the journey. The following year he presented Mehmet with a book of 147 pages on astronomy entitled *Risala al-Fathiya*, the *Book of Conquest*. The originals of both books, bound together, are still preserved in the library of Haghia Sophia.

Domenico Hierosolimitano, a Jewish convert to Christianity who had served as personal physician to Sultan Murat III in Topkapı Sarayı, wrote a description of Topkapı Sarayı in which he claimed that Mehmet II had collected ancient Greek and Byzantine works that included 120 manuscripts from the library of Constantine the Great. A study of the Conqueror's Greek scriptorium by Julian Raby in 1983 revealed only fourteen manuscripts that could be shown, by their watermarks, to have been acquired during his reign. Two more manuscripts in Western libraries, one in Paris and the other in the Vatican, were also shown by Raby to have been taken from the Conqueror's scriptorium.

The most notable work identified by Raby in the Conqueror's scriptorium was the *History of Mehmed the Conqueror* by Kritoboulos of Imbros, which was translated into English by Charles T. Riggs and published in 1954. This work, which covers the Conqueror's life from his accession in 1451 until the end of 1467, begins with a dedicatory epistle to the sultan: 'To the Supreme Emperor, King of Kings, the fortunate, the victor, the winner of trophies, the triumphant, the invincible, Lord of land and sea, by the will of God, Kritoboulos the islander, servant of thy servants.'

Western contemporaries of Mehmet, including those who, such as Niccolo Sagundino, met with him soon after the conquest of Constantinople, report on his interest in ancient history, particularly the story of Alexander the Great. Since Kritoboulos compares Mehmet to Alexander the Great one might expect that the Conqueror possessed a biography of Alexander. Scholars had presumed that Mehmet knew the history of Alexander through the Islamic version of his romance, either that of Nizami in Persian or Ahmedi in Turkish. But Raby's study of Mehmet's scriptorium turned up a copy of Arrian's *Anabasis*, the standard Greek biography of Alexander, which bore the same watermarks and was written by the same scribe as the Kritoboulos manuscript, and thus presumably would have prepared for the Conqueror.

Another Greek manuscript found in Mehmet's scriptorium is an anonymous work, the *Deigesis*, known in English as *On the Antiquities of*

Constantinople and the Church of Haghia Sophia, dated 1474 and written by the scribe Michael Aichmalotes. This cannot be directly associated with the Conqueror, but a source known as the *Anonymous Chronicles* records that Mehmet questioned 'Rum and Frankish' scholars on the history of Constantinople and Haghia Sophia. Also, both Persian and Turkish versions of a work entitled *Tarihi Ayasofya* (*History of Haghia Sophia*) were found in the Conqueror's scriptorium, indicating that Mehmet was interested in the history of the Great Church and the city he had conquered.

The Paris manuscript that Raby traced to Mehmet's scriptorium is a copy of Homer's *Iliad* made by John Dokeianos, who is known as a scholar of the late Byzantine period. Dokeianos is believed to have acted as tutor to Princess Helen, daughter of Demetrius Palaeologus, the Despot of the Morea. When Demetrius surrendered to the Conqueror in 1460 he was given an appanage in Edirne, as may be recalled, and Helen entered Mehmet's harem. Dokeianos seems to have accompanied Demetrius and Helen to the Ottoman court, and was probably employed by Mehmet as a scribe. His copy of the *Iliad* is dated by circumstantial evidence to 1463. Mehmet is known to have read the *Iliad*, as evidenced by the section in his biography where Kritoboulos writes: 'How the Sultan examined the tombs of the heroes, as he passed through Troy, and how he praised and congratulated them.' According to Kritoboulus, Mehmet visited Troy in 1462, the year before Dokeianos completed his copy of the *Iliad*, which can hardly be a coincidence.

Raby points out that Mehmet's knowledge of ancient Greek history 'must have been colored by the long-standing Western conceit, which had gained currency as early as the seventh century, that made the Turks, like the Franks, the descendants of the Trojans'. In the case of the former, this belief stemmed from the confusion between the *Teucri*, identified by Homer as the ancestors of the Trojans, and the *Turci*, or Turks. According to the Greek historian Laonicus Chalkokondylas, the fall of Constantinople was seen in Rome as revenge for the fall of Troy, and Kritoboulos has Sultan Mehmet taking the same view in his visit to Troy in 1462.

The Vatican manuscript from Mehmet's scriptorium is a Greek translation from Latin by Dimitrius Kydones of the *Summa Contra Gentiles* by St Thomas Aquinas. This manuscript must have been prepared before 1475, for it is included in the inventory of the Vatican library for that year. Mehmet's possession of a work by Thomas Aquinas, the leading Christian interpreter of Aristotle, supports the statement by Kritoboulos that the

Conqueror 'held philosophical discussions' with scholars in his court 'about the principles of philosophy, particularly those of the Peripatetics [i.e. Aristotelians] and the Stoics'.

Mehmet's interest in geography, indicated by the map that George Amiroutzes created for him from Ptolemy's *Geographia*, is also evidenced by another work that Raby found in the Conqueror's scriptorium. This is a Greek translation of the *Liber Insularum Archipelagi* (*The Islands of the Archipelago*), published in 1420 by the Florentine geographer Cristoforo Buondelmonti. Buondelmonti's book contains charts of the eastern Mediterranean and its hinterland, including the earliest extant map of Constantinople and the only one from before Mehmet's conquest of the city in 1453. Later editions of his book exist up to 1480, with the map of Constantinople in the latest showing some of the earliest Ottoman buildings in the city, including the Mosque of the Conqueror and Topkapı Sarayı.

Other Greek manuscripts in the Conqueror's scriptorium include Hesiod's *Theogony*; Oppian's *Halieutika*; *Miscellany* by Planudes, including a *Life of Aesop* and the *Fables of Aesop*, *The Prophecies of Hippocrates Discovered in his Grave*, and *The Art of the Lyre*; Antonios Monachos, *Bible Lexicon*, attributed to Cyril of Alexander; an anonymous work *On Precious Stones and the Properties of Animals*; Manuel Moschopoulos, *Grammar*; an anonymous work on *Grammar, Declension and Conjugation of Verbs*; Pindar's *Olympiaka*; Eudemos Rhetor, *Lexicon*; and an anonymous work *On the Testament of Solomon*.

Raby points out that the *Testament* 'seems to have been designed as one of a pair for the sultan's library, although its companion was not a Greek work but an Arabic translation from the Syriac'. The companion volume is *Kitab Daniyal al-nabi* (*Book of the Prophet Daniel*), preserved in the library of Haghia Sophia. According to Raby, both books were magical treatises that served for prognostications, and he has shown that both were dedicated to Mehmet II.

Aside from the sixteen Greek manuscripts that can be traced to the Conqueror's scriptorium, there are other works in the Topkapı collection that can be dated to his reign. One of these, according to Raby, is 'a Hebrew commentary by Mordechai ben Eliezer Comtino on Maimonides' *Guide to the Perplexed*, which is codicologically comparable to the Greek series in the Saray and which is dated 10 Kislev 5241, that is 12 November A. D. 1480'. Raby goes on to note that 'Mordechai Comtino (1420–pre-1487) was born in Constantinople and lived in Edirne for a time in the 1450s. He was a leading member of the Jewish intellectual community in

Constantinople/Istanbul and was celebrated as a Talmudist, Commentator, Mathematician, and Astronomer.' Comtino is known to have had contacts with Muslim scholars in Istanbul, and since one of his works was in the Conqueror's scriptorium it would seem that he was a member of Mehmet's intellectual circle.

Sultan Mehmet was also interested in the work of George Gemisthus Plethon (c. 1355–1452), the great neo-Platonist philosopher, whom Sir Steven Runciman has called 'the most original of Byzantine thinkers'. Plethon was educated in Constantinople and taught there until c. 1392. He then went to Mistra in the Peloponnesos, which at the time was ruled by the despot Theodore Palaeologus, second son of the emperor Manuel II. Plethon taught there for the rest of his days, except for a year he spent as a member of the Byzantine delegation at the Council of Ferrara-Florence. Plethon's teaching was dominated by his rejection of Aristotle and his devotion to Plato, who inspired his goal of reforming the Greek world along Platonic lines. His religious beliefs were more pagan than Christian, as evidenced by his treatise *On the Laws*, in which he usually refers to God as Zeus and writes of the Trinity as consisting of the Creator, the World-mind and the World-soul. George Trapezuntios writes of a conversation he had at Florence with Plethon, who told him that the whole world would soon adopt a new religion. When asked if the new religion would be Christian or Mohammedan, Plethon replied, 'Neither, it will not be different from paganism.'

A manuscript in the Topkapı collection is evidence of Sultan Mehmet's interest in Plethon's writings. According to Raby, this work 'contains an Arabic translation of Plethon's *Compendium Zoroastreorum et Platonicorum dogmatum*, Plethon's entire collection of that fundamental neo-Platonic text, the *Chaldean Chronicles*, and fragments of his *Nomoi*, which included a hymn to Zeus!'.

Mehmet was noted as a patron of literature, and during his reign he supported some thirty poets and scholars, according to contemporary Turkish sources. The sixteenth-century Turkish historian Hoca Sadeddin writes that Sultan Mehmet was held in high regard by all his subjects,

> particularly by those who had distinguished themselves in letters and science during his reign, because of the marks of esteem and consideration they had received from him in the shape of liberalities... The protection he had extended to men of letters has resulted in the production of innumerable works of value, the majority of which are

dedicated to him... He also collected several thousand manuscripts, in most instances autograph copies of the rarest and most valuable commentaries and exigeses on Islamic law and religion, and caused them to be distributed in each of the mosques which he had built for the use and convenience of the teachers residing in these mosques. In short he forgot none of the good works he could do in this world.

Persian was the language of literature in the Ottoman Empire of Mehmet's time, while works in Islamic theology were written in Arabic. But although Mehmet had studied both Persian and Arabic, when he himself wrote it was mostly in colloquial Turkish. Writing under the pseudonym Avni, he left a collection, known as a *divan*, consisting of some eighty poems in Turkish, interspersed with a few Persian verses called *gazels*, which were merely paraphrases of works by the great Iranian poet Hafız. One of the frequently quoted love poems from Mehmet's *divan* reveals his utter lack of originality.

> When the rosebud in the garden dons its coat
> It fashions the buttons from rosebuds.
> When in speech the tongue weaves roses and buds together
> Its words are as nothing compared to her sweet lips.
> When you stroll through the garden with a hundred coy deceits
> The jasmine branches are so amazed at the sight that they sway with you.
> When the dogwood sees the roses strewn in your path
> Then it too strews its roses before you.
> Until that rose-cheeked beauty comes to see the garden,
> O Avni, may the ground be always damp with the tears of your eyes!

The most notable poet in Mehmet's court was Ahmet Pasha, a decendant of the Prophet Mohammed, but even his work is lacking in originality. The same is true of two women poets of Mehmet's reign, Zeynep Hatun and Mihri Hatun. Zeynep Hatun, who was notorious for her many scandalous love affairs, wrote a *divan* in Turkish and Persian that she dedicated to Mehmet II. Mihri Hatun, known as 'the Sappho of the Ottomans', wrote love poems that her contemporary biographer Aşık Çelebi described as purely platonic, for 'not the slightest cloud darkened her reputation for virtue'. 'Despite this poetic love,' he writes, 'this woman of the world ceded to the desires of no one, no lover's hand touched the treasure of her maidenly charms, and no arm excepting her amber-scented necklace embraced her pure neck, for she lived and died a virgin.'

Several Italian artists were at one time or another resident at Mehmet's court in Topkapı Sarayı. Early in 1461 Mehmet entered into correspondence with the condottiere Sigismondo Pandolpho Malatesta, lord of Rimini, whom Pope Pius II called the 'prince of wickedness'. Mehmet asked that an artist be sent to do his portrait, and Malatesta sent the painter and medallist Matteo de'Pasti of Verona, a student of Pisanello who had long been resident at his court in Rimini. Matteo set off for Istanbul in September 1461, bearing with him two presents from Malatesta for Mehmet. One of these was a manuscript of *De re militari*, an illustrated work on warfare by Roberto Valturio, a humanist scholar in Malatesta's court; the other was a detailed map of the Adriatic. Matteo's ship was stopped off Crete by the Venetians, who arrested him and brought him to Venice, where the Council of Ten questioned him about his purpose in going to Istanbul, for Malatesta was suspected of planning to form an alliance with the sultan. Matteo was freed by the Venetians and by early January 1462 he was back in Rimini, having been prevented from reaching Istanbul. Nevertheless, Matteo did do a medallion portrait of Mehmet, in collaboration with the Burgundian painter Jean Tricaudet, though there is no evidence that either of the artists was ever in Istanbul.

Late in the 1470s Mehmet corresponded with King Ferrante of Naples, asking him to send an artist to do his portrait. Ferrante sent the painter Costanzo da Ferrara, who arrived in Istanbul in 1477 or 1478, remaining for a year or two. Costanzo did two versions of a medallion portrait of Mehmet, the first of which is now at the National Gallery in Washington, DC. The obverse of this medallion, dated 1481, is a bust of the sultan and the reverse shows him on horseback, both in left profile. The second version, which is the same except for minor details, was reproduced in many castings.

During the summer of 1479 Mehmet wrote to Doge Giovanni Mocenigo, inviting him to the circumcision of one of his grandchildren and also requesting that the Venetians send him 'a good painter'. The doge politely declined the invitation to the circumcision, but, in consultation with the Signoria, he sent the painter Gentile Bellini to Istanbul. Apparently, Bellini's visit to Istanbul was prompted by a letter written by Giovanni-Maria Angiolello, who writes in his *Historia turchesca* of the great pleasure that Sultan Mehmet took in looking at paintings. Angiolello says, 'It was I who wrote to the illustrious government of Venice that they should send one of their best painters to Constantinople, and there was sent Gentile Bellini, a very expert painter, whom Muhammed [Mehmet] used to see freely.'

Bellini arrived in Istanbul in the autumn of 1479 and remained until the beginning of 1481. The only authenticated work from his stay is his famous portrait of Sultan Mehmet the Conqueror, now in the National Portrait Gallery in London. The portrait shows Mehmet in three-quarters left profile, with deep-set brown eyes, a particularly long and thin scimitar of a nose projecting over his tightly shut thin red lips, reminding one observer of 'a parrot about to eat ripe cherries', a reddish-brown beard pointed at the chin, his head covered by a multi-layered white turban with a red conical top, wearing a red kaftan with a broad fur collar.

Other works attributed to Bellini and dated from his stay in Istanbul include a double portrait of Mehmet and a young man, now in a private collection in Switzerland, and sketches of a janissary and a young woman, now in the British Museum. An album in the library of Istanbul University contains a miniature of the Virgin and Child that may have been painted by Bellini, since it is similar to a painting in the Berlin Museum signed by Bellini. Anecdotal evidence indicates that Bellini painted frescoes on the walls of a pavilion that Mehmet had erected in Topkapı Sarayı, probably the Fatih Köşkü in the Third Court, but these have vanished.

The Florentine artist Bertoldo di Giovanni was commissioned by Lorenzo de'Medici to do a medallion portrait of Sultan Mehmet, which was completed in 1480. The obverse shows Mehmet in left profile and may have been copied from Bellini's portrait of the sultan. The reverse shows the figure of the sultan riding in a chariot drawn by two horses led by the running god Mars. The sultan is holding a rope that encircles three nude women carried on the rear of the chariot, each of them wearing a crown, inscriptions identifying them as Asia, Trebizond and Greece, the three empires conquered by Mehmet. The inscription on the obverse reads 'Mehmet, Emperor of Asia, Trebizond and Greater Greece', the latter term meaning the European dominions of the Byzantine Empire in its prime.

The Topkapı Sarayı Museum has a miniature watercolour portrait of the Conqueror ascribed to the Turkish artist Sinan Bey, who is believed to have studied with an Italian master. The portrait shows Mehmet in left profile seated in the oriental fashion, grasping a handkerchief in his left hand and with his right hand holding a rose up to his nose, the faintest of smiles lighting up his face.

Mehmet's chief architect, known in Turkish as Atik Sinan, was probably a Greek known as Christodoulos. Mehmet commissioned him to build Fatih Camii, the Mosque of the Conqueror, whose plan derived from that of the

Great Church of Haghia Sophia, basically a cube covered by a dome. Mehmet's interest in other styles of architecture besides Turkish is evident in a remark of Angiolello, who says that the Conqueror built in the gardens of the Saray three pavalions, 'one in the Persian-Karaman style, another *alla turchesca*, and a third *alla greca*'. The second and third of these can no longer be identified, but the first is certainly Çinili Köşk, the Tiled Pavilion, a building entirely Persian in its design and decoration.

Mehmet wrote to Sigismondo Pandolpho Malatesta asking for the services of the builder and sculptor Matteo de'Pasti, a follower of the great architect Leon Battista Alberti. When de'Pasti was prevented from reaching Istanbul by the Venetians, Mehmet contacted other disciples of Alberti, including Antonio Averlino, known as Filarete. It is possible that Filarete may have been involved in the design and construction of some of the buildings in Topkapı Sarayı. The Italian humanist Francesco Filelfo wrote to George Amiroutzes on 30 July 1465 to say that Filarete was about to sail to Istanbul, where he may have stayed on, since Italian sources do not mention him after that time. The symmetrical plan of Topkapı Sarayı resembles that of Filarete's Ospedale Maggiori in Milan, which appears in his *Trattato di architettura*, a copy of which was found in the library of King Matthias Corvinus. Mehmet also invited the Bolognese architect Aristotele Fioravanti to Istanbul, but the Italian went instead to Moscow, where he worked on the Kremlin.

Mehmet's grand vezir Mahmut Pasha rivalled the sultan himself as a patron of literature, though in Islamic letters rather than in Greek classics. As Hoca Sadeddin wrote of Mahmut Pasha, referring to the *ulema*, or learned class of the empire: 'The books and treatises written with his name bear witness to his inclination and care for the *ulema*.' The works of only two of the scholars he supported have survived, those of the poet Enveri and the historian Şükrüllah.

Enveri composed a work entitled *Düsturname* (*Book of the Vezir*), completed in 1464, which he dedicated to his patron: 'For the exalted Mahmut Pasha/I composed the *Düsturname*.' The book is a verse epic in three parts, with the first giving the history of Muslim dynasties from the Prophet to the Ottomans, the second recounting the reign of the fourteenth-century emir Umur Bey of Aydın, and the third a history of the Ottoman sultans up to 1464, the last two sections devoted to the exploits of Mahmut Pasha. Enveri also wrote another work entitled *Teferrücname*, probably an account of the Ottoman campaign in Wallachia in 1462, but this has not survived.

Şükrüllah composed a world history in Persian entitled *Behcetü't-Tevarih* (*The Beauty of Histories*), which he dedicated to his patron Mahmut Pasha, 'the beam of the pillars of the kingdom, the flame in the skies of the Vezirate, the one who repairs the affairs of men, the Sultan of Vezirs in the world, the advisor of Beys and Sultans...'. The book is divided into twelve sections, giving the history of the world since the Creation, with emphasis on Muslim dynasties, the last section devoted to the Ottoman Empire.

The historian Tursun Beg, author of *The History of Mehmed the Conqueror*, also enjoyed the patronage of Mahmut Pasha. Tursun served as Mahmut's secretary for twelve years, which he says 'were the most pleasant of my life and passed with the fruits of [Mahmut Pasha's] culture and the profits of his company'. Tursun was always at Mahmut's side in the many campaigns that the grand vezir commanded, which gave him a unique perspective in describing these expeditions. He also served as secretary of the Divan, so that he had an insider's view of internal politics in the reign of Mehmet the Conqueror. Halil Inalcık and Rhoads Murphey, in their translation of *The History of Mehmed the Conqueror*, write that 'Tursun Beg's history was written in the official literary prose style which was in the process of development in Ottoman government circles at that time; it can thus be regarded as one of the first and most important examples of fifteenth-century Ottoman historical writing'.

Other scholars who benefited from Mahmut Pasha's patronage included the poets Hamidi, Halimi, Saruca Kemal, Hayati, Nizami and Cemali, all of whom wrote works in praise of the grand vezir. Mahmut Pasha also patronised distinguished scholars and promising students, particularly through the schools he founded, one of his protégés being the future grand vezir Karamani Mehmet Pasha. Tursun Beg, in the introduction to his history, quotes Mahmut Pasha as saying: 'It is said that the best morals for Sultans, which are necessary for happiness in this and the next world and for proximity to God, prescribe the welcoming of and proximity to scholars and mystics.'

Mahmut Pasha founded two libraries, one attached to the *medrese* of his mosque complex in Istanbul and the other at his estate in Hasköy, twelve miles east of Edirne. The library of Mahmut Pasha's *medrese* was one of the first two Ottoman libraries in Istanbul, the other being that of Sultan Mehmet at his mosque complex in Eyüp.

Theoharis Stavrides, in his biography of Mahmut Pasha, writes: 'The contents of the libraries of his schools were geared towards the curriculum of that educational institution, which put emphasis on religious and legal studies, as well as on science and philosophy.' One of the extant manuscripts known to have been in Mahmut Pasha's personal library is *al-Aǧrad at-Tibbiya ve'l-mahabis al-Alaiya*, a book on medicine by Ismail ibn Huseyin al-Jurjani (d. 1136), copied in AH 862 (AD 1458). According to Süheyl Ünver, several of the books from Mahmut Pasha's personal library had gilded labels and headings as well as decorations, indicating that he was a collector of beautiful volumes. Mahmut Pasha wrote under the pen name of Adni in his *Divan*, which contains poems in both Turkish and Persian. His poetry is in the form of *gazels*, poems of five or more distichs, such as this example from the *Divan*:

> She made her lock of hair, as dark as the night, a curtain over her moon face.

> Is there a day in which she does not turn the lover's morning into night?

Both the sultan and the greatest of his grand vezirs were men of culture and patrons of the arts, and the Conqueror's court in Istanbul rivalled in its brilliance that of Western princes of the European Renaissance. The Florentine humanist Giannozzo Manetti, writing two years after the Conquest, hailed Mehmet as 'the young leader of the Turks, young in age, great in spirit, even greater in power'.

The Conqueror's court reached its peak in 1465, which Mehmet spent taking his ease in the House of Felicity. After his description of Mehmet's activities during his vacation from the wars he had fought in since his childhood, Kritoboulos concludes the account of this pleasant and fruitful year, the only tranquil period in the Conqueror's tumultuous life, by noting: 'While the Sultan busied himself and was occupied with this and similar studies, the whole summer passed, and the autumn; and so was ended the 6973rd year in all, being the fifteenth of the Sultan's reign [AD 1465].'

9 *The Conquest of Negroponte*

After his year's rest in Istanbul, Mehmet resumed his march of conquest in the spring of 1466, leading a campaign into Albania, where Skanderbeg, with Venetian reinforcements, was still holding out in his mountain fortress at Kruje. Kritoboulos describes the devastating total war waged by Mehmet in attacking the Albanians, whom he calls Illyrians.

> He himself with the whole army moved in first into their lower lands, where the cavalry could act. This region he entirely overran and plundered...devastating the country, burning the crops or else gathering them in for himself, and destroying and annihilating. And the Illyrians took their children, wives, stocks and every other movable up into the high and inaccessible mountain fastnesses.

According to Kritoboulos, Mehmet ordered his light infantry and spearmen up into the mountains to pursue the Albanians, followed by the heavily armed units, until they finally trapped their quarry on the heights.

> Then, with a mighty shout, the light infantry, the heavy infantry and the spearmen charged the Illyrians, and having put them to flight, they pursued with all their might, and overtook and killed them. And some they captured alive. But some of them, hard pressed by the heavy infantry, hurled themselves from the precipices and crags, and were destroyed... A very great number of the Illyrians lost their lives, some in the fighting, and others were executed after being captured, for so the Sultan ordered. And there were captured in these mountains about twenty thousand children, and women, and men. Of the rest of the Illyrians, some were in

the fortresses, and some in other mountain ranges where they had fled with their leader, Alexander [Skanderbeg].

The advance guard of the Ottoman army under Balaban Bey then laid siege to Kruje, whose citadel was defended by 1,000 men under Baldassare Perducci and Gian-Maria Contarini, the Venetian commander in Albania, while Skanderbeg occupied a fortified camp near the lower city. Balaban's troops suffered heavy losses in several assaults on the citadel, while at the same time they were attacked from the rear by Skanderbeg's men.

When Mehmet arrived with the main Turkish army he saw that he would not be able to take Kruje without a prolonged and bloody campaign. And so he left Balaban to continue the siege while he withdrew with the main army to build a fortress some thirty miles to the south at Elbasan, which would be used as the main Turkish base for future campaigns in Albania. Mehmet then headed back to Edirne with the main army, leaving a garrison of 400 of his best troops in Elbasan.

A flood of Albanian refugees fleeing to southern Italy led to false reports that Skanderbeg had been defeated by Mehmet, who supposedly put thousands of Albanians to the sword and enslaved the rest. These reports prompted Pope Paul II to make another appeal to the Christian princes of Europe to unite against Mehmet, and late in 1466 he wrote to Duke Philip of Burgundy.

> My dearest son: Scanderbeg, stalwart athlete of Christ, ruler of the great part of Albania, who has fought for our faith for more than twenty years, has been attacked by vast Turkish forces and now defeated in battle, stripped of all his dominions, and driven defenselesss and destitute to our shores. The Albanians, his fellow warriors, have been put to the sword, some of them reduced to abject slavery... Evils without number encompass them, but the Turkish ruler, victorious, proud, monstrous, equipped with greater forces than before, rushes forward to claim one land after another.

Late in the autumn of 1466 Skanderbeg made a hurried trip to Italy in search of aid against the Turks, particularly from the Pope. On 12 December the Mantuan ambassador reported the Albanian prince's arrival in Rome: 'The lord Scanderbeg arrived here Friday, and the households of the cardinals were sent out to meet him. He is a man of advanced age, past sixty; he has come with a few horses, a poor man. I understand he will seek aid.'

The Milanese ambassadors to Rome reported that the Pope was reluctant to give the Albanian prince substantial aid against the Turks while there was the threat of internal war in Italy, and they noted that Paul had asked Skanderbeg to write to his envoy in Venice of 'how the pope refuses to give him any subvention to be used against the Turk in Albania unless he first sees such security in Italy that there is no likelihood of war here, and that all the other Italian powers are in accord on this, except that the Vatican seems rather to be holding back'.

On 7 January 1467 Cardinal Francesco Gonzaga wrote to his father, Marquis Lodovico II of Mantua, to report that he had attended a secret consistory that morning on the matter of aid to Skanderbeg, to whom the Pope was willing to give only 5,000 ducats. Cardinal Gonzaga wrote to his father again five days later to report that he had been to another consistory that morning, at which the Pope had discussed 'the affairs of Scanderbeg, to whom will be given only the five thousand ducats'. Gonzaga went on to note that the Pope's reluctance to give more aid was due to his uncertainty concerning internal affairs in Italy, and also because he was waiting to see how much help Skanderbeg would get from King Ferrante in Naples. Meanwhile, according to Gonzaga, Skanderbeg was waiting in Rome in hope of a larger contribution from the Pope, 'but his Holiness wants to see what shape the affairs of Italy are going to take, for if there is to be a war, he intends that his first expenditure should be for his own protection... In the meantime Skanderbeg is much aggrieved and well nigh desperate.'

Skanderbeg finally left Rome on 14 February 1467, according to Lorenzo da Pesaro. Pesaro noted that 'Scanderbeg departed today in despair, for he had not received any money from the pope. A cardinal gave him two hundred ducats... In jeering tones he said to a cardinal the other day that he would rather make war against the Church than on the Turk.' Five days later Pesaro wrote that Skanderbeg left Rome 'saying that he did not believe one could find greater cruelty anywhere in the world than among these priests!'. It seems that Skanderbeg's departure from Rome was delayed because he could not pay his bill at the inn where he had been staying. After he had received 200 ducats from the cardinal he paid his bill, which left him only forty ducats when he set out for Naples. But at the last moment the Pope had a change of heart and gave Skanderbeg 2,300 ducats, 'and so he went away'.

Skanderbeg fared somewhat better in Naples, where King Ferrante immediately gave him a small subsidy along with provisions and arms. He then returned to Albania, where he raised a force for the relief of Kruje, which was still being besieged by Balaban. Early in the spring of 1467

Skanderbeg defeated and killed Balaban, whose forces fled in disorder, after which he went on to put the Turkish fortress at Elbasan under siege.

Meanwhile, the Venetians had taken advantage of Mehmet's absence in Albania to renew their offensive against the Turks, sending a fleet into the Aegean under Vettore Capello in 1466. Capello attacked and occupied the islands of Imbros and Lemnos, after which he sailed back and put Patras under siege. Ömer Bey, Mehmet's commander in Greece, led a force to relieve the Turkish garrison in Patras, where he was was initially defeated by the Venetians and forced to flee. But then Ömer turned on his pursuers and routed them, forcing the Venetians to lift their siege of Patras and abort the rest of their campaign.

Their defeat at Patras led the Venetians to seek peace with Mehmet, and in December 1466 they sent Giovanni Capello to Istanbul, where he entered into negotiations with Mahmut Pasha. Mahmut demanded the return of Imbros and Tenedos as well as the payment of an annual tribute by Venice, and when Capello rejected this demand he was dismissed and returned to Venice.

Mehmet launched another expedition into Albania early in the spring of 1467. The campaign stemmed from the sultan's rage when he learned that Skanderbeg had forced the Ottoman army to lift its siege of Kruje, according to Kritoboulos. He writes that when Mehmet arrived in Albania 'he ravaged the whole of it rapidly, and subdued its revolted people, killing many of them. He devastated and plundered whatever he could get hold of, burning, devastating, ruining, and annihilating.' Kritoboulos goes on to tell of how Mehmet pursued Skanderbeg, 'who took refuge in the inaccessible fortresses in the mountains, in his customary retreats and abodes in the hills... The Sultan gave his soldiers permission to plunder and slaughter all the prisoners, and he sent up into the mountains the largest and most warlike part of the army, under Mahmud. He himself with the rest of the army, went on ravaging the rest of the country.' But Skanderbeg, 'when he learned that the mountains had been captured by the army, hastily fled, nor have I learned whither. And the Sultan, after ravaging and plundering the countryside, marched again to Kroues [Kruje]. On reaching there he camped before it, dug a trench, and completely surrounded the town with his army, placed his cannon in position, and besieged it.'

Mehmet withdrew his forces in the late summer of 1467, leaving Kruje and four other fortified towns – Shkoder, Drisht, Lezhe and Durres – in the hands of the Albanians and their Venetian allies. Skanderbeg made his way to Lezhe (Alessio), on the northern coast of Albania, where following a brief illness he died on 17 January 1478, after which he was buried in the church of St Nicholas. According to tradition, Skanderbeg's last words were a plea to Venice, his 'most loyal and powerful ally', to protect Albania as well as his young son John.

Mehmet's return to Istanbul was delayed by a terrible outbreak of the plague in the southern Balkans, which Kritoboulos writes of at the very end of his *History of Mehmed the Conqueror*, leading to the supposition that he himself was a victim of the epidemic.

> As he found that the country around Nikopolis and Vidin was healthful and had a good climate, he spent the entire autumn there. But after a short time he learned that the disease was diminishing and that the City was free of it, for he had frequent couriers, nearly every day, traveling by swift relays, and reporting on conditions in the City. So at the beginning of winter he went to Byzantium. So closed the 6975th year in all [AD 1467], which was the seventeenth year of the reign of the Sultan.

Mehmet then focused his attention on Anatolia, which he had neglected during his year of inactivity and in the two years following because of his Albanian wars. The political situation in Anatolia had been destabilised since the death on 4 August 1464 of Mehmet's vassal, Ibrahim Bey of Karaman. Ibrahim had left seven sons, the eldest of whom, Ishak, was the child of a slave woman, while the other six – Pir Ahmet, Kasım, Karaman, Nure Sufi, Alaeddin and Süleyman – were children of Sultan Hatun, a sister of Murat II, and thus cousins of Sultan Mehmet. Ishak had always been the favourite of Ibrahim, who in his latter days conferred upon him the town of Silifke, on the Mediterranean coast. Ibrahim's six other sons were enraged by this and besieged their father in his capital at Konya. Ibrahim managed to escape to the mountain fortress of Kevele, south of Akşehir, where he died soon afterwards.

Pir Ahmet, the oldest of Ibrahim's six sons by Sultan Hatun, took possession of Konya and the northern part of Karaman, the richest and most fertile part of the emirate. Two of his brothers – Süleyman and Nure Sufi, appealed to their cousin Sultan Mehmet, who gave them fiefs within Ottoman territory in central Anatolia. A third brother – Kasım – fled first to Syria and then to Cairo, where he was given refuge by the Mamluk sultan Koshkadem.

Ishak entered into negotiation with the Akkoyunlu chieftain Uzun Hasan, who gave him funds and troops to support him against Pir Ahmet.

The Egyptian chronicler Ibn Taghriberdi gives a summary of this campaign, in which both Ishak and Uzun Hasan apparently recognised the sovereignty of the Mamluk sultan over Karaman.

> Hasan Beg went with his troops from Diyarbakır to the land of Karaman to assist Ishak of Karaman in fighting his brothers. Together with Ishak, he fought the aforementioned until he had defeated them and driven them from Karaman, and pursued them to the sea-coast. He seized their goods and provisions, and took back from them Kayseri, Akşehir, Develi, Beyşehir, Konya and Aksaray, and delivered these cities to emir Ishak.

Ishak then sent an envoy to Istanbul to seek the support of Mehmet, who rejected his request and sent an army against him under Hamza Bey. Hamza Bey, accompanied by Pir Ahmet, defeated Ishak's forces in a battle near Mut, in southern Karaman. Ishak was forced to take refuge with Uzun Hasan, leaving his wife and children behind in Silifke. Pir Ahmet gave Silifke to the young son of Ishak, while he added the rest of his half-brother's territory to his own realm except for the towns of Akşehir and Beyşehir, which he handed over to his cousin Mehmet, acknowledging his status as the sultan's vassal. Meanwhile, Ishak died in Diyarbakır in August 1465, so that Uzun Hasan no longer had a stake in the sovereignity of Karaman.

During the winter of 1467–8 there were two successive usurpations in the Mamluk sultanate in Egypt. The second of these regime changes brought to power Kaitbey, who proved to be one of the greatest of all the Mamluk sultans. The instability in Egypt prompted Mehmet to launch a campaign against the Mamluks in the spring of 1468. Pir Ahmet was supposed to join the expedition as an Ottoman vassal, but he reneged, and so Mehmet attacked him instead of proceeding against the Mamluks. Tursun Beg describes the campaign.

> The Ottoman troops overran Karaman, and Pir Ahmed fled to Taş-Ili. The Sultan took Kevele, Konya, the capital of the Karamanids, and Larende, and gave the responsibility for the administration of the province to Prince Mustafa. When the Sultan reached Kara-Hisar on his way back to Istanbul he dismissed Grand Vezir Mahmud Pasha. The ostensible reason for his dismissal was that Mahmud had pledged for Pir Ahmed's loyalty, assuaging the Sultan's doubts that Pir Ahmed would be present for service. This affair took place in the year 872 [1467–8]. In the spring of 873 [1469], the Sultan remained in Istanbul and sent an army into Karaman to clean up the rebels.

Other Turkish sources say that when Mahmut Pasha was dismissed as grand vezir his tent was suddenly collapsed on his head, apparently an old Turkish tribal custom. After his dismissal Mahmut withdrew to his estate at Hasköy. He remained there until late in 1469, when he was appointed *sancakbey*, or provincial governor, at Gelibolu on the European shore of the Dardanelles, a position that also made him chief admiral of the Ottoman fleet.

Meanwhile, Mahmut was replaced as grand vezir by Ishak Pasha, who held the office until 1471, when he in turn was replaced by Rum Mehmet Pasha. Rum Mehmet, as his first name implies, was of Greek origin, having converted to Islam when he joined the sultan's service. The Turkish sources all agree that the downfall of Mahmut Pasha was largely due to the machinations of Rum Mehmet Pasha.

Mehmet's absence from Europe on his Anatolian campaign led the Venetians to think that this was the opportune time to launch an expedition against the Turks. On 3 June 1468 Doge Cristoforo Moro wrote in this vein to Jacopo Loredan, the Venetian Captain-General of the Sea.

> Never, in everyone's judgment, has there been a more promising and favorable period than at present for embarking upon an expedition against the Turk, the fierce enemy of our faith. The opportunity has been divinely granted to us at the time when, beside the poor conditions in his domains and especially the plague, he is far away in distant lands in Asia, from which he cannot return for many days and months. His whole army, furthermore, will probably come back in poor condition. Consequently...you must consider embarking upon such an expedition as you shall deem both honorable and expedient.

Arrangements were made for Loredan to recruit men from Crete, Corfu and other Venetian territories, while troops and warships would be sent to him from the republic's strongholds in the Adriatic. Meanwhile, Turkish raiders had been attacking as far afield as Zara and Senj on the upper Adriatic, while an Ottoman fleet in the Agean sacked the Venetian-held island of Andros.

Reports then began arriving in Venice that Mehmet was preparing a huge fleet and army for a campaign in the Aegean, probably against the Venetian strongholds of Negroponte and Nauplia in Greece. This led the Senate to appoint Niccolo da Canale to be both Captain-General of the Sea and *provveditore* of Negroponte. During the summer of 1469 Canale commanded a Venetian fleet that brutally sacked and burned the port-city of Enez, north of the Gallipoli peninsula, carrying off around 2,000 prisoners, including some 200 Greek women. He then did the same at Yeni Foça on the Aegean coast of Asia Minor. These attacks were occasions for rejoicing in Venice, but they had no military significance and did nothing more than enrage Mehmet and provoke him into launching an expedition against the Venetians.

The Venetians had been trying to convince Pope Paul II that they were in imminent danger of being attacked by the Turks, and that they desperately needed help. On 7 July 1470 the Senate wrote to the Venetian ambassadors in Rome telling them to seek an immediate audience with the Pope, and to inform him 'that the Turk has sent a fleet of three hundred and fifty sail under Mahmud Pasha out from the Dardanelles, and that he himself has also come with a huge and powerful army to lay siege to Negroponte'.

The Ottoman fleet sailed out of the Dardanelles on 3 June 1470 under the command of Mahmut Pasha, while at the same time Mehmet led the main army from Thrace down the east coast of Greece. As Mahmut sailed through the northern Aegean he attacked the Venetian-held islands of Imbros, Limnos and Skyros, while the Venetian fleet under Niccolo da Canale followed at a safe distance, not daring to attack because of its much inferior numbers and firepower. The Venetian captain Geronimo Lungo, observing the Ottoman armada at Skyros, wrote, 'At first I judged it to be of 300 sail. Now I believe there are 400... The sea looked like a forest. It seems incredible to hear tell of it, but to see it is something stupendous! [...] Negroponte is in danger, and if it falls, our whole state in the Levant will be lost as far as Istria.'

The Ottoman fleet sailed around the south end of Euboea and entered the Euripos channel, anchoring near Negroponte on 15 June, disembarking the troops aboard the transports on the shore of the island south of the fortress. Mehmet arrived with the main army three days later, leading his troops down from the hills to the Euripos, where the Venetians had destroyed the bridge connecting the island to the mainland. One Venetian observer estimated that there were 70,000 troops aboard the transports, with another 120,000 in the main army, although modern authorities hold that the total number of men was about 100,000.

Niccolo da Canale anchored his flotilla of thirty-six galleys and six freight vessels off Akri Mandilli, the southernmost cape of Euboea, refraining from an attack on the Turkish fleet until he received reinforcements. He sent a fast galley to Candia in Crete to order the Venetian *provveditore* there to send him

116

as many ships and troops as possible. Geronimo Lungo was sent to Venice via Corfu, bearing a message from Canale that he would attack the Turks when he had a fleet of 100 galleys and ten round-ships.

The Senate received Canale's letter on 24 June, whereupon they outfitted fourteen great galleys and fourteen round-ships that had been under construction in the Venetian Arsenale. Meanwhile, Canale sailed his flotilla off to Candia, where the *provveditore* had outfitted seven round-ships on receiving the admiral's letter.

A Venetian observer, Fra Giacomo Pugiese, reported that the Ottoman fleet had entered the Euripos channel on 14 June, and 'on 15 June came before Chalkis and prepared to build a bridge from St. Chiara on the mainland with forty-five galleys and seven armed round-ships'. When the bridge of boats was complete Sultan Mehmet crossed to Euboea with one-half of the main army, leaving the remainder on the mainland. He then set up mortar batteries at four points around Negroponte, from which they could fire over the outer walls of the fortress and into the town of Chalkis itself.

Negroponte was one of the strongest fortresses in the Venetian maritime empire. The overall command was in the hands of Paolo Erizzo, the *bailo* of Negroponte, while the garrison was under the joint command of Captains Alviso Calbo and Giovanni Bandumier.

Before beginning hostilities Sultan Mehmet sent an emissary to the defenders on 25 June proposing that they surrender under what he thought were generous terms. The sultan offered the inhabitants of Negroponte ten years' exemption from taxes; those who possessed a villa would be given an extra one; while the *bailo* and the two co-captains of the garrison were offered high positions in the Ottoman court, for Mehmet knew they could never return to Venice if they surrendered to him. The *bailo* turned down the offer contemptuously, saying to the Ottoman emissary: 'Tell your lord to eat swine's flesh, and then come and meet us at the fosse!'

As soon as the emissary returned Mehmet ordered his forces to attack. According to one Turkish chronicler, 'Mahmud Pasha with the marines and many brave men went from the side of the sea and shot with cannons and guns, making breaches in the walls.' At the same time, Mehmet sent 2,000 cavalry to raid the countryside around Negroponte, where they killed or enslaved all who lived outside the walls and cut off the city from the rest of the island. But the attackers were unable to break through the city walls, and Fra Giacomo estimates that 14,000 of them were killed. Mehmet ordered another attack five days later, but that too failed, with 16,000 of his men killed and thirty of his galleys sunk, in Fra Giacomo's account. Two more unsuccessful attacks followed, with 500 Turks killed on 5 July and 15,000 on 8 July, according to Fra Giacomo, though here again modern authorities say the numbers are highly inflated.

The Venetian fleet commanded by Niccolo da Canale finally returned from Crete on 11 July, when it anchored in the Euripos channel three miles north of the bridge of boats connecting the island to the mainland. The arrival of the Venetian fleet caused panic in the Ottoman camp, for it was thought that Canale would destroy the bridge of boats and cut them off from the mainland. Mehmet at first thought to withdraw his forces, but Mahmut Pasha persuaded him to press on with the siege.

Canale remained at anchor despite signals from the defenders urging him to attack, which he answered by saying that he was waiting for reinforcements. One of his galleys, commanded by Antonio Ottobon, disregarded orders and made its way through the Ottoman armada into the fortress harbour, but when others thought to follow, Canale prevented them from doing so, and thus left Negroponte to its fate.

The final assault began later that same day, when Mahmut Pasha's cannons opened a breach in the fortress walls, after which he led the Ottoman troops as they broke into the city in the early hours of 12 July. The defenders fought valiantly, with the two co-captains, Alviso Calbo and Giovanni Bandumier, killed in the hand-to-hand battle within the city. Paolo Erizzo surrendered to Mahmut Pasha on the promise of safe conduct for him and his fellow defenders, but Sultan Mehmet had them all executed, supposedly having the *bailo* tied between two boards and sawn in half through the waist.

Giovanni-Maria Angiolello, one of the few Venetians to survive the fall of Negroponte, says in his memoir that he was presented to Mehmet by his captor and was inducted into the sultan's service, possibly as a janissary. According to Angiolello, Mehmet rounded up virtually all the populace of Euboea and either executed or enslaved them. Then, after leaving a garrison in Negroponte, Mehmet led his army back to Istanbul, where he arrived on 4 September, according to Angiolello.

Meanwhile, Mahmut Pasha took the Ottoman armada back to Gelibolu in the Dardanelles, shadowed the whole way by the Venetian fleet under Niccolo da Canale. According to the seventeenth-century French historian Guillet de Saint-Georges, writing of Mahmut Pasha's reaction to his

Venetian escort, 'It is related that the Vezir, seeing the Christian fleet finally retiring peacefully, said laughing that the Venetians were treating him like one of their good friends, and that in order to keep exactly the rules of civility, they had escorted him from their place to his.' Mahmut Pasha also sent a cynical message to Doge Cristoforo Moro via the Venetian *bailo* in Istanbul. Referring to the annual ceremony celebrating the symbolic maritime marriage of Venice, the 'Bride of the Sea,' he said, 'You can tell the Doge that he can leave off marrying the sea; it is our turn now.'

After the Turkish fleet left the Aegean, Niccolo da Canale made an attempt to recapture Negroponte, landing troops on Euboea to attack the fortress. But his troops were virtually annihilated by Turkish cavalry. The Venetian chronicler Domenico Malipiero noted that the failure was inevitable because 'no one in the armada gave them any help'.

Soon afterwards an Ottoman army under Hass Murat Pasha swept through the Morea, capturing the Venetian fortress at Vostitsa [Aegeion] on the Gulf of Corinth and other places. According to Malipiero, this led to the surrender of the Venetian fortresses at Belvedere, Chilidoni and Kalamata.

The Venetians reacted with shock and consternation when news of the fall of Negroponte, the 'glory and splendor of Venice', reached the lagoon on 27 July, as the Milanese ambassador reported to his duke: 'All Venice is in the grip of horror; the inhabitants, half dead with fear, are saying that to give up all their possessions on the mainland would have been a lesser evil.' But the republic was determined to fight on against the Turks, as the Senate declared in a letter sent on 31 July to all the Christian princes of Europe.

> Today the report has been brought to us from Naupactus, our city in Aetolia, that Christ's monstrous enemy the Turk has finally taken by storm the city of Negroponte, to which he had laid siege with an army of incredible size, and that he visited every form of cruelty upon his victims, in keeping with his foul and fearsome character. Nevertheless, we are neither shattered by this loss nor broken in spirit, but rather we have become the more aroused and are [now] determined with the advent of these greater dangers to augment our fleet and to send out fresh garrisons in order to strengthen our hold on our other possessions in the East as well as to render assistance to the other Christian peoples, whose lives are threatened by the implacable foe.

Writing of the fall of Negroponte, Malipiero observed: 'Now it does indeed seem that the greatness of Venice has been brought down, and our pride has been swept away... The fall of Negroponte had terrified all the princes of Italy, but especially the King [Ferrante of Naples], because he possessed the coast of Apulia, exposed to all the Sultan's force.'

A letter sent by the commune of Florence to the Pope on 8 August 1470 warned of the extent of Mehmet's imperial ambitions, saying that what interested the sultan was 'dominion over the globe and not only Italy and the Urbs [Rome]'.

Meanwhile, Venice had been using its network of informers, some of them in contact with members of Mehmet's court, to try and stop the relentless Ottoman advance. Franz Babinger, Mehmet's modern biographer, writes of two such episodes dating from soon after the fall of Negroponte, when the Venetians tried to bribe high Ottoman officials to betray the sultan.

The first episode involved Mesih Pasha, who at the time was in command of the Ottoman fleet at Gelibolu in the Dardanelles. According to Babinger, Mesih sent word to the Venetians through one of their agents that he was prepared to surrender his fleet to them, provided that he received 40,000 ducats and was made ruler of the Morea. But the Council of Ten answered that 10,000 ducats should be enough, making no mention of the Morea, and the plot came to nothing. It would appear that Mesih Pasha's offer was an Ottoman subterfuge, for he retained high office throughout the Conqueror's reign, and was thrice grand vezir under Mehmet's son and successor Beyazit II.

The second episode involved Maestro Iacopo of Gaeta, an Italian Jew who was Mehmet's personal physician and constant companion. The Venetians conspired with Iacopo to poison the sultan, offering him a huge bribe and Venetian citizenship for him and his descendants. But nothing came of the supposed plot, which may also have been an Ottoman scheme, for Maestro Iacopo continued as the sultan's physician and companion through the remainder of Mehmet's reign.

Mehmet in the meanwhile rested on his laurels in Istanbul, sending two of his generals on campaign in Anatolia, while he received ambassadors from the powers of both Europe and Asia, as Tursun Beg writes in describing the sultan's activities after his conquest of Negroponte: 'The Sultan did not accompany the army on campaign in 875 (1470–1). First Rum Mehmet Pasha and then Ishak Pasha were sent to complete the conquest of Karaman. In that year ambassadors came from far and near, from Iran, Bohemia, Hungary and other places, and great festivities were held.'

10 *Victory over the White Sheep*

The two expeditions that Mehmet sent into Anatolia in 1470–1 were due to uprisings in Karaman, first by Pir Ahmet and then by his brother Kasım Bey, both of whom tried to take advantage of the sultan's preoccupation with the siege of Negroponte.

Pir Ahmet, who had taken refuge with Uzun Hasan, tried to regain the territory in Karaman he had lost to the Ottomans. At the same time Kasım Bey, acting independently of his brother, attacked Ankara with some 5,000 troops and laid waste the surrounding countryside. The local Ottoman commanders mustered a force of 5,000 cavalry to drive off the attackers, but they were ambushed by Kasım and lost several hundred men.

When news of this defeat reached Mehmet he appointed Daud Pasha as *sancakbey* in Ankara and sent an army from Istanbul under Rum Mehmet Pasha to put down the rebellion. At the beginning of the campaign Rum Mehmet retook all of Karaman north of the Taurus Mountains, after which he headed south to attack the Varsak Türkmen tribe led by Uyuz Bey. But the Türkmen warriors ambushed the Ottomans and forced Rum Mehmet to retreat and abandon the campaign for the rest of the year.

The following spring Mehmet sent an army under Ishak Pasha to resume the campaign in Karaman against Pir Ahmet and Kasım Bey. Pir Ahmet was forced to flee and take refuge with Uzun Hasan, but Kasım, although defeated by Ishak Pasha's army, eluded capture and continued his rebellion.

Then in the summer of 1471 Mehmet launched another campaign into southern Anatolia by both land and sea to attack the Mediterranean port of Alanya, which was held by the Türkmen emir Kılıç Arslan. Rum Mehmet Pasha led an army across Anatolia to besiege Alanya, while the Ottoman fleet sailed around the Mediterranean coast to attack it from the sea, forcing Kılıç Arslan to surrender.

The capture of Alanya gave the Ottomans control of the Mediterranean shore as far east as Silifke, which was still in the hands of the Karamanid dynasty, along with the fortified coastal towns to its east. Mehmet mounted an expedition to this region in the summer of 1472 under his son Prince Mustafa and Gedik Ahmet Pasha, who took Silifke and the other Karamanid strongholds to its east without resistance.

A Turkish chronicler reports that the Ottoman victory had left Kasım Bey 'fleeing like a bandit from mountain to mountain'. But after the Ottoman army withdrew Kasım persuaded the Varsak Türkmen to recapture Silifke and another stronghold to its east. When Mehmet learned of this he ordered Prince Mustafa and Gedik Ahmet Pasha to march back to Silifke, which they recaptured only after stiff resistance.

Meanwhile, Venice and other European powers were trying to regroup their forces after the fall of Negroponte. Two months after its fall, in mid-September 1470, Pope Paul II wrote to the princes of Italy in an effort to form an anti-Turkish league. 'Beloved sons, there must be no delay, because our enemy, who seems to desire nothing more than the bloody extermination of all Christendon, [is] already at our throats, grows stronger every day, and fresh from the victory he has, he is strengthened in his resolve, so that every slightest delay affords him the opportunity for our common destruction.'

Meanwhile, the Venetian Senate learned of a diplomatic initiative that had been made by Mara Branković, Mehmet's stepmother, and her sister Catherine. The sisters had contacted Sultan Mehmet, who was devoted to Mara, and he indicated to them that he would be receptive to a Venetian embassy to discuss peace terms. On 16 October 1470 the Senate sent a note to the Venetian ambassador in Rome about this development so that he could inform the Pope, concluding with a note of caution. 'Add also that we understand very well that this is one of the usual cunning stunts of the Turk, in whom we believe that absolutely no trust should be placed, for he yearns for the destruction of our faith and religion. Considering the present state of affairs, however, it has seemed best to us to play his own game of pretense and to go along with him.'

The Senate appointed two envoys – Niccolo Cocco and Francesco Capello – and sent them to Istanbul in the hope of negotiating peace terms with Sultan Mehmet. They were instructed to tell the sultan 'that although fortune, in whose grasp lies the determination of all human affairs, has allowed that we should have been drawn into war with his Excellency, nevertheless our intention always has been and is sincerely to live at peace with his Excellency, as we have done for many generations with his most illustrious forebears'. The basic principle for peace could be 'that each should hold and possess what he holds and possesses at present…', and the peace should include 'all the lords of the Aegean archipelago as well as the most serene king of Cyprus; the most reverend lord, the grand master of Rhodes, with the Order [of the Hospitallers]; and the most illustrious lord of S. Maura'.

Then on 22 December 1470 a general defensive alliance of the states of Italy against the Turks was agreed upon, reviving the so-called Italian League that had been created after the Peace of Lodi in 1454. Two days later Pope Paul wrote to the papal governor of Bologna to inform him that 'we have concluded, renewed, blessed, and entered into a league of all the powers in Italy, placing our hope in the Lord that from this confederation, union and league there will come an expedition against [the Turk], the monstrous common enemy of the Christian faith, so that this great peril and crisis may be met by combining our strength'.

But then on 26 July 1471 Pope Paul quite unexpectedly passed away. Eight days later he was succeeded by Cardinal Francesco della Rovere, who became Pope Sixtus IV. The new Pope was very much aware of the imminent danger posed by the Ottomans, and on 23 December he despatched four cardinals as envoys to enlist the various Christian rulers of Europe in an anti-Turkish crusade. Bessarion was sent to France, Burgundy and England, Rodrigo Borgia (the future Pope Alexander VI) to Spain, Marco Barbo to Germany, Hungary and Poland, and Oliverio Carafa to the Kingdom of Naples. Pius reached agreements with both Naples and Venice, giving each of them 72,000 florins annually for two years to launch a papal fleet to be commanded by Cardinal Carafa.

Eight days later Sixtus published an encyclical calling for the united action of Christendom against the common enemy, expressing his deep regret that the 'most truculent race of the Turks, followers of the impious dog Mohammed, had risen rapidly against the Christian faith', capturing Constantinople and other cities and regions of the Byzantine Empire.

The Venetian peace mission was a failure, for the Senate was not willing to accept the terms offered by Mehmet, who for his part had turned down all their proposals. The Venetian envoys were then recalled, but Francesco Capello died in Istanbul, whereupon Niccolo Cocco proceeded homeward via Corfu. There Cocco conferred with another Venetian envoy, Marco Aurelio, who was being sent to Istanbul for further negotiations with the sultan.

But at that point the Senate also recalled Aurelio, for they had learned that Mehmet was preparing a great expedition against Uzun Hasan, chieftain of the Akkoyunlu, or White Sheep, whom the Venetians had long sought as an ally in their struggle with the Ottomans. Instead, the Senate sent Caterino Zeno as an envoy to Uzun Hasan, proposing that a Venetian fleet should attack the Ottomans in the Aegean while the Akkoyunlu fought them in Anatolia.

The Senate had first contacted Uzun Hasan at the beginning of the Venetians' war against the Ottomans. On 2 December 1463 the Senate agreed to seek an alliance with the Akkoyunlu, and soon afterwards the Venetians sent Lazzaro Querini as their envoy to Uzun Hasan's court in Tabriz. Querini returned from Persia to Venice in February 1471, bringing with him an envoy named Murad from Uzun Hasan. Two years earlier Uzun Hasan had defeated Jihanshah, chieftain of the Karakoyunlu, or Black Sheep, thus adding Persia to the domain of the Akkoyunlu, which already comprised eastern Anatolia, Iraq and Syria. Murad Beg delivered a message from Uzun Hasan declaring that he had 'eradicated and expelled Jihanshah, the lord of Persia…and acquired the great dominions of the lord Abu Said…which occupied the greater part of Persia, as far as Baghdad… Now no other obstacle remains, save the son of the Ottoman Turk, Mehmed Bey, and it is an easy thing to abase and eradicate his dominion and lordship.'

Caterino Zeno was chosen as the Venetian envoy to the Akkoyunlu court because of his familiarity with the East and his family links with Uzun Hasan. Caterino had spent years in Damascus with his father Dracone, while his wife Violante was a niece of Uzun Hasan's wife Despina Hatun, originally known as Theodora Comnena, an illegitimate daughter of the late Emperor John IV Comnenus of Trebizond.

Zeno left Venice in the autumn of 1471 in the company of Murad Bey, and after spending several months on Rhodes he crossed over to Anatolia, finally arriving at Tabriz on 30 April 1472. There he was presented to Despina Hatun, to whom he gave rich presents from Venice, after which he was lodged in the royal palace and dined with Uzun Hasan.

At the end of August a Türkmen envoy named Hacı Muhammed arrived in Venice, where he delivered a letter from Uzun Hasan asking for artillery, for the Akkoyunlu had no cannon to face the heavy guns of the Ottoman army. Soon afterwards another Türkmen envoy arrived, an unidentified Sephardic Jew, who delivered a message from Uzun Hasan saying that he was marching westward into Anatolia and would not cease until he had defeated Sultan Mehmet. The envoy then went on to deliver the same message to the Pope and King Ferrante of Naples, and while in Rome he was baptised and converted to Christianity.

Zeno's arrival in Tabriz encouraged a nephew of the late Emperor John IV Comnenus who had taken refuge with Uzun Hasan to recapture Trebizond. Aided by Uzun Hasan and the Georgians, the prince mounted an expedition and besieged Trebizond, but the fierce resistance of the Turkish garrison and the arrival of an Ottoman flotilla of eight galleys forced him to abandon his campaign, the very last attempt to restore a fragment of Byzantium.

After the loss of Negroponte Pietro Mocenigo replaced Niccolo da Canale as Captain-General of the Sea and began rebuiding the battered Venetian navy, which he led on a few minor raids on Ottoman possessions. Then early in 1472 he was approached by a Sicilian named Antonello, who had been captured by the Turks at Negroponte and taken to the headquarters of the Ottoman fleet at Gelibolu on the Dardanelles, where he escaped and made his way back to Italy. Antonello told Mocenigo that he was willing and able to blow up the Turkish arsenal at Gelibolu, which contained arms and ammunition for more than 300 galleys. Mocenigo provided a small ship for Antonello and six of his companions, who landed at Gelibolu on 13 February 1472. That night they made their way into the arsenal and set it on fire, destroying it completely. Antonello and his companions were caught and brought before Sultan Mehmet, who was prepared to torture them in order to find out who was behind them, for he was sure that it was the Venetians. According to Domenico Malipiero, Antonello said that it was his own idea.

> And with great courage he added that he, the sultan, was the plague of the world, that he had plundered all his neighbor princes, that he had kept faith with no one, and that he was trying to eradicate the name of Christ. And that was why he [Antonello] had taken into his head to do what he had done... The Grand Turk listened to him with great patience and admiration. But then he gave orders to behead him and his companions.

Meanwhile, the crusader fleet had been launched and sailed to Rhodes, where the various contingents assembled in June 1472. The fleet comprised eighty-five galleys and fifteen transports, commanded by Cardinal Carafa and two Venetian *provveditori*, Luigi Bembo and Marin Malipiero, with Pietro Mocenigo commanding the Venetian contingent. The galleys included thirty-six from Venice, twelve from the Venetian-controlled cities on the Dalmatian coast, eighteen from the papacy, seventeen from Naples, and two from the Knights of St John on Rhodes. Mocenigo received a letter on Rhodes that Caterino Zeno had written from Tabriz, recommending that the Christian armada attack the fortresses held by the Ottomans on the Mediterranean coast of Anatolia, so as to divert Mehmet when Uzun Hasan began his offensive against the sultan.

Mocenigo thereupon attacked and took Silifke and two other fortresses to its east, which he handed over to Kasım Bey. The entire crusader fleet then sailed to Antalya in August 1472, breaking through the chain that blocked the entrance to the fortified port and landing troops, who laid waste the environs of the city. But the crusaders were unable to break through the powerful Roman walls of the fortified city, and so after a brief siege the fleet sailed back to Rhodes.

At that point the Neapolitan leaders, who had been in continual disagreement with Mocenigo and the other Venetian commanders, withdrew their contingent from the armada and sailed back to Naples. The rest of the crusader fleet attacked Izmir (Smyrna) on 13 September 1472, and after a bloody battle with the Ottoman defenders the city was sacked and burned to the ground.

Uzun Hasan sent an army into Anatolia in the late summer of 1472 under the command of his *beylerbey* Emir Bey and his nephew Yusuf Mirza, who took with them the Karamanid princes Pir Ahmet and Kasım Bey, as well as Kızıl Ahmet, the son of the dispossessed Türkmen emir of Sinop. Caterino Zeno, the Venetian ambassador in Tabriz, also accompanied the expedition with a force of 500 Croatian cavalrymen. Zeno estimated the size of the Akkoyunlu army to be 50,000 men, while other estimates range up to 100,000.

The Türkmen troops commanded by Emir Bey and Yusuf Mirza captured and sacked Tokat. Uzun Hasan then reinstated Pir Ahmet as emir of Karaman, where Prince Mustafa was provincial governor. Prince Mustafa, who at the time was with Gedik Ahmet Pasha on campaign in southern Karaman, received instructions from his father not to engage the Akkoyunlu forces until he had joined forces with Daud Pasha. Mehmet then personally led the main Ottoman army into Anatolia, whereupon he ordered Prince Mustafa and Daud Pasha, who now commanded an army estimated to comprise 60,000 troops and cavalry, to attack the Akkoyunlu. The two forces met near Carallia on the south shore of Lake Beyşehir, a battle described by Tursun Beg.

> The Ottoman prince Mustafa, who was at the time in charge of the province of Karaman, advanced against them with a contingent of the Anatolian forces and subjected them to a defeat, taking Mirza Yusuf and two hundred other influential *begs* prisoner. Some of those who attempted to escape were put to the sword while others who managed to escape the Ottomans were taken prisoner by the Varsak tribe. Out of an army of twenty thousand men, scarcely a thousand escaped with their lives. The captured *begs* were sent to Fatih [Sultan Mehmet]. The Sultan threw Mirza Yusuf, the son of Uzun Hasan's sister, into jail, and the others were put to the sword.

Uzun Hasan was undeterred by this defeat, and in the autumn of 1472 he widened the conflict by sending an army to invade the territory of the Mamluk sultan Kaitbey in south-eastern Anatolia. The Akkoyunlu army captured Malatya and then went on to attack Aleppo, where it was defeated by the Mamluk emir Yashbak and forced to withdraw, ending the invasion.

Mehmet took advantage of the invasion to send an envoy to Yashbak, offering to form an alliance against Uzun Hasan. The Egyptian chronicler Ibn Iyas records that the emir Yashbak responded by sending an embassy to Istanbul 'bearing copious gifts and letters, so that friendship should be established between the Ottoman and Mamluk Sultans, on account of Uzun Hasan'.

Mehmet was now determined to crush Uzun Hasan once and for all, and so early in September 1472 he restored Mahmut Pasha as grand vezir, realising that he 'was the most valiant and practical man that he had in his court'. At the same time, Mehmet summoned the Ottoman troops of Rumelia to muster in Edirne on 20 September, and then on 12 October the sultan and his pashas led the army across the Bosphorus to Üsküdar, ready to march eastward to attack Uzun Hasan. But at the last moment Mahmut Pasha persuaded Mehmet to postpone the expedition till the following spring. The Turkish chronicler Hoca Sadeddin paraphrases the arguments that Mahmut Pasha presented to the sultan: 'The violent winter season of the land of Karaman is approaching... The victorious army is not prepared. What is fitting to do is to wait until spring and prepare the victorious army and the equipment for the campaign, and now send to the *beylerbeyi* of Anatolia an order to hurry for the annulment and extinguishing of the fire of the disorders of these villains.'

The Ottoman campaign against Uzun Hasan finally got under way the following spring, when Mehmet crossed over into Anatolia with his army. Mehmet's youngest son, Prince Jem, who was then only fourteen, was left with a small force to defend Edirne in case of a European incursion.

A letter written by an Italian diplomat on 15 May 1473 notes: 'The *beylerbeyi* of Rumeli [Hass Murat Pasha] crossed from Istanbul to Gelibolu with all the host of the Grand Turk, and on Palm Sunday, the Grand Turk, with all his court crossed from Istanbul to a place called Anichvari.' Mehmet had entrusted overall command of the expedition against Uzun Hasan to his young favourite, Hass Murat Pasha, with the grand vezir Mahmut Pasha serving as his adviser.

The various contingents of the Ottoman army assembled near Amasya, the total force numbering more than 260,000, according to the Turkish chronicler Kemalpaşazade. Hass Murat Pasha was in the vanguard with the Rumelian army, Prince Beyazit on the right wing with the troops from the province of Sivas and Amasya, Prince Mustafa on the left with those from Karaman, and Daud Pasha in the rear with the Anatolian army, while Mehmet himself, with some 30,000 troops, was in the centre.

The situation in Uzun Hasan's camp is known from a letter written by Caterino Zeno to the Doge of Venice on 12 July 1473, in which he writes that 'at present we are in the district of Erzincan. According to the most recent roll-call, there are 300,000 in the field...and the lord intends to have 500,000 by the end of the month.' He goes on to write that 'forty camels laden with money' had arrived from Tabriz, 'wages were paid...and all are in good spirits to go against the common enemy'. The numbers seem to have been inflated, for when Uzun Hasan first caught sight of the Ottoman army, on the opposite bank of the Euphrates, he saw that it was as large as his own, and Zeno heard him exclaim: 'Son of a whore, what an ocean!'

Tursun Beg describes the first battle of the campaign, which took place near Tercan on 4 August 1473, when Hass Murat impetuously crossed the Euphrates with the vanguard of the Ottoman army, only to be ambushed by Uzun Hasan.

Mahmud Pasha asked Hass Murad Pasha to gather his forces at a given place and wait. He himself decided to attack the enemy in their hiding place. Hass Murad's soldiers, complaining that, should the enemy attack be turned back, Mahmud Pasha would get all the credit, broke ranks again and charged their horses against the enemy. Thereupon Uzun Hasan suddenly attacked Mahmud Pasha from his hiding place. A fierce and closely fought battle began. Mahmud managed to withdraw with great difficulty to the place where Hass Murad's troops had been but was unable to join up with them again. Hass Murad had fallen on the battlefield; and Fenarıoğlu Ahmed, Turahanoğlu Ömer and Aydın Beyoğlu Hacı Beg were all taken prisoners.

The news of Uzun Hasan's victory reached Venice through two letters written in October 1473, one from Ragusa and the other from Lepanto, both of which exaggerated the extent of the Ottoman defeat, the former even saying that Mehmet himself had been killed. The letter from Ragusa says: 'At this time came a man from Edirne, who secretly told me about the Grand Signor, how he was defeated and about his death. It is not known for certain about the Pasha [Mahmut], and very bad things are said about the *Sancakbeys*. I believe that maybe it was worse for them than we think.' The letter from Lepanto states: 'It is said that the son of the Turk was routed and several *Sancakbeys*, the *Beylerbeyi* of Rumeli and Ömer Bey were killed, and fifty thousand men died, all the flower of the camp of the Turk. And all these bands of Turkey were in great terror, may God, in his mercy, confound them totally.'

The two armies met a week later at Otluk Belli, in the mountains north of Erzincan. The Ottoman army, led by Mehmet himself along with Mahmut Pasha and Daud Pasha, utterly defeated the Akkoyunlu, commanded by Uzun Hasan's sons Ughurlu Mehmet and Zeynel, forcing Uzun Hasan to flee for his life. The Akkoyunlu are estimated to have lost some 10,000 men, the Ottomans only about 1,000. Both Turkish and Venetian chroniclers agree that the Akkoyunlu lost because of their lack of artillery, which they had never before encountered.

Meanwhile, Prince Jem had been holding the fort in Edirne, under the supervision of his advisers Nasuh Bey and Karıştıranlı Süleyman Bey. At one point during the campaign against the Akkoyunlu there was no word from Sultan Mehmet for forty days, and the rumour spread that he had been defeated and killed by Uzun Hasan. When Jem heard this he decided to usurp the throne, but then when he learned that his father was alive and had defeated Uzun Hasan he fled from Edirne. When Mehmet returned to Istanbul he forgave Jem for his rash action, probably because he saw in him something of the impetuosity that he himself had often exhibited in his youth. He put the blame on his son's advisers, severely punishing Nasuh Bey and Karıştıranlı Süleyman Bey, while Jem himself was sent to Kastamonu as provincial governor.

Mehmet also dismissed Mahmut Pasha as grand vezir, replacing him with Gedik Ahmet Pasha. Mahmut Pasha then retired to his estate at Hasköy, a place that Hoca Sadeddin says 'he made the envy of towns, having built a mosque and *medrese* there'. The sources give various reasons for Mahmut Pasha's dismissal, one being that Mehmet blamed him for the death of Hass Murat. According to Angiolello: 'The Turkish *Signor* was angry that Mahmut Pasha withdrew...and did not give help to Murat, and it was suspected that he had done that on purpose, because he was not his friend.' Another possible reason is that that he had advised the sultan not to pursue Uzun Hasan after the Battle of Otluk Belli, which allowed Mahmut Pasha's enemies to accuse him of being in league with the enemy.

Uzun Hasan, despite his defeat at Otluk Belli, had lost little territory, and he sent an envoy to tell the Venetians that he fully intended to continue his war against the Ottomans. He also sent an emissary to Pope Sixtus IV, with a message asking 'that the Christians attack the Turks with a land army, and promises, if this is done, that he will again descend upon the Turk with a powerful army, and that he will not give up the war until the Turk is destroyed'.

The Pope wrote to Lodovico II Gonzaga, Marquis of Mantua, on 2 October 1474, appealing to him to send an envoy to confer in Rome with representatives of the other Italian states, to whom he had sent a similar message concerning the financing of another expedition against the Turks. Sixtus said: 'And would that we could bear this weight alone, because we would burden no one. Our resources are not sufficient however, and therefore it is necessary that we have recourse to your Excellency and other Italian powers.' He urged that plans should be made quickly, 'so that we may know how to give a definite reply to the [Türkmen] envoy and his prince'.

Lodovico answered on 23 October, saying that he was appointing his son, Cardinal Francesco Gonzaga, as his envoy concerning the anti-Turkish expedition. Similar responses were received from other Italian states, but the expedition never materialised.

Uzun Hasan refused to admit defeat, and he sent a message to the Signoria in Venice proposing that they should 'ride against the Ottomans together'. At the same time he sent Caterino Zeno back to Venice, with a message to the princes of Christendom that he had not abandoned his war against the Ottomans, but would muster a powerful army the following spring to march against Mehmet.

The Signoria responded on 10 December 1473 by sending Ambrogio Contarini as an envoy to Tabriz, with a message telling Uzun Hasan that Venice would commit its fleet to an expedition against the Ottomans, and urging him to attack Mehmet as soon as possible. Contarini, who served as Venetian ambassador at Tabriz in the years 1474–6, describes Uzun Hasan's appearance at the time: 'The king is of a good size and very lean, with a pleasant countenance, having somewhat of the Tartar appearance, and seemed to be about seventy years old. His manner is very affable, and he conversed familiarly with every one around him, but I noticed that his hands trembled when he raised the cup to his lips.'

Contarini goes on to write: 'His eldest son Ughurlu Mehmet was much spoken of when I was in Persia, as he had revolted against his father.' When news of this rebellion reached Istanbul, Mehmet knew that he no longer had to fear an invasion by the Akkoyunlu. Uzun Hasan died in Tabriz on 6 January 1478, and with his passing the Akkoyunlu literally disappeared from history, the domains of their tribe absorbed by those around them, leaving the Ottomans as the supreme power in the region.

11 Conquest of the Crimea and Albania

Mehmet remained in Istanbul throughout the year 1474, taking his ease in Topkapı Sarayı after the rigours of his victorious campaign against Uzun Hasan. His three sons were all serving as provincial governors in Anatolia, with Mustafa residing in Konya, the capital of Karaman, while Beyazit was in Amasya and Jem in Kastamonu.

Mustafa spent the autumn boating on Lake Beyşehir and hunting in the surrounding countryside. Towards the end of the year he sent his officer Koçi Bey to attack the mountain fortress of Develi Karahisar, south-west of Kayseri, which was still held by the Karamanid. The garrison commander refused to surrender to Koçi Bey, insisting that he would negotiate only with Prince Mustafa himself. Mustafa had in the meanwhile become seriously ill, and he was able to reach Develi Karahisar only with great difficulty. His condition then deteriorated to the point where his advisers decided to take him back to Konya, sending a courier to inform Sultan Mehmet of the situation.

Mehmet immediately ordered Gedik Ahmet Pasha to Develi Karahisar with an army of 30,000, while at the same time he sent his Jewish physician Maestro Iacopo to Konya to treat Prince Mustafa. But Mustafa died en route at Bor, near Niğde, probably in June 1474, according to Giovanni-Maria Angiolello, who was in the prince's entourage at the time. Mustafa's companions embalmed his body and brought it to Konya, where it was laid out in a mosque while a courier was sent to Istanbul to inform Sultan Mehmet.

When the news of Mustafa's death reached Istanbul the only one who had the courage to inform the sultan was Hoca Sinan Pasha, Mehmet's old tutor. Hoca Sinan dressed in black robes and obtained an audience with Mehmet, who realised at once that he was death's messenger. Angiolello describes the sultan's inconsolable mourning for Mustafa, who had always been his favourite son.

> The carpets which were spread on the ground were lifted, and standing on the dirt, he was lamenting his son. He gathered the dust and placed it over his head, as a sign of great sorrow. And he was beating his face, his chest and his thighs with his palms, and he groaned greatly. And he remained this way for three days and nights... The entire city was filled with loud lamentation because Mustafa was especially beloved of his father and of all those who had dealings with him.

Mehmet had Mustafa buried in the Muradiye at Bursa, in a magnificent *türbe* that he erected for him near the tomb of Murat II. Angiolello writes of the extraordinary eulogy delivered by Mustafa's daughter, Princess Nergiszade, whom he calls Herzisdad.

> [Her funeral oration] lasted more than an hour, in which she praised his virtues and mentioned by name some of the people who had been brought up with him, saying that, had he survived, the world would have known much better his good will towards his followers; and that death was the common lot of all. She said many other things which made her hearers all to weep. Even Herzisdad herself was obliged to stop and weep at suitable moments, which she did with very decorous movements and gestures, showing at the same time a great audacity. For all that she said and did she was much praised, as much for her wisdom as for her erudition in Arabic literature and expert knowledge on every subject pertaining to a woman of her condition. So that her fame spread as far as Constantinople, and even in other countries people talked of the qualities and virtues of this young woman.

Mehmet then transferred Jem from Kastamonu to Konya, to replace Mustafa as provincial governor of Karaman, where he would remain for nearly a decade.

The death of his beloved son apparently embittered Mehmet against Mahmut Pasha, whom he seems to have held responsible for Mustafa's death, according to both Western and Turkish sources. All the sources agree that there was deep enmity between Mahmut and Mustafa, though they differ on the reason for this hatred. Several sources suggest that Mustafa had seduced or raped Mahmut's wife, and some say that the grand vezir took his revenge by poisoning the prince. The Turkish poet Muali, in his epic *Hünkârname*, writes that Mustafa's dying words were a request that Mehmet be told who was responsible for his death: 'My last request from my father is this: let him ask Mahmut Pasha about this disaster that befell me. He did this evil to me because of his enmity. Let the truth be known to you.'

According to Muali, Mahmut Pasha went from his place of retirement in Hasköy to offer his condolences to Sultan Mehmet at Topkapı Sarayı, although his old tutor Kürt Hafız advised him not to go. At the palace gate Mahmut met his former slave Teftin Ağa, who gave him the same advice. But Mahmut went ahead and shed tears for Mahmut in Mehmet's presence, wearing black robes as was customary for mourners. His enemies told the sultan that Mahmut was only feigning grief, and that he had been in good humour shortly afterwards, as Hoca Sadeddin writes in his chronicle: 'The spy that they sent entered suddenly and unexpectedly in the gathering of the honorable Pasha [Mahmut] and he saw the Pasha dressed in white, seated in a cheerful gathering and playing chess. He took off the mourning clothes before the Sultan and the army did.'

Shortly afterwards Mehmet had Mahmut Pasha arrested and taken to the Castle of the Seven Towers in Istanbul, where he was executed by strangulation on 18 July 1474. According to Muali, the sultan justified the execution by saying: 'It is impossible that Mustafa's enemy should remain alive.'

Such was the end of Mahmut Pasha, who by all accounts was the greatest of all the early Ottoman grand vezirs. Kritoboulos, in praising Mahmut Pasha, writes: 'From the time that he took charge of the affairs of the great Sultan, he gave everything in this great dominion a better prospect by his wonderful zeal and his fine planning as well as by his implicit and unqualified faith in and goodwill toward his sovereign. He was thus a better man than them all, as shown by his accomplishments.'

Gedik Ahmet Pasha, who had replaced Mahmut Pasha as grand vezir, was sent on an expedition into Anatolia to regain all the places in Karaman that had been lost by the Ottomans during the war with Uzun Hasan. He recaptured Ermenek and Minyan on the central plateau, as well as Silifke and other coastal fortress towns to its east that had been taken by the Christian allies of Uzun Hasan. He then called all the Türkmen tribal chieftains of Karaman to a meeting, at which he entertained them with a great feast before having almost all of them killed, enslaving their families and followers. Only a few of the Türkmen chiefs escaped to their remote mountain fortresses, where they continued to hold out into the early sixteenth century before they were finally conquered by the Ottomans.

The final conquest of Karaman freed Mehmet to resume his march of conquest in southern Europe. There the sultan's principal foe was still Venice, whose fortresses in Albania and elsewhere along the eastern coast of the Adriatic were preventing him from advancing deeper into Europe.

King Matthias Corvinus was also a foe to be reckoned with, and in the autumn of 1473 Mehmet sent Mihailoğlu Ali on a raid into Hungary. The raiders met no opposition and returned with some 16,000 captives, according to the Turkish chronicler Oruç.

Early in the spring of 1474 Mehmet launched an expedition into Albania under the command of Hadım Süleyman Pasha, the *beylerbey* of Rumelia. A Bosnian by birth, Süleyman had been captured as a youth and castrated, becoming a *hadım*, or eunuch, serving in the harem of Topkapı Sarayı, where he became a favourite of Sultan Mehmet and quickly advanced to the highest levels in the Ottoman bureaucracy.

The goal of the expedition was the fortress of Shkoder (Scutari, Albanian Scodra), on the lake of the same name in northern Albania, which flows into the sea through the river Bojana. The Venetians were expecting an attack on Shkoder, and had garrisoned the mighty fortress there with 2,500 troops under the command of the valiant Antonio Loredano.

Süleyman Pasha set out with an army of 80,000 troops, including 8,000 janissaries, whom he marched across Serbia and Macedonia to northern Albania. His advance guard of 10,000 arrived before Shkoder on 17 May 1474 and immediately attacked the town, hoping to catch the defenders unprepared. But Loredano sent out his garrison and they were able to drive back the attackers, with heavy casualties on both sides.

When news of the attack reached Venice the Senate sent a fleet under the joint command of Triadan Gritti and Piero Mocenigo, who sailed seven of their galleys up the Bojana to Shkoder, leaving the rest on patrol off the Albanian coast. Leonardo Boldu, the Venetian *provveditore* of Albania, also enlisted the local Montenegrin warlord John Chernojevich to aid in the defence of Shkoder with his Albanian warriors, some 8,000 of whom were ferried south across the lake to the fortress.

When Süleyman arrived with the main army on 15 July he surrounded Shkoder and put it under siege, bombarding the fortress with his heavy artillery. At the beginning of the siege he set out to built a barricade across the mouth of the Bojana to trap the Venetian ships upriver. But the Venetian commanders sailed their galleys down the Bojana, and after a battle with the Ottoman troops defending the barricade they broke through into the Adriatic and joined the fleet cruising off the coast.

When the Ottoman bombardment and infantry attacks failed to take the fortress Süleyman offered generous terms of surrender to Loredano, who contemptuously refused them. Süleyman then ordered another infantry attack, which was turned back after an eight-hour battle in which some 3,000 to 6,000 Ottoman troops were killed, according to the various sources. This led Süleyman to abandon the siege, and on 28 August he withdrew his army and began the long march back to Istanbul.

The victory over the Ottomans at Shkoder was marked with a gala celebration in Venice. But the Signoria knew that it was just a matter of time before Mehmet launched another expedition against Albania. Reports soon reached Venice that Mehmet was preparing a huge fleet, and so the Signoria decided to increase the Venetian fleet to 100 galleys.

On 2 November 1474 Venice agreed with Florence and Milan to ally themselves for twenty-five years in a war against the Turks, with Ferrara subsequently joining the pact. Pope Sixtus refused to join the league, which he saw as an attempt to limit his freedom of action, and instead he formed a separate alliance with King Ferrante of Naples. Venice was angered by this and withdrew its ambassador from Rome, so 'that the world may know what manner of shepherd it is who looks calmly on as his flock is being devoured and does not come to its help'.

After Süleyman Pasha returned from Shkoder to Istanbul he disbanded his army, but then Sultan Mehmet ordered him to prepare for another campaign early the following year, this time against Count Stephen the Great, voyvoda of Moldavia.

Two years earlier, during the Ottoman campaign against Uzun Hasan, Stephen had taken advantage of Mehmet's absence in Anatolia to invade Wallachia, which at the time was ruled by the sultan's vassal Radu, brother and successor of Vlad the Impaler. Stephen defeated Radu at Cursul Apei (Rimnicu Sarat) in a three-day battle on 18–20 November 1473. Stephen then deposed Radu as voyvoda of Wallachia and replaced him with his own man, Laiot Basaraba, who subsequently went over to the Ottomans after he was defeated by them. This led to a confused two-year struggle, which Mehmet sought to end by sending an expedition into Moldavia against Stephen and restoring Laiot Basaraba as voyvoda of Wallachia.

Süleyman Pasha's army crossed the Danube into Wallachia early in January 1475. On 10 January they were ambushed by Stephen's army and totally routed, with some 40,000 killed out of a total force of 90,000, according to the Venetian Paolo Ogniben.

Another Venetian source, Domenico Malipiero, writes that Mara Branković, Mehmet's stepmother, told Geronimo Zorzi, the Venetian ambassador to Istanbul, 'that the Turks had never suffered a greater defeat and had exhorted him to continue his journey in good spirit, because the Turk had good reason to make peace, and he would never have a better opportunity to negotiate'. But when Zorzi reached Istanbul, where he had an audience with an unidentified pasha, he found that peace terms offered by the Ottoman government were unacceptable.

Raiders under Malkoçoğlu Bali Bey, the Ottoman commander at Smederova in northern Serbia, crossed the Danube on 6 February 1474 and penetrated deep into Hungary, plundering and killing before they withdrew with all the captives they could handle. At the beginning of June a horde of Turkish horsemen from Bosnia raided into Croatia and penetrated as far as southern Austria, before withdrawing with their captives. On 22 June a force of 20,000 Turks made their way into Venetian territory in Friuli, at the head of the Adriatic, plundering and killing before they departed. The Venetians were forced to raise a militia of 60,000 together with 500 cavalrymen to defend Friuli against future Turkish incursions.

Another mounted Turkish horde crossed the Danube from Serbia into Hungary in August and penetrated as far as the river Koros in Transylvania before they were driven back by a Hungarian force. The constant Turkish threat forced King Matthias Corvinus to conclude a truce with King Casimir IV of Poland and to interrupt his war with Bohemia.

The Ottoman fleet whose construction had been reported to the Signoria was not directed towards Venice, as they expected, but against the Genoese colony of Kaffa (Feodosiya) in the Crimea, where a struggle for succession in the Tatar khanate gave Mehmet an opportunity to intervene.

The Tatars were Ottoman vassals, but had special status because their ruling dynasty claimed direct descent from Genghis Khan. The Tatars living in and around Kaffa were governed by an official of their own race known as a *tudun*, who the Khan of the Crimea appointed after consultation with the Genoese *Ufficio della Campagna*. When the *tudun* Marmak died in 1473 he was succeeded by his brother Eminek. But Marmak's widow tried to have her son Sertak appointed as his father's successor, and a bitter dispute

1. Mehmet II, portrait attributed to Sinan Bey, c. 1480

2a. Mehmet II and a youth who may be Prince Jem, portrait attributed to Gentile Bellini

2b. Mehmet II, portrait attributed to Constanza da'Ferrara

3a. Rumelı Hisarı (right) and Anadolu Hisarı (left) on the Bosphorus

3b. The Theodosian walls leading down to the Golden Horn

4a. The original Mosque of the Conqueror dominating
the skyline above the Golden Horn

4b. Topkapı Sarayı above the point at the confluence
of the Bosphorus and the Golden Horn

5. Kapalı Çarşı, the Covered Bazaar

6a. The Golden Horn viewed from the cemetery of Eyüp

6b. Yedikule, the Castle of the Seven Towers

7. Interior of Haghia Sophia as a mosque

8a. Court and fountain of Haghia Sophia

8b. Third Court of Topkapı Sarayı

ensued. The Genoese committee consulted Mengli Giray, Khan of the Crimean Turks, who at first agreed to accept Sertak, but then changed his mind to name his own favourite, Kirai Mirza.

When Mengli Giray tried to install Kirai Mirza as *tudun* in Kaffa there was strong resistance, particularly from Sertak's mother, who bribed one of the Genoese committee, Oberto Squarciaficio, to support her son. Oberto put pressure on Mengli Giray by threatening to release his rebellious brothers, who had been imprisoned by the Genoese after they contested the khanate with him when their father Hacı Giray Khan died. Mengli Giray gave in and named Sertak as *tudun*, but most of the Tatar notables supported Eminek, and they sent an emissary to Sultan Mehmet asking him to intervene.

The Ottoman fleet left Istanbul on 20 May 1475 under the command of Gedik Ahmet Pasha, comprising 280 galleys, three galleons, 170 freighters and 120 ships carrying horses for his cavalry. The fleet reached Kaffa on 1 June, and on the following day it began bombarding the city. The defenders, most of whom were supporters of Eminek and favoured Turkish intervention, surrendered on 6 June, while Mengli Giray fled to his capital at Kekri with 1,500 loyal cavalry.

Gedik Ahmet had promised the townspeople that he would spare their lives if they paid the customary Ottoman *haraç*, or head tax. But in the next six days the conquerors seized all the wealth of the locals and plundered Kaffa, capturing some 3,000 of the townspeople as slaves. On 8 July Gedik ordered all the Italians in Kaffa, most of them Genoese, to board his fleet under pain of execution. The Italians were then resettled in Istanbul around the Seventh Hill of the city, where the census of 1477 recorded that they occupied 277 houses and had two churches.

Mengli Giray was captured and taken to Istanbul, where Mehmet pardoned him and sent him back to the Crimea as his vassal Eminek was installed as *tudun* in Kaffa, but now under Ottoman rather than Genoese rule. The Ottoman fleet then went on to capture all the other Genoese possessions in the Crimea, as well as the Venetian colony of Tana (now Azov) in the Sea of Azov. This ended the long Latin presence in the Crimea and its vicinity, which for the next four centuries remained under the control of the Ottomans, extending their dominions around most of the Black Sea.

That same year Malkoçoğlu Bali Bey led another Turkish raid from Serbia into Hungary, again plundering the countryside and killing or enslaving the local populace. A Hungarian force tried to cut the raiders off on their way back to Serbia, but Bali's men virtually annihilated them, taking back several hundred severed heads that were sent to Sultan Mehmet in token of their victory. This seems to have provoked King Matthias Corvinus into mounting an expedition against the Ottomans, and on 15 February 1476 he took their fortress at Shabats in Serbia, capturing 1,200 janissaries, then advanced as far as Smederova, where he built three fortresses to blockade the city before he withdrew.

Mehmet himself led an expedition against Count Stephen of Moldavia in the spring of 1476. Hadım Süleyman Pasha led the advance guard, while the main army was commanded by Mehmet, a total of 150,000 troops, including a contingent of 12,000 Vlachs under Laiot Basaraba, whom the sultan intended to restore as voyvoda of Wallacha. Stephen commanded an army of 20,000 men, whom he positioned in a fortified wooded area on the expected Ottoman line of march, so that he could ambush them.

The two armies met on 26 July 1476 at the Battle of Rasboieni, during the first phase of which Stephen attacked the Ottoman vanguard under Süleyman Pasha. According to Angiolello, who was with the Ottoman army, Stephen's troops charged out of the forest where they were hiding 'and put Süleyman Pasha's guards to flight... The Pasha mounted his horse and attacked. Some were killed on both sides but, because Süleyman Pasha had more men..., Count Stephen was forced to retire within his fortified wood, where he stood firm and defended himself with artillery, damaging the Turks, who withdrew to the outside.'

When Mehmet heard of this engagement he led the main army to attack Stephen, who tried to stop them with his artillery, but to no avail, as Angiolello writes in describing the course of the battle that ensued. 'We put Count Stephen to flight, seized the artillery, and followed him into the wood. About two hundred were killed and eight hundred taken prisoner. If the wood had not been so dense and dark because of the height of the trees, few would have escaped.'

That effectively ended the campaign, as Tursun Beg notes in describing the aftermath of the battle. 'The Prince [Stephen] fled and his camp was plundered by the Ottoman attackers. The Sultan pursued the fleeing Prince, pillaging and plundering his country and capital. Raids were carried out against Hungary, and then the army returned to Edirne laden with booty.'

Mehmet restored Laiot Basaraba as voyvoda of Wallachia, leaving him behind with his 12,000 Vlach troops. Matthias Corvinus sent an army into Wallachia after the Ottomans withdrew, and on 16 November 1476 the

Hungarians deposed Laiot Basaraba and replaced him as voyvoda with the infamous Vlad III, the Impaler.

When Mehmet returned to Edirne he learned that Matthias Corvinus had invaded Serbia and blockaded Smederova by building three fortresses around the city. He realised the danger posed by the Hungarian incursion, and within ten days he turned his army around and headed for Serbia, 'disregarding the fact that the soldiers and horses were exhausted by the journey and the hunger', according to Angiolello.

When the Ottoman army arrived at Smederova the garrisons of two of the Hungarian fortresses around the city fled. But those in the third fort stood firm, and when the Ottomans attacked it they lost around 500 men. Mehmet then put the fortress under siege, which he knew he could not keep up for long because of the bitter winter weather. According to Angiolello, Mehmet had his troops cut down trees and throw them into the moat of the fortress until they were piled higher than its walls. He then prepared to set fire to the timber so as to burn down the fortress, but at that point the garrison agreed to surrender on promise of a safe conduct. Mehmet agreed, and for once he kept his word, allowing the 600 men of the garrison and their commander to leave the fort and set out on the road to Belgrade. Mehmet destroyed all three forts and then set his army back on the road to Istanbul.

Thus ended what came to be known as 'the Winter War with Hungary'. Tursun Beg, after describing this difficult expedition, writes: 'Out of consideration for the hardships to which his soldiers had been subjected during this winter campaign, in the following year, 882 [1477], Fatih did not go out on campaign.'

But, although Mehmet did not go to war himself in 1477, at the beginning of spring that year he sent Hadım Süleyman Pasha off on a campaign in Greece, his goal being to capture the Venetian fortress at Naupactos on the northern shore of the Gulf of Corinth. Süleyman's forces besieged Naupactos for three months, during which time a Venetian fleet of twelve galleys under Antonio Loredano kept the city supplied with food and ammunition. Finally, after informing the sultan that he was unable to take the fortress, Süleyman lifted the siege on 20 June 1477, after which he returned to Istanbul. Mehmet then dismissed him as *beylerbey* of Rumelia, replacing him with Daud Pasha, who had been *beylerbey* of Anatolia, a post that was then given to Süleyman Pasha.

That same year Mehmet also sent an army of 12,000 men under Evrenosoğlu Ahmet to besiege the Albanian fortress city of Kruje,

Skanderbeg's old stronghold. The defenders were on the point of accepting surrender terms when a Venetian relief force arrived, forcing the Ottoman army to withdraw. The Venetians began plundering the enemy camp, but then the Ottoman army counter-attacked and defeated them, forcing them to take refuge within the fortress, which continued to hold out against the besiegers.

Meanwhile, a large force of Turkish *akincis* under Iskender Bey, the Ottoman *sancakbey*, or provincial governor, of Bosnia penetrated into Friuli beyond the river Tagliomento, which took them to within forty miles of Venice. The Venetian commander in Friuli, Geronimo Novello, gave battle to the *akincis* at the Tagliomento, but he and most of his men were killed. The Venetian chronicler Domenico Malipiero writes of the terror that gripped all of Friuli before the raiders suddenly withdrew.

> There was great fear in the country. All the towns between the Isonzo and the Tagliomento were burned by the Turks. Three days after the battle, when they had collected the booty, the Turks pretended to leave. Then suddenly they turned round and put all the land on both sides of the river to fire and sword. Then, because there was a rumour that great preparations against them were in hand by land and sea, they collected their baggage and hastily left Italy.

The Venetian Senate decided to send 2,000 infantry and 6,000 cavalry to Friuli, as well as arming an additional force of 20,000 troops to defend Venetian territory against Turkish raids. But the Turkish attacks continued nonetheless, one *akinci* force penetrating as far as Pordenone, pillaging and destroying everything in its path, the smoke of burning villages clearly visible to observers atop the campanile of the basilica of San Marco in Venice. According to Malipiero, the Venetian nobleman Celso Maffei cried out in despair to Doge Andrea Vendramin, 'The enemy is at our gate! The axe is at the root. Unless divine help comes, the doom of the Christian name is sealed.'

The Senate decided in February 1478 that they would send Tomaso Malipiero as an envoy to Istanbul to seek a peace agreement with Sultan Mehmet. Tomaso returned on 3 May and reported that he had made no progress, since the terms proposed to him were unacceptable.

It soon became clear why Mehmet was not interested in a settlement, when word reached Venice that the sultan himself was leading an expedition against Shkoder, the Albanian fortress city whose capture had eluded him for years, along with Kruje. Gedik Ahmet Pasha had advised against trying

142

to capture Shkoder, for he thought the fortress was invincible, and so Mehmet dismissed and imprisoned him, appointing Karamanı Mehmet Pasha to replace him as grand vezir.

Mehmet first stopped at Kruje, which Evrenosoğlu Ahmet had been besieging for a year, sending Daud Pasha on to Shkoder with most of the Rumelian army.

According to Angiolello, the defenders at Kruje had used up all their food supplies and had been reduced to eating cats, dogs, rats and mice, but still they would not give in. On 15 June 1478 the defenders sent emissaries to Mehmet to negotiate terms of surrender, and he agreed to give safe conduct to all who wished to leave and to allow those who remained to live in Kruje as Ottoman subjects. But when they surrendered only those who could pay a large ransom were allowed to leave unharmed, all the rest being beheaded. Mehmet then took possession of Kruje, thereafter known as Akhisar, which thenceforth remained in Ottoman hands until 1913.

Meanwhile, Daud Pasha and his Rumelian army had reached Shkoder on 18 May. They were joined there on 12 June by the Anatolian army under Mesih Pasha, the new *beylerbey* of Anatolia, brother of the late Hass Murad Pasha. The Ottoman artillery, which had been transported by camel caravan, was in place by 22 June, when the siege of Shkoder began with a heavy bombardment of the fortress.

Mehmet arrived from Kruje with his contingent on 2 July, by which time Shkoder had been bombarded daily by the artillery, while the Ottoman archers had been firing a constant hail of arrows at the defenders on the fortress walls. On 22 July Mehmet ordered an attack by his infantry, 150,000 strong, and when that was driven back he ordered another assault the following day, but that failed as well. Then at daybreak on 27 July the entire Ottoman army attacked the fortress, but the defenders once more drove them back.

The failure of this third attempt convinced Mehmet that Shkoder could not be taken by direct assault, and so he left a number of troops to continue the siege of the city, while he used the rest of his army to attack other Venetian-held fortresses in northern Albania. Mehmet sent Daud Pasha with the Rumelian troops to attack Zhabljak, on the northern shore of Lake Shkoder, while the Anatolian soldiers under Hadım Süleyman Pasha were to take Drisht (Drivasto), six miles east of Shkoder. Zhabljak surrendered with little resistance, while Drisht held out for sixteen days before it was taken by storm, whereupon its inhabitants were herded to Shkoder and beheaded in front of its walls to persuade the defenders there to surrender.

Mehmet then ordered Süleyman and Daud to attack Lezhe, where Skanderbeg had died in 1468, and after taking the town they burned it to the ground. They then went on to attack Bar, on the coast of what is now Montenegro, where the defenders under the Venetian governor Luigi da Muta put up such a determined fight that the Ottoman commanders finally abandoned the siege. Mehmet then ordered his army to withdraw from Albania, leaving enough troops behind with Evrenosoğlu Ahmet to continue the siege of Shkoder.

The Turkish raids in Friuli and the Ottoman advance in Albania, coming after sixteen years of warfare, finally convinced the Signoria to come to terms with Mehmet. The secretary of the Senate, Giovanni Dario, a Venetian who had been born on Crete, was sent to Istanbul late in 1478, empowered to make an agreement without receiving further instructions. The result was a peace treaty signed in Istanbul on 28 January 1479 ending sixteen years of war between the Venetian Republic and the Ottoman Empire. The Venetians ceded to the Ottomans Shkoder and Kruje in Albania, the Aegean islands of Lemnos and Euboea (Negroponte), and the Maina (Mani) peninsula in the south-west Peloponnesos. The Ottomans for their part agreed to return within two months some of the Venetian possessions they had taken in the Morea, Albania and Dalmatia. The Venetians promised to pay within two years a reparation of 100,000 gold ducats, agreeing also to an annual payment of 10,000 ducats for the right of free trade in the Ottoman Empire without import and export duties. Venice in return was allowed to maintain a *bailo* in Istanbul, with civil authority over Venetians living and doing business in the Ottoman capital. In addition, both parties were to appoint an arbiter to define the boundaries between the two states.

Dario returned to Venice on 16 April 1479 with one of the Ottoman negotiators, Lutfi Bey, accompanied by a party of twenty. Domenico Malipiero writes that forty Venetian noblemen went out into the Bacino San Marco in gilded vessels to meet the envoys, while 'the Doge and the College stood at the window of the Hall of the Great Council'. Then on 25 April, the feast day of St Mark, Lutfi Bey took an oath to confirm the peace in the presence of Doge Giovanni Mocenigo, who swore to it and proclaimed it to the Signoria.

The Greek text of the treaty and a Latin translation are preserved in the state archives of Venice, where one can read Sultan Mehmet's oath of agreement, dated 25 January 1479: 'By the God of Heaven and earth, by our great Prophet Mohammed, by the seven copies of the Koran which we Moslems possess and profess, by the 124,000 prophets of God by the faith which I believe and profess, by my soul and the soul of my father, and by the sword with which I am girded.'

The war between Venice and the Ottoman Empire, which had lasted for sixteen years, was at last over. But the Serenessima paid a great price for the peace, for which she was reviled by her fellow Christian states, as the nineteenth-century historian Horatio Brown pointed out in his history of Venice:

> Thus after sixteen years of continuous warfare, Venice secured a ruinous peace which deprived her of a large part of her Levantine Empire, and rendered her tributary to the new lords of Constantinople. She had undertaken the war at the request of Europe and encouraged by promises of support; she had been deserted at the very outset; she struggled on with great bravery, spending men and money till she could endure no further drain; she made the best peace she could, and instantly all of Europe attacked her for her perfidy to the Christian faith...

12 *The Siege of Rhodes*

Venice was severely criticised for coming to terms with Mehmet, most notably by King Matthias Corvinus and Pope Sixtus IV, who felt that the Venetians had betrayed the Christian cause. But the overwhelming power of the Ottomans soon led other Italian states to cultivate friendly relations with Mehmet, particularly those who were doing business in Istanbul.

The first to do so was Florence, where the ruling Medici family was engaged in a struggle with the rival Pazzi clan, who were backed by Pope Sixtus. On Sunday 26 April 1478, at High Mass in the Duomo in Florence, Lorenzo de'Medici and his brother Giuliano were attacked by a group led by Francesco da'Pazzi and Bernardo Bandini de'Baroncello. Giuliano was killed, but Lorenzo was only slightly wounded, and he led his supporters to put down the attempted coup. All the conspirators were slain except for Bernardo Bandini, who escaped and made his way aboard a Neapolitan galley to Istanbul, where he took refuge with relatives in Galata.

When Sultan Mehmet learned of Bandini's presence in the city he had him arrested and imprisoned, after which he informed Lorenzo Carducci, the Florentine consul in Galata. Carducci's associate Bernardo Peruzzi sent the news to the Signoria in Florence 'of the arrest of... Bernardo Bandini, impious parricide and rebel against us'. The Signoria's letter responding to Carducci, dated 18 June 1479, is full of praise for Sultan Mehmet as a friend of Florence.

> By letters of Bernardo Peruzzi we have learned with great pleasure how that most glorious prince [Mehmet] has seized Bernardo Bandini, most

heinous parricide and traitor to his country, and declares himself willing to do with him whatever we may want – a decision in keeping with the love and great favor he has always shown toward our Republic and our people as well as with the justice of his most serene Majesty...

Antonio de'Medici was sent to Istanbul to pick up Bandini, who was placed in his custody and brought back to Florence. There on 29 December he was hung from a window of the Palazzo del Bargello, as Leonardo da Vinci, watching from the square below, sketched his dangling body. Lorenzo de'Medici expressed his gratitude to Mehmet by commissioning the sculptor Bertoldo di Giovanni to make a medallion honouring the sultan.

After the Venetians signed their agreement with the Ottomans they made every effort to keep the peace, acting with great restraint in cases of Turkish aggression. The situation was still very critical, for in the summer of 1479 an Ottoman fleet assembled at Valona (Vlore) in Albania, directly across the Strait of Otranto from the heel of the Italian peninsula, and there was fear that Mehmet was planning a large-scale invasion of Italy.

The fleet was commanded by Gedik Ahmet Pasha, the former grand vezir, whom Mehmet had released from prison and appointed as captain-pasha of the Ottoman navy. Gedik Ahmet sent an envoy to the Signoria, with an astonishing proposal that they join him in an invasion of the Kingdom of Naples, saying that King Ferrante and the Pope were common enemies of the Venetians and the Ottomans. The message went on to say that Sultan Mehmet was ready to attack Naples with or without Venetian help, but the Senate diplomatically turned down the proposal.

As it turned out, the Ottoman fleet was not intended for an invasion of Italy but for an attack on some of the Ionian Islands, the archipelago lying along the north-western coast of Greece. The islands that Gedik Ahmet had been ordered to attack were Santa Maura (Lefkas), Cephalonia, Ithaka (Ithaki) and Zante (Zakynthos). All these islands, as well as the town of Vonitsa on the Greek mainland, were ruled by Duke Leonardo III Tocco, who had been Despot of Arta in north-west Greece during the last years of the Byzantine Empire.

The Ottoman fleet's course took it from Valona through the strait between the mainland and Corfu, northernmost of the Ionian Islands, a possession of Venice. While passing through the Strait of Corfu, according to a Venetian report of 7 September 1479, Gedik Ahmet's ships encountered the republic's Captain-General of the Sea 'with some of our galleys.' Because of the peace treaty that had been signed earlier that year the Venetian flotilla did not interfere with the Ottoman fleet, but simply observed it as it went on to attack Leonardo Tocco's island domain. According to the report:

> He [Gedik Ahmet Pasha] was saluted and honored by our aforesaid captain, as he passed by on his way to the lord Leonardo's state, and he went first to S. Maura, which he found abandoned by the aforesaid lord, and garrisoning [the fortress] with Turks, he then continued on to Cephalonia, took the island, then the fortress, pillaging everything. He burned and destroyed the castello, leaving the whole island deserted...

After Gedik Ahmet took the castle on Cephalonia he enslaved the islanders and destroyed their homes, according to the Venetian chronicler Stefano Magno, who adds: 'He also laid waste the island of Ithaki and other small islands nearby, which belonged to the said lord [Leonardo Tocco].'

Gedik Ahmet sailed on from Cephalonia to Zante, where 40 per cent of the population were Venetian subjects, and which was garrisoned by 500 Venetian *stradiots*, or cavalry. When the Ottoman forces landed on 8 September they were opposed by the *stradiots*, who inflicted casualties on them, while the Turks in turn killed a number of the Venetian residents of the island when they refused to surrender.

The Venetian captain-general Antonio Loredano was then sent to Cephalonia to protect the Venetian subjects there, while Gedik Ahmet wrote back to Istanbul for instructions. A courier from Istanbul arrived on 23 September, with instructions that the Venetian subjects were free to leave, but that the island belonged to the Ottomans, and Sultan Mehmet wanted to destroy it and resettle its Greek inhabitants elsewhere in his empire. The Venetian subjects left aboard Loredano's ships, along with the *stradiots*, and the civilians were resettled in the republic's possessions in the Morea. Gedik Ahmet then slaughtered all Leonardo Tocco's officials on the island, after which he took the Greek population off to be resettled on the islands in the Sea of Marmara.

Meanwhile, Leonardo Tocco had taken refuge with King Ferrante, who gave him two fiefs in the Kingdom of Naples. Leonardo's brother Antonio made an attempt to retake the Tocco possessions, hiring an army of Catalan mercenaries with whom he briefly occupied Cephalonia and Zante in 1480, before he was driven out by the Venetians and finally murdered.

That same year Mehmet mounted a small expedition to the eastern end of the Black Sea under Hızıroğlu Mehmet Pasha, who captured three Georgian fortresses. Mehmet Pasha then sailed his fleet across the eastern end of the Black Sea, where he took two fortresses of the Circassians, whom

Mehmet wanted to reduce to subjects of the Tartar Khan of the Crimea, his vassal.

Throughout 1479 there were also numerous raids by Ottoman *akincis* into Hungary, Transylvania, Croatia and even Austria. The raids into Hungary brought a reprisal from King Matthias Corvinus, who sent an army of 7,000 troops to attack the Ottomans in Sarajevo, which they looted and burned. A Turkish force under Daud Pasha cut off the Hungarians on their homeward march and, after heavy casualties on both sides, forced the invaders to abandon their loot and flee.

Mehmet then turned his attention to Rhodes, where, now that the Venetians had come to terms, the Knights Hospitallers of St John were the only Christian power in the eastern Mediterranean that still refused to pay tribute to the Ottomans. The Knights had been plundering Muslim merchant ships and Mehmet was determined to end their piracy, according to the Turkish chronicler Kemalpaşazade. Mehmet was also anxious to open up the south-eastern Mediterranean to his navy, for he seems to have been planning a major expedition against the Mamluks of Egypt, and to do that he first had to subjugate the Knights of Rhodes.

The Order of the Knights Hospitallers of St John had been founded in Jerusalem in the eleventh century. One of its original purposes was to build and operate hospices and hospitals for the Christian pilgrims who came to visit the Holy Land, and another was to fight in the crusades. Their emblem, the white cross of St John on a red field, contrasted with the red cross on white of the Knights Templars and the black cross on white of the Teutonic Knights, the latter two being solely military crusading orders.

The Knights of St John moved frequently during the Middle Ages, from Jerusalem to Lebanon in 1188, to Palestine in 1191, to Cyprus in 1291. Then, after taking Rhodes from the Byzantines in 1309, they established their headquarters in the principal town of the island, at its eastern end, where they built a powerful fortress opposite the south-western coast of Asia Minor. The Knights also captured and fortified several other islands in the Dodecanese, as well as building a great fortress on the south-western coast of Asia Minor at Halicarnassus, Turkish Bodrum. During the fourteenth and fifteenth centuries the Knights of Rhodes fought against both the Ottomans and Mamluks at sea as well as on land, sometimes alone and sometimes in coalitions with other Christian powers, one notable instance being their participation in the crusading expedition that was defeated by Murat I at Nicopolis in 1396.

At the time when Mehmet was considering an expedition against Rhodes the grand master of the Knights of St John was Pierre d'Aubusson, a French knight who had been fighting against the Turks for a quarter of a century. He had distinguished himself in the attack on Rhodes by the Ottoman admiral Hamza Bey in 1455, during which he personally led the defence, fighting hand to hand with the Turks even after he had been wounded five times. According to a contemporary historian, d'Aubusson was 'of fine person and acute intelligence and easily captured the friendship of anyone who met him and whose affection he studied to win'. At the time of his election as grand master, on 17 June 1476, he had been given dictatorial powers to prepare the defences of Rhodes against what the Knights saw as the inevitable Turkish attack on their island fortress.

D'Aubusson began discussions with Kaitbey, the Mamluk Sultan of Egypt, who was also threatened by Mehmet, and on 28 October 1478 they signed a peace treaty. Then, to gain more time to strengthen the defences of Rhodes, d'Aubusson entered into negotiations with Sultan Mehmet, who was only too pleased to do so, since he needed some months to fully prepare his army and navy for an expedition against the Knights.

Normally such negotiations would have been conducted by the grand vezir or one of the other pashas. But on this occasion Mehmet entrusted the task to Prince Jem, his youngest son, who was summoned from Konya to head the negotiations with the Knights. The negotiations were successful from the points of view of both parties, and in the late summer of 1479 a truce was signed between the Ottomans and the Knights of St John.

Earlier that summer Mehmet had sent out invitations to celebrate the circumcision of his nine-year-old grandson, the future Selim I, son of Prince Beyazit. Now that Venice was at peace with the Ottomans, an envoy was sent with an invitation for Doge Giovanni Mocenigo to attend the circumcision feast, but he politely declined.

The envoy also delivered a letter containing Mehmet's request that the Venetians send him 'a good painter' (*un buon pittore*). The Signoria chose Gentile Bellini, who at the time was restoring the paintings in the Hall of the Great Council in the Doge's Palace. Gentile accepted the commission, while his younger brother Giovanni replaced him in the work of restoration in the council chamber. Gentile, accompanied by two assistants, left Venice on 3 September 1479 aboard the galley of Melchiore Trevisano, which arrived in Istanbul at the end of the month.

Gentile remained in Istanbul for about sixteen months, departing for Venice around mid-January 1481. During that time he did the celebrated portrait of Sultan Mehmet the Conqueror now in the National Portrait Gallery in London, and probably several other works as well, though none of the latter have been definitely attributed to him.

Another portrait that may have been painted by Gentile Bellini during his stay in Istanbul was discovered around 1950 in a private collection in Switzerland. The painting shows Sultan Mehmet on the left facing a beardless young man on the right, both figures in half profile. An old label on the back identifies the painter as Gentile Bellini and the subjects as *Maometto Secondo i suo Figlio* ('Mehmet II and his Son'). The young man would appear to be Prince Jem, who was about twenty at the time, for Mehmet's only other son, Prince Beyazit, was thirty-two, appreciably older than the youth in the painting. Both brothers were at that time serving as provincial governors in Anatolia, Beyazit in Amasya and Jem in Konya, and so, when the painting was discovered, it was thought that neither one of them could have been the youth shown with Mehmet, since Bellini did the painting in Istanbul. Jem did return to Istanbul in 1479, however, when his father recalled him to take charge of the negotiations with Pierre d'Aubusson, and so he may have been living in Topkapı Sarayı for at least part of the time that Bellini was working there.

The fact that Mehmet chose Jem rather than Beyazit to conduct the negotiations with d'Aubusson was commented upon by insiders in the Ottoman court, who concluded that the sultan had decided to groom his younger son as his successor. Jem was by far the more attractive and charismatic of the two brothers, his generous and outgoing nature having made him a great favourite in Karaman, the central Anatolian region that he governed from the provincial capital at Konya. He was an enthusiastic sportsman and hunter, as well as an accomplished poet in both Persian and Arabic, presiding over a brilliant circle of poets and musicians in Konya, where stories of his love affairs eventually passed into legend.

Beyazit, by contrast, was dour and withdrawn. During the years that he served as provincial governor in Amasya, near the Black Sea coast of Anatolia, he had little contact with the local people, preferring to spend his time in study. He became a member of the Halveti dervishes, a contemplative order who believed that their hereditary sheikhs had the power of divination. The Halveti skeikh at the time, Muhyidden Mehmet, told Beyazit that he would succeed his father as sultan. This gave great comfort to Beyazit, who felt, with good reason, that Mehmet had already decided on Jem as his successor. From early in his youth Beyazit had been an opium addict. When Sultan Mehmet learned of this from Gedik Ahmet Pasha, who was grand vezir at the time, he was furious, though Beyazit assured his father that he took opium only as medicine during a period of illness. The grand vezir also told Mehmet that the troops under Beyazit's command were poorly organised and undisciplined. Beyazit denied this charge too, and Mehmet decided to let the matter pass, but it obviously added to his reasons for preferring his younger to his older son. Beyazit knew this, and from then on he was determined that one day he would take his revenge on Gedik Ahmet Pasha.

Sultan Mehmet's inactivity in 1479–80 was due in part to his declining health. This was remarked upon by the French statesman and historian Philippe de Commines, who ranked Mehmet II along with Louis XI of France and Matthias Corvinus of Hungary among the greatest rulers of the fifteenth century. Commynes observed, however, that Mehmet overindulged in '*les plaisairs du monde*' and noted that 'no carnal vice was unknown to this voluptuary'. Mehmet had from his early manhood suffered from gout, as Angiolello observed, as well as a number of other ailments that may have been brought on by his excesses. The sultan had a huge swelling and abcess in one of his legs that had first appeared in the spring of 1480. None of his physicians were able to explain or cure this malady, but Commines remarks that they looked upon it as divine punishment for the sultan's great gluttony ('*grande gourmandise*'). Commines goes on to say that the sultan's illness kept him confined to his palace, for he was loath to show himself in public in such a condition: 'Lest people notice his sorry state and his enemies despise him, he seldom allowed himself to be seen and remained secluded in his *serai*.'

Meanwhile, Pierre d'Aubusson had used the truce with the Ottomans to strengthen the defences of Rhodes, which included the great fortress that surrounded the island capital as well as the coastal castles of Pheraclus, Lindos and Monolithos. He considered the castle on Mount Phileremus too difficult to defend, and so he left it to be taken by the Turks, though he removed a sacred icon of the Virgin from a monastery there and brought it to the capital.

The acropolis of the ancient city of Rhodes was on Mount St Stephen, which rises to the west of the modern town. The town of Rhodes has since classical times had two artificial harbours, created by building moles out into the sea. The northernmost is Porto del Mandraccio, or Galley Port, now known as Mandraki, enclosed on its seaward side by a long mole extending north to a fortress called the Tower of St Nicholas. The southern harbour, the Porto Mercantile, or Commercial Port, was protected on its seaward side by a long mole stretching north to the Tower of St Angelo. A shorter transverse mole guarded at its outer end by the Tower of Naillac extended eastward towards the Tower of St Angelo. At times of siege, chains could be stretched from the Tower of St Angelo to the Tower of Naillac and the Tower of St Nicholas, thus closing off the inner and outer parts of the Commercial Port.

The town was protected by a circuit of defence walls some two and one-half miles in circumference, which also extended around the semicircular shore of the Commercial Port between the moles leading out to the Tower of Naillac and the Tower of St Angelo. Outside the land wall there was a fosse 30–45 metres wide and 15–20 metres deep, in some places hollowed out of the living rock, backed by strong earthworks that in places divided the moat into two ditches. The walls were studded with a score of towers. The most notable of these were the Bastion of St Paul and the Tower of St Peter in the north wall; the Bastion of St George, the Tower of Aragon and the Tower of St Mary in the west; and the Koskinou Bastion and the Italian Tower on the south. The principal entryways were St Paul's Gate and St Peter's Gate on the north; D'Amboise Gate on the west; St Anthony's Gate and Koskinou Gate on the south; and along the shore St Catherine's Gate, the Marine Gate and the Arsenal Gate.

The town comprised two distinct and separate sections, Kastello and Chora. Kastello, the Castle of the Knights, was the smaller of the two. This was the preserve of the Order of the Hospitallers of St John of Jerusalem, its principal buildings being the Palace of the Grand Master, the hospital, and the auberges, or inns of the order, which lined the main thoroughfare in Kastello, the Street of the Knights. Kastello was separated by an inner wall from the Chora, or main town, which included the commercial centre and the residential quarters of the Greeks, Jews and western Europeans.

Each of the inns housed knights from one of the *langue*, or tongues, into which the order was divided by nation. There were originally seven *langue*, these were, in order of seniority: Provence, Auvergne, France, Italy, Aragon and Catalonia, England and Germany. Then in 1462 an eighth *langue* was formed that included both Castile and Portugal. (Pope Pius II wrote of the English *langue*, to which the Scots and the Irish also belonged, that 'there was nothing the Scots liked better than abuse of the English'.)

Beneath the Grand Master in the hierarchy of the order was a network of bailiffs, also known as 'grand crosses'. There were three categories of bailiffs: conventual, capitular and honorary. The conventual bailiffs were the elected heads of the eight inns at Rhodes, each holding important posts in the military hierarchy of the order. The bailiff of the *langue* of Provence was the grand commander and president of the treasury, comptroller of the expenditure, superintendent of stores, governor of the arsenal and master of the ordinance. The bailiff of Auvergne, Pierre d'Aubusson, was the Grand Master and commander of the armed forces, both military and naval. The bailiff of France was the grand hospitaller, serving as director of the hospitals, infirmaries and hospices. The bailiff of Italy was grand admiral, acting as second in command to the Grand Master. The bailiff of Aragon was commissary-general, while the bailiff of Germany was chief engineer. The bailiff of England was Turcopolier, chief of the light cavalry, the so-called *turcopoles*, who were sons of Turkish fathers by Greek mothers. The *turcopoles* were brought up as Christians and were hired to serve as cavalrymen in the order; they dressed in Islamic fashion and were familiar with the ways of Turkish warfare. The English knight John Kendal was appointed Turcopolier in 1477 and led his *turcopole* cavalry in the defence of Rhodes when it was besieged by the Ottomans in 1480. Kendal was subsequently appointed to be one of the Order's ambassadors to the papacy. Guillaume Caoursin, vice chancellor of the Hospitallers, also served as private secretary to the Grand Master Pierre d'Aubusson, whom he often quotes in his account of the Ottoman siege of Rhodes in 1480.

Meanwhile, Mehmet had appointed Mesih Pasha to command the expedition against Rhodes. During the winter of 1479–80 the army mustered in Üsküdar and marched across western Anatolia to Physkos (Marmaris), a port on the Mediterranean coast eighteen miles from Rhodes. Mesih Pasha set sail early in December 1479 from the Dardanelles with the first ships of the fleet, which eventually comprised more than 100 vessels. After failed attempts at landings on the north coast of Rhodes and on the nearby island of Telos he finally anchored in the harbour of Physkos, where the army, numbering some 70,000 troops, had set up its winter encampment.

D'Aubusson had been kept informed of the Ottoman expedition by his observers, and he had ordered the country people of Rhodes to withdraw within the fortified capital and the other fortresses on the island, bringing with them their animals and supplies. They were also ordered to harvest their grain and bring that with them too, and to cut down their fruit trees, so as to leave nothing for the invaders. D'Aubusson had also been stocking the capital with arms and munitions, as well as enough food to last through a two-year siege. The preparations for the siege are described by the Augustinian monk Fra de Curti in a letter to his brother in Venice: 'The city is well provided with grain, oil, cheese, salted meat and other foodstuffs ...many crossbows and both heavy and light guns and earthenware fire-pots and receptacles for boiling oil and Greek fire and pots full of pitch lashed together...and there is a continuous watch day and night of select companies of crosssbowmen and hand-gunners and 100 cavalry.'

The defenders in the capital numbered only about 600 knights and servants-at-arms of the Order, along with some 1,500 mercenaries and local militiamen. Shortly before the siege began reinforcements arrived in the company of d'Aubusson's nephew Antoine, Count of Monteil, who, though he was not a member of the Order, was appointed Captain-General of the City.

After 29 April 1480 no ships were allowed to leave the harbour of Rhodes, as word reached d'Aubusson that the Ottomans were making their final preparations across the Rhodian strait in Physkos. Then, shortly after sunrise on 23 May, a sentinel on Mount St Stephen gave the alarm that the Ottoman fleet was headed towards Rhodes. Fra de Curti writes: 'The sea was covered with sails as far as the eye could see.' The fleet landed troops, who occupied the hill of St Stephen, after which some of the ships went back to pick up more soldiers at Physkos.

By dawn the following day there were about 60,000 Ottoman soldiers on Mount St Stephen, where Mesih Pasha set up his tent and his artillery park of sixteen cannon. According to d'Aubusson, this battery included 'three great bronze basilisks of incredible size and power, capable of firing balls of nine palms [about seven feet] in circumference'.

Mesih sent his herald before the walls of the town to call upon the defenders to surrender, promising them an amnesty. When the offer was ignored Mesih ordered his artillerymen to begin firing. The gunners concentrated their bombardment on the Tower of St Nicholas, which Mesih intended to destroy so that he could land troops on the mole that it defended.

D'Aubusson, in a letter to Emperor Frederick III, reported that within a few days the Ottoman bombardment severely damaged the Tower of St Nicholas and eight other towers, as well as the Palace of the Grand Master. Fra de Curti told his brother that during the bombardment 'the ground trembled under his feet…no one from any nation had ever before seen such cannon… Had you been here, you would certainly have taken refuge in a cave!'

Shortly before dawn on 28 May a deserter from the Ottoman forces appeared under the Tower of St Peter, where he called up to the lookout and asked to be admitted into the city. When he came to the gate he was identified by a soldier who had been a prisoner of the Turks in Istanbul as Master George of Saxony, a cannon founder and master bombardier, who had once lived on Rhodes and had joined the Ottoman service. One of the German knights interviewed him, and he said that his conscience had moved him to desert the Muslim service and join his fellow Christians in their time of need. D'Aubusson was sceptical of the deserter's motives, but he decided to make use of his services, appointing a bodyguard of six knights to keep a constant watch on Master George and report on his every move.

That same day d'Aubusson wrote a circular letter to the Knights of St John throughout Europe, appealing to them to come to the aid of their Order. The letter, which was sent off on a fast galley, concluded with a defiant pledge that the brethren on Rhodes would resist the Turks with all their might, sustained by their faith.

> We resist with all our power and energy and with courage sustained by our Faith in the Mercy of God who never abandons them whose hope is in Him and who fights for the Catholic Faith… We are no make-believe soldiers in fine clothes. Our men are no effeminate Asiatics. Their fidelity is proved and we have abundant cannon and bombards and good store of munitions and victuals. We will continue to confront the enemy while we await the aid of our Brethren. Above all we are sustained by our loyalty to the Holy Religion.

Four days later a ship from Sicily managed to elude the Turks and made its way into the harbour of Rhodes, carrying grain as well as 100 troops. Mesih Pasha realised by now that he had to control access to the harbour to make his siege effective, and to do that he first had to capture the Tower of St Nicholas, which he had been bombarding constantly for a week.

D'Aubusson had about 1,000 labourers working day and night repairing the Tower of St Nicholas and the mole on which it stood. A company of knights under Fabrizio Del Carretto was assigned to defend the tower in case Mesih attempted to take it by landing troops on the mole. The first attempted landing took place early in June after an intense bombardment that lasted for ten days. The Turkish troops boarded triremes that had been converted into landing craft, some of which mounted light cannons. As they approached the knights shot at them with crossbows and other weapons, including the incendiary liquid known as 'Greek fire', blowing up one of the triremes, and as the ships drew closer they were bombarded by guns from the defence towers. When the Turks tried to land on the mole the knights cut them down with their swords, forcing them to flee under a hail of arrows. Two other such attacks were made in the following days, the second on 9 June, when the Ottomans lost 600 men, according to Caoursin.

On 13 June the Turkish artillery began a furious bombardment of the mole and the tower that continued for four days and nights. On the fourth night a party of Turks in rowing boats began building a wooden pontoon bridge from the foreshore out to the mole, using a hawser to attach it to a grapnel they dropped into the sea by the base of the tower. An English sailor named Robert Jervis heard the sound of their oars, and after they rowed away, paying out the hawser as they went, he dived in and cut through the rope, carrying back the grapnel to present to d'Aubusson, who rewarded him with a bag of gold coins.

Mesih Pasha made another attempt to land on the mole on the night of 18–19 June, but this was also repelled. Some 2,500 Ottoman troops were killed, according to Caoursin, who writes that 'for three whole days their corpses kept being washed up by the sea, glittering with gold and silver and rich raiment. Others could be seen on the bottom of the harbour, swaying with the currents as if put there by nature... Not a few of our men collected the spoils, to their great profit.' Fra de Curti told his brother that 'the heads of many Janissaries were displayed on our towers and the sea was red with their blood'.

Meanwhile Mesih Pasha had also been bombarding the southern part of the walled city, the densely populated Jewish quarter, badly damaging the Italian Tower and the south-eastern section of the defence walls. Seeing that the outer fortifications were being reduced to rubble by the bombardment, d'Aubusson set everyone to work on building an inner fortification, demolishing the houses in the Jewish quarter and using their stones to erect a new defence work. Caoursin writes of the dedication with which the populace went about their work, undeterred by the constant bombardment.

Neither did the Grand Master, the Bailiffs, Priors, citizens, merchants, matrons, brides, maidens, spare themselves; but all carried on their backs stones, earth and lime, having no thought of personal gain but each thinking only of the safety of all… The great projectiles from the mortars terrified the people who saw them flying through the air… We ourselves were not a little anxious, particularly at night…which was spent in cellars, near the more robust doors, or under the arches of Churches…snatching some restless sleep…

D'Aubusson himself led the defenders in the Jewish quarter, sleeping on the walls at night so that he would be ready if there was an attack. During the night of 18–19 June, when Mesih Pasha attempted to land on the mole, d'Aubusson rushed there to help, killing a janissary with his own hands, while he himself was almost killed when a piece of shrapnel shattered his helmet. Fabrizio Del Carretto, who was in charge of the defenders on the mole, implored him to take shelter, and d'Aubusson replied, 'My place is the place of danger, if I should be killed, you will be able to worry about your own future and not mine.'

A rumour spread among the Italian knights that Sultan Mehmet himself was headed towards Rhodes with an army of 100,000 fresh troops. The Italians prevailed upon Gian Maria Filefio, the Grand Master's secretary, to suggest to him that the knights abandon Rhodes before it was too late. D'Aubusson called in the Italian knights and told them if they wanted to leave Rhodes they were free to do so, and he would cover their departure, but if they remained there was to be no talk of surrender, under pain of death, to which they had no recourse but to agree and beg the Grand Master's forgiveness.

Mesih Pasha had a herald call out to the defenders that he was requesting a safe conduct for his envoy to offer the knights terms of surrender. D'Aubusson said that the envoy could not enter the city, but would have to deliver his message from the counterscarp in front of the defence walls. According to Caoursin, the envoy, Süleyman Bey, said that Mesih Pasha offered to allow the knights to continue living in Rhodes as vassals of the sultan if they surrendered. But if they did not give in, he said, 'The city will be devastated, the men slaughtered, the women ravished and consigned to ignominy.'

Caoursin then quotes the response given by d'Aubusson's spokesman, Fra Antoine Gualtier, castellan of the city of Rhodes, who concluded by saying: 'Take your armies home and send us ambassadors. Then we will talk of peace as equals; but as long as you stand armed before our city, do your duty as a soldier, and, with the help of God, we will give you our answer. You do not have to do with effeminate Asiatics, but with Knights of proven valour.'

After the refusal of his proposal Mesih Pasha resumed his bombardment of the city, pleased by the arrival of two shiploads of fresh janissaries. At this point Master George of Saxony, the German bombardier who had defected from the Ottoman forces, fell under suspicion and was summoned before the Council of Knights. When the question was put to him under torture, he admitted that he had been secretly communicating with Mesih Pasha, whereupon he was condemned and hanged.

On 24 June the knights celebrated the feast day of St John the Baptist, their patron saint, with the usual Solemn Mass in their conventual church. A few days later a Christian ship made its way into port with reinforcements, a company of troops under Benedetto della Scala of Verona, greatly improving the morale of the defenders.

D'Aubusson sent envoys to Rome, who arrived there at the beginning of July, bringing with them an appeal to the Pope for aid against the Turks. Pope Sixtus agreed to send two large ships to Rhodes with troops, ammunition and supplies, and King Ferrante of Naples promised to send two more vessels. On 3 July Sixtus convened a meeting of the ambassadors resident in Rome, and it was agreed that the expenses for this relief expedition were to be met by imposing a so-called Rhodian defence tax (*tassa per defesa de Rodi*). The assessments they agreed upon were: the Pope 10,000 ducats, the King of Naples 20,000, the Duke of Milan 15,000, the Signoria of Florence 8,000, the Duke of Ferrara 4,000, the Signoria of Siena 4,000, the Marquis of Mantua 1,000, the Marquis of Montferrat 1,000, the Signoria of Lucca 1,000, and the Duke of Savoy 3,000 – a total of 67,000 ducats. Venice was not included in the assessment, because of the republic's peace treaty with the Ottomans. But Sixtus hoped that when the Venetians saw the other Christian powers preparing for a crusade they would scrap their treaty and join in the struggle against the Turks.

Meanwhile, the siege on Rhodes continued unabated, the Turks bombarding the Jewish quarter day and night, eventually destroying the Tower of Italy and opening a breach in the defence walls. At dawn on 27 July, after a night of particularly heavy bombardment, Mesih Pasha ordered his entire army to attack the breach in the walls of the Jewish quarter. He first sent in his shock troops, the *başıbozuks*, who charged over the mound of rubble and up onto the ruins of the Tower of Italy, where they planted the Turkish standard. They were followed by the janissaries and *sipahis*, some of whom made their way into the town and began slaughtering the townspeople. By then d'Aubusson had led the knights up onto the tower, where a janissary severely wounded him with a spear so that he had to be carried away. But the knights outfought the attackers and forced them to withdraw, cutting them down in droves as they fled in disorder and slaughtering those who were cut off inside the town. The knights pursued their enemies as far as the Ottoman camp on Mount St Stephen, where they captured the sultan's gold and silver standard, triumphantly returning to town with the severed heads of Turks on their pikes and lances.

According to Caoursin, 3,500 Turks were killed in the attack on the Jewish quarter, including 300 janissaries. He writes: 'There were corpses all over the city, on the walls, in the ditch, in the enemy stockades and in the sea...they had to be burned to avoid an infectious disease.'

At first it was thought that d'Aubusson would die from his wound, for the spear had punctured his lung, but he made a remarkably rapid recovery. He reported that 'many of our Knights and Bailiffs fell, fighting to the last wherever the combat was thickest. We and others of our comrades sustained many wounds.' Fra de Curti noted that in the battle in the Jewish quarter ten knights of the Order lost their lives, 'including the Bailiff of Germany'. According to other sources, seven of the ten knights who died were English: Thomas Benn, John Wakelyn, Henry Hales, Thomas Plumpton, Adam Tedbond, Henry Battesby and Henry Anlaby. Marmaduke Lumley, who later became Grand Prior of the Order in Ireland, was gravely wounded but subsequently recovered. Other English knights who fought in the battle and survived were Leonard Tybert, Walter Westborough, John Boswell, who was a Scot, and John Roche, an Irishman.

The failure of his assault on the Jewish quarter convinced Mesih Pasha that he was unable to take Rhodes, and on the following day he ordered his troops to lift the siege and begin preparations for withdrawing from the island. It took ten days for them to strike their camp, and the last of the troops were taken aboard the Ottoman fleet late in the afternoon of 7 August.

Just as the Ottoman fleet departed, headed for Physkos, observers on Rhodes saw two ships approaching, a carrack and a brigantine, one flying the flag of the Pope and the other that of the King of Naples. Mesih Pasha sent a squadron of twenty galleys to attack the Christian ships, a shot from one of their guns carrying away the mainmast of the brigantine. But the heavily armed carrack, the *Santa Maria*, captained by a Spaniard named Juan Poo, covered the brigantine until it was able to make its way into the harbour of Rhodes before nightfall. The *Santa Maria* was unable to enter the harbour because of heavy seas, and the next day it was attacked by the Ottoman galleys, which it fought off in a three-hour battle in which the Turkish squadron commander was killed. The *Santa Maria* then entered the harbour under full sail, unloading fresh troops and supplies, including 800 barrels of wine, as well as letters from Pope Sixtus and King Ferrante for Pierre d'Aubusson, whose life still hung in the balance.

The siege had left the city of Rhodes in ruins, with the Grand Master's palace and many of the churches destroyed along with the Tower of St Nicholas and much of the defence walls. About a half of the knights were killed during the siege, including seven of the fourteen English, Scottish and Irish knights, along with a similar proportion of the other Christian defenders, not to mention the civilians who were slain when the Turks broke into the Jewish quarter.

The Ottoman casualties, according to Christian sources, probably amounted to 9,000 killed and 15,000 wounded, about a quarter of Mesih Pasha's force. Mesih Pasha kept his fleet in Physkos for eleven days before sailing homeward, after unsuccessfully trying to take the fortress that the Knights of St John had built at Halicarnassus. When the fleet arrived at Gelibolu, Mesih Pasha was relieved of his command on the orders of Sultan Mehmet, who is reported to have said that if he himself had led the expedition Rhodes would have been taken. When the defeated fleet reached Istanbul, according to Angiolello, its crews and troops arrived in silence, 'not sounding instruments of joy, as they were accustomed to do on such occasions when the fleet came home'.

Meanwhile, the Christian victory was celebrated joyously all over Europe, particularly in the city of Rhodes itself. When the celebration was over Guillaume Caoursin, vice chancellor of the Order, sat down to write his famous account of the siege 'for praise of God, exaltation of the Christian religion, and the glory of the knights of Rhodes'. Entitled *Obsidionia Rhodiae Urbis Descriptio*, Caoursin's account was first published at Venice in 1480. It was then translated into English by John Kay, laureate to King Edward IV, and published by Caxton in 1496 as *The Derlectable newess & Tithyngs of the Gloryoos Victorye of the Rhodyns Agaynst the Turke*.

13 *The Capture of Otranto*

Although Pierre d'Aubusson had been seriously wounded during the siege, immediately after it was over he set out to rebuild the ruined city of Rhodes and its defence walls and towers. Three days after the Ottoman withdrawal the Grand Master and the council met and decided to send an envoy to Italy to inform Pope Sixtus and King Ferrante of their victory over the Turks, and also to request further aid, 'for it is of course assumed that the enemy proposes to come back'. By the beginning of October 1480 d'Aubusson decided that the Ottoman fleet had finally left the region and was not likely to return in the immediate future. The council therefore decided to allow the departure of the galleys and mercenaries that had been sent by King Ferrante. But they decided to retain the 100 men of arms who had come to Rhodes with the prior of Rome, because the knights had suffered such heavy casualties during the siege that their garrison needed reinforcements.

Mehmet's expedition against the Ionian Islands in 1479 had given him possession of Santa Maura, Ithaka, Cephalonia and Zante, the former possessions of Leonardo III Tocco, who had taken refuge with King Ferrante of Naples. Corfu, the northernmost of the Ionian Islands, remained in the possession of Venice, which because of its peace treaty with the Ottomans remained neutral when Gedik Ahmet Pasha conquered the other islands in the archipelago.

On 2 July 1480 the Senate wrote to Vettore Soranzo, the Captain-General of the Sea, who at the time was on Corfu, informing him that the Ottoman fleet had left the Dardanelles and had divided into two parts, the larger one headed for Rhodes (where the siege had already begun on 23 May) and the other bound for the Adriatic.

As soon as Soranzo received the letter he left Corfu with twenty-eight galleys for Methoni, in the south-west Peloponessos, which together with nearby Methoni were called the 'Eyes of the Republic', for they surveyed all maritime traffic between the eastern Mediterranean and the Adriatic. Soranzo's instructions were to avoid any conflict with the Ottoman forces, but if they attacked any Venetian possessions he was to oppose them. At Methoni, Soranzo met with an Ottoman envoy, who requested safe passage for a Turkish flotilla headed into the Adriatic, along with provisions. Soranzo agreed to the envoy's requests, and he followed with his squadron as the Turkish ships headed towards the Adriatic to join Gedik Pasha's fleet at Valona in Albania.

On 24 July 1480 Naples, Milan, Florence and Ferrara renewed their alliance for twenty-five years, an alignment designed to counter the pact between Venice and the papacy. Pope Sixtus IV immediately summoned envoys of the Italian states to Rome in order to gain their cooperation in sending help to Rhodes. The envoys expressed their concern that internecine war in Italy would make it difficult or impossible to help the Rhodians, and they asked the Pope to give them reassurance in this matter. Sixtus responded on 27 July with a circular letter to the states of Italy, making an impassioned appeal to keep the peace and take united action against the Turks before it was too late.

> We think of nothing else than how the Italian states may with a unity of purpose resist the terrible power of the Turks... [Now] we have the enemy before our very eyes. He has already been sighted, poised to strike at the province of Apulia with a large fleet. If he should seize Ragusa or Rhodes (which God forbid!), nothing would be left of our safety... Hear our paternal voice, consider the common peril, and judge for yourself how great is the need to quicken our pace...

Meanwhile, Gedik Pasha's fleet had left Valona on 26 July, headed across the Adriatic to southern Italy. The Venetian squadron under Soranzo remained at Corfu and made no move to interfere with the Ottoman fleet, which comprised forty large galleys, sixty smaller galleys and forty freighters, carrying some 18,000 troops and 700 horses for the cavalry.

The original plan was for the expedition to land near Brindisi, but, having learned from the sailors on a captured Italian freighter that the coast further to the south was undefended, Gedik Ahmet decided to head for

Otranto. On the morning of 28 July he landed a squadron of cavalry without opposition near the castle of Roca, and the horsemen rode through the countryside as far as Otranto, on the heel of the Italian peninsula, capturing many of the locals and their cattle. The garrison at Otranto made a sortie and drove off the Turks, killing many of them and freeing some of the prisoners.

By that time Gedik Ahmet had landed the rest of his army, estimated to number 18,000. He then sent an Italian-speaking envoy into Otranto offering terms of surrender, and when these were rejected the pasha threatened the city with 'fire, flame, ruin, annihilation and death'. Gedik Ahmet then positioned his siege guns and began bombarding the city, which was only lightly defended, its small garrison having no artillery to fire back at the Ottomans, while at the same time his cavalryman laid waste the surrounding countryside, putting all they encountered to the sword.

Word of the Ottoman attack quickly reached the court of King Ferrante at Naples, where it was feared that this was the beginning of a full-scale Turkish invasion of Italy. Niccolo Sadoleto, the Ferrarese ambassador to Naples, wrote on 1 August to inform Duke Ercole I d'Este of Ferrara.

> This morning four horsemen have come [to Naples], riding at breakneck speed from Apulia and the region of Otranto. They have gone to find the lord king at Aversa, where he went yesterday evening, and they have brought him the news of how the Turks have landed at Otranto with 150 sail, and have made three assaults upon the castle. The news is all over Naples. I have no certain information, however, except that the lord king has in fact returned posthaste from Aversa within the hour.

Soon afterwards Sadoleto added in a postscript that the report of the Ottoman landing was true, and that 'the number of ships is uncertain, but the armada is so great that it is believed to contain all the vessels that were at Rhodes!'. That same day Sadoleto wrote to Duke Ercole saying that he thought that King Ferrante would soon ask all his allies to help him to repel the invaders, who besides attacking Otranto had taken three villages in the vicinity. He reported that a horseman had arrived from Taranto 'who says that there are more than 350 vessels, and that the Turks have attacked the castle of Otranto and ranged as far as Lecce, burning villages, taking prisoners and killing little children as though they were dogs…'.

Luca Landucci, a Florentine apothecary, viewed the Turkish attack on Neapolitan territory as a blessing to his native city. He noted in his diary that Duke Alfonso of Calabria, son of King Ferrante of Naples, had intended to do much evil against Florence but 'by a great miracle it happened that on the sixth of August [sic], the Turkish army came to Otranto and began to besiege it; so it was necessary to leave our neighborhood, at the king's command, and return to defend the kingdom...'.

On 2 August King Ferrante wrote to summon home Duke Alfonso, who was with his troops in Siena, which the Neapolitans had been trying to take. Ferrante then wrote to inform Pope Sixtus that the enmity between the various Italian states must be put aside because of the common danger posed by the Turkish invasion. Otherwise, he warned, he would throw in his lot with the sultan and work for the destruction of all the other states in Italy.

The Signoria of Venice had been making efforts to maintain peace with the Ottomans. On 3 June 1480 the Senate had instructed Zaccaria Barbaro, their new ambassador to Rome, to avoid Venetian involvement in the anti-Turkish alliance then under discussion among the Italian states. At the same time the Signoria was trying to avoid attempts by the Ottomans to involve Venice in an invasion of Italy. On 23 August 1479, during the Tuscan War, the conflict between the Kingdom of Naples and its allies against those of the papacy, Gedik Ahmet Pasha had sent an envoy to the Senate suggesting that the Venetians join him in an attack against King Ferrante and the Pope, both of whom he declared to be the worst enemies of Venice. The Senate politely declined the suggestion, remarking that 'Venetian merchants had suffered no losses either in the papal states or in the Neapolitan kingdom'.

The defenders at Otranto were able to hold out only until 11 August, when the Ottoman infantry poured through a breach in the walls and took the city by storm. All the older men of the city were put to the sword, while the younger men and women were enslaved, 8,000 of them being shipped off to Albania. It is estimated that 12,000 of the 22,000 inhabitants of Otranto were killed by the Turks. The aged archbishop of Otranto, Stefano Pendinelli, remained to the last in the cathedral of Otranto, praying for divine deliverance as the Ottoman soldiers slaughtered his congregation. One Italian chronicler says that the Turks sawed the archbishop in two on the high altar of his cathedral, although a more reliable source suggests that he died of fright. The Italian chronicler goes on to say that Gedik Ahmet Pasha had 800 of the townspeople beheaded when they refused to convert to Islam, leaving their remains unburied on the eminence now known as the Hill of the Martyrs. All the martyrs were canonised in

1771 under Pope Clement XIV, and their skulls are still displayed in the cathedral.

After the fall of Otranto the Ottoman cavalry plundered the surrounding region, which was abandoned by all the Italian men capable of bearing arms, leaving only women, children and old men, many of whom were slaughtered. The cavalry extended its raids as far as Taranto on the west and northward to Lecce and Brindisi, so it appeared that Gedik Ahmet was going to use Otranto as his base for a wider invasion of Italy.

King Ferrante, after sending a courier to inform the Pope of the Turkish invasion, quickly mustered an army, which left Naples for Apulia on 8 September. His son, Alfonso, withdrew his troops from Tuscany, and by the end of the month he too headed for Apulia. By the time the Neapolitan forces reached Apulia the Ottoman troops had withdrawn from the surrounding countryside and retired within the walls of Otranto. By then Gedik Ahmet Pasha had returned to Valona with a large part of his army, leaving a garrison of only 6,500 infantry and 500 cavalry in Otranto under Hayrettin Bey, the *sancakbey* of Negroponte, a Greek convert to Islam who was fluent in Italian. When Ferrante tried to negotiate with Hayrettin Bey he was told that the sultan was not only going to keep Otranto, but that he also demanded Taranto, Brindisi and Lecce. Hayrettin went on to say that if these demands were not met the sultan himself would appear the following spring, leading an army of 100,000 troops and 18,000 cavalry, along with a powerful artillery corps, with which he would conquer all of Italy.

News of the fall of Otranto and rumours of a coming Turkish invasion caused panic throughout Italy. According to Sigismondo de'Conti, the papal secretary, the Pope was so terrified that he contemplated fleeing to Avignon.

> In Rome the alarm was as great, as if the enemy had already encamped before her very walls... Terror had taken such hold of all minds that even the Pope meditated flight. I was at the time in the Low Countries, in the suite of the Cardinal Legate Giuliano, and I remembered that he was commissioned to prepare what was necessary at Avignon, for Sixtus IV had decided upon taking refuge with the French, if the state of affairs in Italy should become worse.

But Sixtus regained his nerve and realised that aid had to be given to the Kingdom of Naples, even though Ferrante had recently betrayed him during the Tuscan war. As Sigismondo writes of the Pope's decision to come to Ferrante's aid:

Sixtus IV would have witnessed with great indifference the misfortunes and losses of his faithless ally, had Ferrante's enemy been anyone but the Sultan, but it was a very different matter when the common foe of Christendom had actually got a footing on Italian soil, and speedily the Papacy and Rome itself were threatened with utter ruin, unless he were promptly expelled... [The Pope] at once sent all the money he could get together, permitted tithes to be levied from all the clergy in the kingdom, and promised a Plenary Indulgence to all Christians enlisting under the banner of the Cross.

Later in the summer of 1480 Sixtus issued a bull calling for united Christian action against the invaders before they took all of Italy: 'How perilous it has become for all Christians,' he wrote, 'and especially the Italian powers, to hesitate in the assumption of arms against the Turk and how destructive to delay any longer, everyone can see...' He went on to warn that 'if the faithful, and especially the Italians, want to keep their lands, homes, wives, children, liberty, and the very faith in which we were baptised and reborn, let them believe us that they must now take up arms and go to war!'.

King Louis XI of France indicated that he would give his support to an anti-Turkish alliance. The Sforza dukes in Milan also offered the Pope their support, but they said that peace had to be established among the Italian states before they sought help from the French kingdom, 'for we confess that we cannot see how we may expect foreign aid if we make light of our troubles at home'.

The anti-Turkish coalition, known as the League of Naples, came into being on 16 September 1480, its members consisting of the papacy, the King of Naples, the King of Hungary, the Dukes of Milan and Ferrara, and the Republics of Genoa and Florence. Representatives of the league gathered in Venice at the beginning of October, and the Neapolitan envoys led the pleas for Venetian help against the Turks. The Republic of Venice was exhorted to join the league, but the Signoria immediately declined, saying that for 'seventeen successive years' they had fought the Turks almost alone, with an unbearable cost in men and money, and now they could do no more.

Sixtus then began preparations to build a papal fleet in Genoa and Ancona, while at the same time he appealed to England, France and Germany to join the coalition. Emperor Frederick III declined because of internal political problems, as did Edward IV of England, who wrote to the Pope that rather than making war against other Christians, as he was forced to do in order to keep his throne, he would have 'preferred being associated with the other sovereigns of Christendom in an expedition against the Turk'. Edward had been fearful of a Turkish invasion, and a year earlier he had said that the Pope should have unified Italy, 'owing to the great perils...for the Christian religion, when the Turk is at the gates of Italy, and so powerful as everyone knows'.

Louis XI assured the Pope that France would participate in the crusade, but only if all the other Christian states shared the burden. The Sforza Dukes of Milan said that aid from northern Europe would be long in coming and that the united Italian states would have to make the effort themselves, even without Venice, 'because we are prepared to strive beyond our strength for the common safety and to defeat in war the barbarous, butcherly and savage Turks'. The private instructions given to their envoys by the Sforzas began with a statement impressing upon them the grave emergency of the situation. 'We do not believe that for many centuries a more grave and perilous thing has befallen not only Italy but all Christendom than this...invasion of Calabria by the Turk, both because of the inestimable power and great cruelty of the enemy and because of the utter shame it brings to our religion and the Christian way of life.'

The Pope and the College of Cardinals agreed to contribute 150,000 ducats towards the crusade, 100,000 of which would be spent equipping twenty-five galleys for the papal fleet, the remainder to be sent to King Matthias Corvinus of Hungary, who was expected to divert Mehmet's attention from Italy to central Europe. In addition, Sixtus was recruiting a force of 3,000 infantry. The ambassadors who convened in Rome agreed that a fleet of 100 galleys should be launched for the crusade, and that 200,000 ducats should be sent annually to Corvinus to support his offensive against the Turks. Since the papacy was assuming such a large financial obligation, it expected the other Christian powers to shoulder their share of the burden and sent briefs informing each of them of their assessment. King Ferrante was to provide forty galleys for the Christian fleet and was to send Corvinus 100,000 ducats; Milan was to contribute 30,000 ducats; Florence, 20,000 ducats; Genoa, five galleys; Ferrara and Siena, four galleys each; Bologna, two galleys; Lucca, Mantua and Montferrat, one galley each.

Louis XI sent envoys to Rome to discuss the situation with Pope Sixtus. The king offered to contribute 200,000 ducats a year for the crusade, and if the Pope permitted him to tax the benifices of the clergy in France 'he would add another 100,000 ducats'. Louis estimated that Italy could easily contribute 40,000 ducats annually for the crusade; Germany, 200,000; 'all the Spains', an additional 200,000; 'and the king of England, who is so powerful and has such rich benifices, 100,000 ducats'. He had been informed 'that the Venetians are willing to declare themselves against the Turks, provided that they are assured that all Italy is going to join in and will not leave them in the lurch'. His envoys were authorised to commit their king to his pledge of 300,000 ducats annually, provided that he was allowed to tax the clergy, and that the other states of Europe support the crusade to the amounts 'of which mention is made above'. Louis also noted his desire for assurances of peace from his neighbours to the east, 'and in making the aforesaid offer he does not discount the fact that he must be safe from the king of England through the duration of the war [against the Turks] and for one year thereafter'. He said that the King of England was 'as good a friend as he had in the world', but the Pope had to realise the responsibilities that Louis had to maintain the security of his own kingdom.

Meanwhile, Emperor Frederick III and King Matthias Corvinus were waging war on one another in Austria. At the same time Turkish *akincis* were raiding in Croatia, Carniola, Carinthia and Styria, some of them even penetrating into Friuli, despite the peace treaty between the Ottomans and Venice.

The Neapolitan army finally went on the offensive during the winter of 1480–1, putting Otranto under siege and containing the Ottoman forces within their beachhead in Apulia. Then in March 1481 the Neapolitan fleet defeated an Ottoman naval force in the Adriatic, cutting off the Turkish garrison in Otranto from the sea and thus intensifying the siege.

On 8 April 1481 Pope Sixtus issued a bull proclaiming a new crusade, summoning all the princes of Europe to arms against the Turks. He imposed a three-year peace on Christendom, beginning on 1 June 1481, lest 'western Europe go the way of Constantinople and the Morea, Serbia and Bosnia, and the empire of Trebizond, whose rulers (and peoples) had all come to grief'.

But a general fear prevailed that, once again, nothing would come of this effort. The classical scholar Peter Schott, canon of Strasbourg, wrote later that month from Bologna that he had gone to take a last look at Rome 'before the Eternal City was taken by the Turks'.

14 *Death of the Conqueror*

Sultan Mehmet spent the winter of 1480–1 sequestered in Topkapı Sarayı, from where rumours leaked into Istanbul that he was in poor health. Then early in the spring of 1481 he began mustering his army on the Asian shore of the Bosphorus in Üsküdar. He had told no one of the goal of the expedition that had taken him out of his sick bed: some thought it would be another attempt to take Rhodes, while others believed that Mehmet intended to conquer the Mamluk Sultanate of Egypt.

On 25 April Mehmet crossed the Bosphorus in his imperial caique to the Asian shore at Üsküdar, after which the grand vezir Karamanı Mehmet Pasha ordered his troops to get under way. The army marched slowly down the eastern coast of the Sea of Marmara, gathering additional forces as it proceeded. By 1 May the army had only reached Gebze, at the head of the Gulf of Nicomedeia (Iznik), where a halt was made at a place called Hünkâr Çayı, or Emperor's Meadow. This was where Hannibal had taken his own life in 183 BC when he was trapped by the Romans, and where the emperor Constantine the Great had died in AD 338, though Mehmet, despite his deep interest in the lives of great conquerors, would hardly have been aware of the historical significance of his campsite.

Mehmet had called a halt here because he had been stricken by severe abdominal pains. His Persian physician, Hamiduddin al-Lari, administered medicine that only made matters worse, and so Mehmet's old Jewish doctor Master Iacopo was called in. Iacopo concluded that the pain was caused by blockage of the intestines, but despite his frantic efforts he was unable to do anything more than alleviate the sultan's agony with powerful doses of opium.

Mehmet lingered on until late in the evening of 3 May 1481, when he passed away at 'the twenty-second hour', according to Giovanni-Maria Angiolello. The sultan was forty-nine when he died, having reigned for more than thirty years, most of which he had spent in war. As Tursun Beg wrote of Mehmet: 'Besides the gracious gift of the conquest of Constantinople, Fatih wrested twenty or more independent lands from the enemies of His High Estate.'

The grand vezir Karamanı Mehmet Pasha tried to keep the sultan's death a secret, and he warned the doctors and all others in attendance to say nothing about it under pain of death. Others outside the imperial tent were told that the sultan was ill and was being taken back to Istanbul for treatment, and so the royal carriage was readied and the horses saddled for the grand vezir and others in his party. Mehmet's body was bundled up and placed in the carriage, and the small caravan headed back to Istanbul in the dead of night surrounded by the sultan's bodyguard.

The Turkish chronicler Nesri was with Mehmet's army when they stopped at Hünkâr Çayı, and after evening prayers he had bedded down near the imperial tent and fallen asleep. But in the middle of the night he was awakened by the sound of wagon wheels and neighing horses, only to find 'the wind whistling where the sultan's tent had been pitched'.

Mehmet's death left Prince Beyazit, the older of the sultan's two surviving sons, as his obvious successor, though there were some who favoured Prince Jem. At the time Beyazit was thirty-three and serving as provincial governor in Amasya, while Jem, who was twenty-one, was governing in Konya, the capital of Karaman. Karamanı Mehmet was one of the few in the uppermost level of the Ottoman government who supported Jem as the successor to the throne. Gedik Ahmet, now the captain-pasha of the Ottoman navy, was sympathetic to Jem and despised Beyazit, but he was at Valona in Albania with the Turkish forces that had captured Otranto. Most others in the government were on the side of Beyazit, including the vezirs Ishak Pasha and Daud Pasha, the *beylerbey* of Anatolia, Sinan Pasha, the *beylerbey* of Rumelia, Hersekzade Ahmet Pasha, and the commander of the janissaries, Kasım Ağa.

Before starting back to Istanbul, Karamanı Mehmet sent three of his slaves on fast horses to Konya with instructions to inform Jem of his father's death, and to urge him to rush back to Istanbul to claim the throne before his brother Beyazit. But Sinan Pasha had ordered checkpoints to be set up on all the roads leading into Konya, and the grand vezir's couriers were intercepted before they could reach Jem. At first the couriers would say nothing, but after Sinan Pasha had one of them impaled the other two revealed the message they were carrying. Sinan Pasha then sent his own courier to inform Beyazit in Amasya, advising him to hasten back to Istanbul to seize the throne before Jem.

By that time Karamanı Mehmet had brought Mehmet's body to Topkapı Sarayı in Istanbul, where he had it packed in ice in a meat locker in the palace kitchens. The army had returned to Üsküdar, where some janissaries seized rafts and crossed over to Istanbul and stormed the palace. After they discovered the sultan's body they beheaded the grand vezir and paraded through the streets of Istanbul with his head on a pike, shouting 'Long live Beyazit!'. The janissaries then took advantage of the absence of authority to sack the Christian and Jewish quarters of Istanbul, before they were finally subdued by Ishak Pasha, who had been left in charge of the city.

Ishak and Davud Pasha then summoned the other members of the government and met at the palace with Beyazit's young son Korkut, who had been living with his mother in the harem of Topkapı Sarayı. Korkut, who was then eleven years old, was raised to the throne as regent for his father, who was expected to arrive in Istanbul soon; meanwhile, the pashas secured the loyalty of the janissaries and other elements of the army by promising them higher pay.

Beyazit was indeed en route, riding westward from Amasya at top speed with a bodyguard of 4,000 *sipahis*. At Izmit he paused in his journey and sent a trusted slave ahead to Istanbul, fearing that he might be riding into a trap. The slave reported that he had seen the sultan's remains, and that Beyazit's son Korkut had been made regent and was waiting to turn the throne over to his father.

Thus reassured, Beyazit proceeded on to Üsküdar, where he arrived on 20 May, having donned a black robe as a sign of mourning for his father. At Üsküdar Beyazit was formally greeted by the pashas and conducted across the Bosphorus in the imperial caique, escorted by a flotilla of galleys and barges. But when he reached the European shore he was confronted by a mob of janissaries and *sipahis*, who demanded that he confirm the promises made to them by the pashas in the name of his son Korkut. Beyazit placated the soldiers by promising them *bahşiş*, or a bribe, as well as a permanent raise in pay, an increase that he had to give to all other units of the army as a result of a second confrontation with a mob of troops near the palace. He was also asked to promise that in the future he would appoint his vezirs only from among the janissaries, *sipahis* and *içoğlan*, the imperial pages, for the soldiers wanted to prevent the rise to power of palace favourites such as Karamanı Mehmet Pasha from the *ulema*, or learned class. Again Beyazit agreed, but when the soldiers made still another demand, that they be given amnesty for their recent sack of the Christian and Jewish quarters, he remained silent and continued on his way to the palace.

The following day Beyazit took turns with the pashas and *ağas* and other dignitaries in carrying the coffin of his father to Fatih Camii, the Mosque of the Conqueror. There Mehmet was laid to rest in the splendid tomb that he had built for himself behind his mosque, the turban that he had worn to his last day placed at the head of his catafalque. The noted cleric Şeyh Vefa then led Beyazit and a crowd of 20,000 mourners in prayer for the repose of Mehmet's soul, many of them continuing their devotions until dawn.

The following day the Ottoman court assembled at Topkapı Sarayı, where the regent Prince Korkut handed over power to his father, who ascended the throne as Beyazit II, the eighth sultan of the Osmanlı dynasty. Beyazit sat enthroned just outside Bab-üs Saadet, the Gate of Felicity, the entryway to the Inner Palace. There he received the homage of the court in the ceremony known as *Biat*, or Allegiance, during which all the notables and functionaries of the empire filed past to kiss the hem of the sultan's robe and swear fealty to him. This was followed by a meeting of the Divan, the Imperial Council, at which Beyazit announced the appointment of Ishak Pasha as grand vezir and of Daud Pasha and Hersekzade Ahmet Pasha as first vezirs. Messengers were sent to governors and other officials throughout the empire to inform them of the new appointments, and all judges were ordered to publish the news of Beyazit's accession.

Some days later Beyazit proceeded to the suburb of Eyüp on the upper reaches of the Golden Horn, where Mehmet had built a mosque and shrine around the tomb of Eba Eyüp, Companion of the Prophet Mohammed. There Beyazit was girded with the sword of his ancestor Osman Gazi, in a ceremony equivalent to a coronation, performed by the Nakib-ül Eşraf, Chief of the Descendants of the Prophet. Following this he visited Mehmet's tomb to offer up his prayers, a pilgrimage that thenceforth became customary for all new sultans upon their accession. He then returned to the palace in a procession lined with the entire populace of Istanbul, who cheered their new ruler with shouts of 'Long live Sultan Beyazit', while he distributed largesse to the crowd as he passed by. When the procession reached Topkapı Sarayı, Beyazit announced an additional increase in pay for the janissaries, the *bahşiş* known as *Cülus Akçası*, or Accession Money, which was now customary for a new sultan to pay to his elite troops before they would agree to serve him. Only then did Beyazit retire to the Inner Palace to receive the congratulations of the women in his harem, which was now headed by his mother Gülbahar, who had become the *valide sultan*, or queen mother.

Jem had by this time learned that his father had died and that his brother had succeeded as sultan. After consulting with his advisers at Konya, he decided to contest the succession. He assembled a mixed army of Anatolian *sipahis*, irregular infantry known as *azabs*, Türkmen warriors from Karaman and from the tribes of Warsak and Turgud, together with dervishes and men of the *ahi*, the craft guilds of Konya and other cities in central Anatolia.

Jem led his forces westward by way of Akşehir, Afyon, Kütahya and Eskişehir. On 27 May his advance guard reached the outskirts of Bursa, where he was joined by a large number of *sipahis* and feudal troops known as *timarcis*, who originally had been mustered to join Mehmet's final campaign, now aborted. This brought Jem's force to about 20,000 troops, which he marshalled below the *kale*, or citadel, of Bursa, the first capital of the Ottoman Empire. The janissaries who garrisoned Bursa refused to open the gates of the *kale* to the rebels, fearing the wrath of Beyazit if they capitulated, and Jem was forced to camp outside the city to the west around the Beyazidiye, the hilltop mosque complex built by his great-great-grandfather Beyazit I.

Beyazit had anticipated that his brother would contest the throne and attempt to establish himself at Bursa, and so he sent orders to all the European provinces to send troops to join the forces he was mustering in Istanbul. He also ordered the Ottoman navy to stop transporting troops to Valona in Albania, where Gedik Ahmet Pasha was waiting to reinforce the Turkish garrison at Otranto. At the same time he ordered the pasha to return to Istanbul with his army to join the imperial expedition against Jem.

Jem's forces made several probing attacks on the *kale* at Bursa, after which his emissaries were able to persuade some of the janissaries in the garrison to come over to their side, the traitors killing those who remained loyal to Beyazit. The people of Bursa then opened the city gates to Jem. Most of Bursa's populace were sympathetic to the rebellion, having also been influenced by a popular astrologer who had predicted that Jem would be the next sultan. Many hoped that under Jem the city might regain its former status as capital of the Ottoman Empire. They believed that with their city as his base Jem could go on to conquer the rest of the empire, or at least force his brother to divide it between them, with Bursa as capital of the Anatolian part of the realm.

On 2 June 1481, a month after his father's death, Jem had silver coins in his own name minted at Bursa, and at the next Friday noon prayer imams in all the mosques of the city praised him as sultan in their *hutbe*, or sermon. These two symbolic acts meant that Jem was the acknowledged ruler of the Ottoman state, if only in the tiny part of it that his troops controlled.

Beyazit had by then crossed the Bosphorus to Üsküdar with the troops of the Istanbul garrison. He sent Ayas Pasha ahead with an advance force of 2,000 janissaries to reinforce the garrison at Bursa. But when Ayas arrived at Bursa he found it already in the possession of the rebels, and after a brief battle he was forced to surrender to Jem. When Beyazit learned that Jem had taken Bursa he sent reinforcements to Ayas under his son Prince Abdullah, provincial governor at Manisa. Abdullah reached Bursa only to find that Ayas had already surrendered, so he had to withdraw his forces. Thus a stand-off ensued, and Beyazit was compelled to wait at Üsküdar for the arrival of Gedik Ahmet and his army from Albania.

Jem chose this moment to send a deputation to negotiate with Beyazit, the principal envoy being his great-aunt Selçuk Hatun, a daughter of Mehmet I, who was accompanied by several members of the *ulema* from Bursa. He proposed that he and his brother divide the empire, with Beyazit ruling the European provinces from Istanbul and Jem reigning over Anatolia from Bursa. But Beyazit rejected the proposal, quoting the old Muslim saying 'There are no ties of kinship between princes', and continued to marshal all the loyal troops in the empire to attack Jem in Bursa. He also sent a secret agent to contact Jem's chamberlain, Astinoğlu Yakup Bey, whom Beyazit had corrupted with an enormous bribe and the promise of being made *beylerbey* of Anatolia. The agent instructed Yakup to come over to Beyazit's side with his troops when an opportunity presented itself, and the chamberlain readily agreed.

As soon as Beyazit received news that Gedik Ahmet and his army from Abania were approaching Istanbul he marched his own troops to Iznik, the Greek Nicaea, thirty miles north-east of Bursa. There he was joined by Prince Abdullah, and together they continued on to Yenişehir, ten miles to the south of Iznik, where they would rendezvous with Gedik Ahmet's army of over 16,000 men. This would bring Beyazit's force to about 40,000 – double the size of Jem's – and these were all troops of the regular army, including the seasoned veterans under Gedik Ahmet, the most capable commander in the Ottoman service. The rebels were for the most part irregulars and Karamanian volunteers, whose commanders included men such as Jem's tutor Nasuh Bey, who had little or no military experience.

Jem met with his commanders to decide upon a plan of action. Most of his officers advised him to hold out in the *kale* of Bursa and not to face the superior forces of Beyazit. But Fenerlioğlu Hasan Çelebi strongly recommended that they take their chances against the imperial army, since they did not have the arms and supplies to withstand a prolonged siege. His view was supported by Astinoğlu Yakup Bey, who knew that a battle in open country would give him the opportunity to switch sides at the right moment. Their advice suited Jem's natural impetuosity, leading him to decide that he would rather fight than be besieged, and so he led his army out of Bursa to do battle with his brother.

Jem led the main body of his army towards Yenişehir, sending a detachment of janissaries under Nasuh Bey to hold a pass near Iznik. Sinan Pasha, the *beylerbey* of Anatolia, was sent by Beyazit to attack Nasuh Bey, whom he quickly drove from the pass. He then marched in to the plain of Yenişehir, where Beyazit's other forces had now converged, including the army from Albania under Gedik Ahmet. Jem's commander, Uzguroğlu Mehmet, led the rebel forces out onto the plain to confront Beyazit's forces early in the morning of 22 June 1481. Jem led the first cavalry charge himself, shouting 'Victory or Death!'.

At the outset of the battle Astinoğlu Yakup Bey rode off with his troops on the pretext of making a flanking attack on the imperial army, but as soon as he was out in the open he switched to the side of Beyazit, who was waiting to welcome him. This quickly turned the tide of battle against the rebels, and by noon Jem's forces had been routed and were in headlong retreat. As the chronicler Nesri wrote of the battle of Yenişehir: 'The Karaman crows scattered like young from the nest when they saw the eagles of Beyazit.' Jem, who was slightly wounded in the battle, fled for his life along with his family and a group of loyal followers. His reign as sultan in Bursa had ended abruptly after only twenty days.

Jem and his companions managed to make their way to Konya, after having been attacked along the way by Türkmen tribesmen who robbed them of all their possessions. They remained in Konya for only three days, leaving when they learned that Beyazit and his army were heading their way.

Jem decided their only chance was to head for south-eastern Anatolia beyond the Taurus Mountains, where they would be in Mamluk territory. Their route took them across the bleakest part of the Anatolian plateau, and as they rode along they were again attacked by Türkmen tribesmen, whom they had to bribe in order to continue on their way. After stopping briefly at Ereğli they left the Anatolian plateau and passed through the Taurus Mountains via the Cilician Gates – the same route that Alexander the Great had taken in 334 BC – descending to the Mediterranean coast at Tarsus, where they entered Mamluk territory. They then made their way by easy stages to Egypt, and on 30 September they arrived in Cairo, where Jem and his companions were given refuge by Sultan Kaitbey.

Meanwhile, Beyazit had led his army eastward to Konya, where he arrived four days after Jem's departure. Beyazit remained in Konya and ordered Gedik Ahmet Pasha to continue in pursuit of Jem. The pasha led the imperial army south-eastward as far as Ereğli, where he gave up the chase, for to continue further would have taken him into Mamluk territory. He then took the army back to Konya and reported his failure to Beyazit, who felt that Gedik Ahmet could have caught Jem had he moved more swiftly, which added to the deep resentment he felt towards the pasha.

There was nothing more that Beyazit could do for the time being. He appointed Prince Abdullah as provincial governor of Karaman, and having ordered Gedik Ahmet to follow him he started back towards Istanbul. As the imperial army proceeded westward the Türkmen tribesmen along the way petitioned Beyazit to absolve them of their taxes, saying that they should be rewarded for having attacked Jem and his followers on their flight after the Battle of Yenişehir. Beyazit would not commit himself and told them to present their case before the Divan in Istanbul. When they did so subsequently, Beyazit had the Türkmen chieftains executed for having interfered in royal affairs.

When Beyazit reached Bursa the janissaries in his bodyguard demanded that they be permitted to sack the city and punish those who had supported Jem. Beyazit restrained them with bribes, but nevertheless they put to the sword a number of dervishes who had been supporters of Jem, as well as killing those janissaries who had gone over to the rebels.

Beyazit then returned to Istanbul, and eight days later Gedik Ahmet Pasha and his army reached the capital. As soon as the pasha arrived he was summoned to Topkapı Sarayı, where Beyazit had him arrested and imprisoned without explanation. Beyazit probably knew that Gedik Ahmet favoured Jem, and he also felt that the pasha had deliberately dallied in pursuing his brother, allowing him to escape. Beyazit had long hated Gedik Ahmet for having maligned him to his father Mehmet, and he had been waiting for the chance to take his revenge.

When news of Gedik Ahmet's arrest spread the next morning the janissaries stormed the palace and threatened Beyazit, demanding that he release the pasha, who was a great favourite of theirs. The old general, who was of Serbian origin, had been taken up in the *devşirme* as a youth and enrolled in the janissaries during the reign of Murat II. He had risen to the rank of vezir under Mehmet II, for whom he had commanded the Ottoman army in a number of victorious campaigns, including the capture of Otranto. He was a heavy drinker but never let this dull his ability as a commander, and he was highly respected by his men, beloved for his generosity and fairness. The troops saw his arrest as another example of Beyazit's disregard for them as common soldiers and his preference for those of the *ulema*, and they were outraged. The violence of their reaction alarmed Beyazit, who was still deeply worried that Jem might gain the support of the military. And so Gedik Ahmet was released from prison, reappointed as vezir and restored as commander-in-chief of the army.

Beyazit had another reason for reinstating Gedik Ahmet, for he was now faced with a serious uprising by the Karamanid Türkmen under Kasım Bey, who had succeeded as emir on the death of his brother Pir Ahmet in 1475. Kasım Bey had attacked an Ottoman force under Ali Pasha, the military governor in Konya. Beyazit sent Gedik Ahmet with an army to aid Ali Pasha and put down the Türkmen revolt in Karaman. Kasım Bey attacked Ali Pasha's forces again near Mut, but on the approach of Gedik Ahmet's army he retreated across the Taurus Mountains to Tarsus. Gedik Ahmet then set up his winter camp near the town of Larende (Karaman), south of Konya, which he used as his headquarters to quell the revolt in central Anatolia and keep an eye on Kasım Bey.

Meanwhile, news of the death of Sultan Mehmet had reached western Europe. The first foreign ambassador in Istanbul to learn of Mehmet's death was Niccolo Cocco, the Venetian *bailo*. Cocco immediately wrote to Doge Giovanni Mocenigo, sending the letter off with the captain of a Venetian galley, which reached Venice on 29 May 1488, twenty-five years to the day after the fall of Constantinople.

When the captain arrived at the Palazzo Ducale he was told that the doge was in conference with the Signoria, but without waiting he burst into the council chamber and cried out: '*La Grande Aquila è morta!* ("The Great Eagle is dead!")'. After the doge read Cocco's letter he gave orders to ring the *marangona*, the great bell in the campanile of San Marco that counted off the Venetian hours and was tolled on special occasions, usually to mark the death of a doge, the appearance of enemy forces or a victory for the republic. The news quickly spread through the city, and soon all the other church bells of the city were tolling along with the *marangona*, as the entire population of Venice celebrated the death of the man they knew as the Grande Turco.

The doge sent a courier to Rome to inform Pope Sixtus, who had cannons fired from Castel Sant'Angelo, the great fortress on the Tiber near the basilica of St Peter and the Vatican. All the church bells of the city were rung to alert the populace, after which the Pope, followed by the College of Cardinals and all the ambassadors, led a procession from St Peter's to the church of Santa Maria del Popolo. As night fell Rome was illuminated by a tremendous display of fireworks; bonfires were lit and services of thanksgiving were held in churches throughout the city, beginning a celebration that lasted for three days. The scenes of jubilation in Venice and Rome were repeated throughout western Europe as word spread of Mehmet's death and the deliverance of Christendom. As the Venetian chronicler Marino Sanudo wrote two centuries later, reflecting on the passing of the Grand Turk: 'It is fortunate for Christendom and Italy that death stopped that fierce and indomitable barbarian.'

Nowhere was the news of Mehmet's death received with more joy than on Rhodes, which was in ruins from the recent Turkish siege, its surviving populace grieving for those who had been killed, many of the knights still nursing their wounds, including the Grand Master Pierre d'Aubusson. On 31 May 1481 the vice chancellor of the Hospitallers, Guillaume Caoursin, addressed an assembly of the surviving knights convoked by the Grand Master, delivering an oration entitled '*De morte Magni Turci*'. His opening words were an expression of fierce joy at the passing of Sultan Mehmet, whose terrible crimes against Christendom led Caoursin to refer to him as 'this second Lucifer...this second Antichrist'.

> If a pen could describe the pleasure in my heart, and speech explain the happiness in my soul, today has certainly provided the occasion..., for lo! not without God's love and the divine judgment, to which all things

are subject, the festering wound of Christendom has been healed, the consuming fire put out…, and we behold the dispatch of the fiercest enemy of orthodoxy. Satan, whose minion he was, has rejoiced at the coming of his lost companion, and the denizens of hell have greeted his advent with great applause – if we can conceive of any joy among them. The grim abode of eternal confusion is the just due of the unspeakable tyrant who has destroyed the souls of so many children whom he compelled to abjure their faith, and thus blinded they have descended into hell. (He had caused virgins and matrons to be defiled, slaughtered young men and old, profaned sacred relics, polluted churches and monasteries, destroyed, oppressed and seized kingdoms, principalities and cities, including Constantinople, which he took for himself and made the scene of unbelievable crimes.)

Caoursin goes on to note that Mehmet's passing had been marked by extraordinary convulsions of nature, including powerful earthquakes that shook Rhodes and western Anatolia on 18 March and 3 May 1481. The latter tremor, which caused a huge tidal wave, occurred on the very day that the Grand Turk had died, indicating to Caoursin that the earth was reacting cataclysmically against receiving the remains of one guilty of such monstrous crimes.

For about the time of his departure from life frequent earthquakes occurred in Asia, Rhodes and the isles roundabout, including two of the most marked severity, which were so great and terrible that they laid low many castles, strongholds, and palaces. Even the sea rose more than ten feet and flooded the shores, and straightaway rolling back into the deep it sank as many feet as it had risen, and finally flowed back to its accustomed level. So abundant was the exhalation [of his corpse], and so great the explosion confined within the caverns of the earth, that seven times it sent through the earth its violent shocks and caused a sudden outflow of the sea. The phenomenon is worth recording, and something the Rhodians have never seen before. Although it is explicable by physical principles, nevertheless it usually portends some great event.

By that time the anti-Turkish crusade proclaimed by Pope Sixtus showed signs of becoming a reality, spurred on by the death of Sultan Mehmet and the war of succession that was distracting the Ottomans. On 4 June 1481 Sixtus wrote to the Marquis of Mantua and others that, through the death of Mehmet and the ensuing civil war, God had indicated the way to salvation from the Turks, 'showing us a light from on high to free us forever from that peril which for years past has struck the Christian commonwealth with so

181

many calamities'. Now was the time to take action, before the Turks could recover from the civil war and the sons of the Conqueror could resume the barbarities of their father. 'We have our fleet ready in Genoa,' he wrote; 'thirty galleys and four ships splendidly equipped will soon be at the Tiber docks; at Ancona also we are arming others, and they will be joined in good course with the royal fleet [of Naples].'

Sixtus knew that interest in the crusade would subside now that the Conqueror was gone. His fears were soon realised when the Bolognese informed him that they wished to withdraw their pledge of financial support for the crusade, for 'with the Turkish tyrant's death necessity presses us no more'. The Pope's envoys in Mantua had already told him that the Marquis Federico was withholding funds that had been collected for the crusade, though Sixtus said that he did not believe this. Sixtus himself tried to set the best possible example by contributing most of his silver plate and sending a large quantity of liturgical vessels to the papal mint to meet his share of the expenses of the crusade.

Sixtus put the papal fleet under the command of Cardinal Paolo di Campofregosa, who had previously been Doge of Genoa, summoning him to Rome along with the papal legate Cardinal Savelli. On 30 June 1481 the Pope and the College of Cardinals went to the church of San Paolo Fuori le Mura for the blessing of the papal fleet. After vespers the Pope held a consistory at which he addressed Cardinal Campofregosa, telling him of the historic importance of his mission. Then, according to the chronicler Volaterranus, Sixtus 'gave him his legate's ring and the banner which he had consecrated for the fleet'. Volaterranus writes of how the captains of the fleet came in, kissed the Pope's feet and were signed with the cross on their breasts.

The Pope and the cardinals then went down to the Tiber, where the galleys of the papal fleet were moored, and they boarded each of them in turn to bestow the apostolic blessing. The crews stood fully armed on the decks and saluted when the Pope came aboard, whereupon, according to Volaterranus, 'weapons were brandished, swords drawn and struck upon the shields, and military evolutions executed as in actual battle; hundreds of hoarse voices shouted the Pope's name amid the thundering of the artillery; it was a feast for both ear and eye'.

On 4 July the papal fleet departed to join forces with the royal navy of King Ferrante of Naples in besieging the Ottoman forces at Otranto, which had been isolated since Gedik Ahmet Pasha had been recalled from Valona by Beyazit. The Ottoman troops in the Otranto garrison fought obstinately, but their shortage of arms and supplies forced them to surrender on 10 September. Ferrante immediately informed the Pope, and Sixtus in turn transmitted the good news to the other Christian princes of Europe.

Sixtus hoped that the recapture of Otranto would be the first step in the reconquest of Christian lands under Ottoman occupation. According to the plan that he had formulated, the papal fleet, joined by the ships of the other Christian powers, would sail across the Strait of Otranto to capture the Ottoman-held port of Valona, and from there the allies would head south to begin the liberation of Greece. The first phase of the Pope's plan was executed that August, when a Portuguese fleet of twenty-five vessels under the command of the Bishop of Elbora arrived to take part in the crusade, whereupon Sixtus began preparations for the attack on Valona.

An important element of the Pope's plan was his ward, Andreas Palaeologus. Andreas was the son and heir of Thomas Palaeologus, former Despot of the Morea and brother of Constantine XI, the last Byzantine emperor. When Thomas Palaeologus died in 1465 Andreas became the pretender to the throne of Byzantium, supported first by Pope Paul II and then by Sixtus IV, who now saw a God-given opportunity to use him as the symbolic leader of his crusade.

On 15 September 1481 Sixtus instructed the Bishop of Elbora to assist Andreas Palaeologus in crossing the Ionian Sea to the Morea, so that the pretender could begin the reconquest of his late father's despotate. Three days later the Pope wrote to all the Christian states of Europe, telling them the glorious news of the recapture of Otranto, 'which we have been waiting for with all of our heart, and which has been most pleasing to us – today we have learned it from our people!'. He then made an eloquent plea for united action: 'This is the time of deliverance, of glory, of victory, such as we shall never be able to regain if it is neglected now. With a little effort the war can now be brought to a successful conclusion which later on can be done only at the greatest cost and with the greatest injury to ourselves.'

At the same time, Sixtus sent a messenger to the commander of the Christian fleet, Cardinal Campofregosa, urging him to swift action 'lest we prove unequal to the chance which heaven has offered us'. But the Pope's plea came to nothing, for dissension in the Christian army at Otranto, along with an outbreak of plague in the papal fleet, led the allied leaders to postpone their campaign indefinitely. King Ferrante informed Sixtus that Campofregosa was about to return with the fleet to Civitavecchia, near

Rome, quoting the cardinal's statement that he had been instructed to do so by the Pope himself. Writing to Ferrante on 21 September, Sixtus replied that he had, on the contrary, intended that the papal fleet should attack Valona directly after the recapture of Otranto. Sixtus then sent strict orders to Campofregosa to set sail for Valona at once.

But by the beginning of October Sixtus learned that the papal fleet had docked at Civitavecchia. The Pope hurried there at once in an attempt to persuade Campofregosa, the Neapolitan ambassador and the ships' captains to turn the fleet around. Campofregosa reluctantly informed Sixtus that the planned invasion of Greece was for the moment impossible for several reasons, namely the outbreak of the plague, an increasingly mutinous mood among the troops and the ships' crews, the advanced season of the year and the escalating cost of the expedition. Sixtus declared himself still resolute and prepared to make every sacrifice, according to Volaterranus, who wrote that, though the Pope 'would, like Eugenius IV, pawn his mitre and sell the rest of his silver plate, all was in vain'.

And so Sixtus admitted defeat for the time being. He returned to Rome on 17 October 1481, bitterly disappointed but consoled by the fact that the Turks were not in a position to invade Italy while the two sons of Mehmet the Conqueror were embroiled in a civil war. But his mood would soon change when he learned that Beyazit had emerged victorious in the war of succession and that Jem was now in exile in Cairo.

Meanwhile, Mehmet's tomb at Fatih Camii had become a place of pilgrimage, where a constant stream of pious Muslims came to offer their prayers at the foot of the sultan's catafalque, a custom that continues to the present day: a form of emperor worship dating back to the earliest Turkish times. Turks still refer to Mehmet as Fatih, the Conqueror, and honour him as the 'Sultan of Sultans', for in their view none of his predecessors or successors in the House of Osman equalled his accomplishments, most notably the conquest of the city that remained the capital of the Ottoman Empire for the remainder of its history.

The view of Mehmet as 'the present terror of the world' endured in the West, where he became the personification of the cruel oriental despot, as Richard Knolles portrays him in the *Generall Historie of the Turkes*, published in 1609–10:

> The death of this mighty man (who living troubled a great part of the world) was not much lamented by those who were nearest to him (who ever living in feare of his crueltie, hated him deadly) than of his enemies,

who ever in doubt of his greatness were glad to hear of his end. He was of stature but low, and nothing answerable to the height of his mind, square set and strong limmed, not inferior in strength (when he was young) unto anyone in his father's court, but to Skanderbeg onely; his complexion was Tartarlike, sallow and melancholy, as were most of his ancestors, the Othoman kings; his looke and countenance sterne, with his eyes hollow and little, sunke as it were in his head, and his nose so high and crooked that it almost touched his upper lip. To be briefe, his countenance was altogether such, as if nature had with most cunning hand depainted and most curiously set forth to view the most inward disposition and qualities of his mind: which were in most parts notable... In his love was no assurance, and his least displeasure was death: so that hee lived feared of all men, and died lamented of none.

15 The Sons of the Conqueror

After remaining in Cairo for nearly six months Jem made a second attempt to take the Ottoman throne from his brother Beyazit in the spring of 1482. He was encouraged to do so by Kasım Bey, former emir of the Karamanid Türkmen, who wanted to regain his emirate from the Ottomans, and offered to help Jem in a renewed war of succession against Beyazit. Jem also received help from the Mamluk Sultan Kaitbey, who had given him refuge after he was defeated in his first war of succession against Beyazit the previous year.

But Beyazit, whose army was commanded by Gedik Ahmet Pasha, easily defeated Jem's forces. Jem and Kasım were forced to flee before the advancing imperial army, taking refuge in the Taurus Mountains above the Mediterranean coast with a small band of loyal followers. Beyazit sent Iskender Pasha to pursue the fugitives with his cavalry, but the imperial troops lost their way in the trackless mountains and soon gave up the chase. For Jem and Kasım had been taken by their Türkmen nomad guides into the highlands of Pisidia, which even Alexander the Great had failed to penetrate when he conquered Asia Minor in 334 BC. There they went to ground early in the summer of 1482, while Beyazit fumed at his inability to find Jem and end the war of succession that had troubled the whole first year of his reign.

Jem at first considered fleeing to Persia, but Kasım persuaded him to seek refuge in western Europe, where the Christian princes would help him regain his throne. Kasım had his own interests at heart in giving this advice, for he knew that if Jem led a European army against the Ottomans then Beyazit would leave Karamania undefended, whereupon he could regain control of his emirate.

Jem first sent a letter to Venice requesting asylum, but the Signoria refused, not wishing to provoke Beyzazit into making war on them. Beyazit learned from his spies of Jem's approach to the Venetians, and he wrote to the Senate reaffirming the peace treaty that had been signed between the Ottomans and the Serenissima, adding that he assumed Venice wished to preserve 'the good and sincere and faithful peace and friendship which we have between us'. The Senate responded by congratulating Beyazit on his 'glorious victory' in the civil war he had been forced to fight against his brother Jem, now a fugitive.

After his rejection by the Venetians Jem sent a similar letter to the Grand Master Pierre d'Aubusson, with whom he had established cordial relations three years beforehand, during the negotiations between Sultan Mehmet and the Knights of St John on Rhodes. D'Aubusson and his council agreed to give Jem refuge, whereupon he and his followers boarded a Rhodian ship at Anamur on the Mediterranean coast of Anatolia. On 22 July 1482 they entered the harbour of Rhodes, where d'Aubusson and his knights gave Jem a royal welcome, showing him around the walled city that his father had failed to conquer less than a year earlier.

D'Aubusson knew that it was just a matter of time before the Ottomans made another attempt to take Rhodes. This was why he had agreed to give Jem asylum, for he wanted to use him as a pawn to keep Beyazit at bay, playing on the sultan's fear that his brother would be used as a figurehead in a war against the Turks.

When d'Aubusson first announced Jem's arival on Rhodes to the Christian princes of Europe Pope Sixtus responded by saying that Christendom would gain much from possession of the pretender, and that they could possibly use him in a crusade to 'rid the world of Mohammed's descendants'. But, privately, d'Aubusson had little confidence that the Christian powers would manage to unite in peace and use Jem in a crusade. So in the meantime he saw no reason why he should not use the pretender to his own advantage.

As soon as Beyazit learned that Jem had taken refuge on Rhodes he began negotiating with the Grand Master about his brother's custody, for he wanted him safely out of the way so as to prevent another war of succession. Eventually their representatives concluded a peace treaty, which contemporary sources refer to as the most favourable ever granted by the Ottomans to the Christians up to that time. As part of the agreement the sultan was to send the knights on 1 August of each year a payment for Jem's upkeep of 40,000 ducats (of which d'Aubusson apparently kept 10,000), and for the present year the same amount was to be paid in forty days.

Soon after the treaty was signed Beyazit attended to some unfinished business, the elimination of Gedik Ahmet Pasha, who had been one of his two principal envoys in the negotiations with the knights, along with Mesih Pasha. Beyazit had Gedik Ahmet executed, ending the career of the greatest Ottoman commander of his time. Beyazit also took the opportunity to order the execution of Jem's two-year-old son Oğuzhan, who had been held hostage in the Ottoman court.

Meanwhile, the Council of Knights had been deliberating about what to do with Jem, and they decided that he could be held more securely in one of their commanderies in France. On 18 August D'Aubusson met with Jem and informed him of the council's decision. Jem readily agreed, and the council decided to inform the Pope and all other Christian princes of this decision. As Caoursin writes, referring to Jem as 'the King': 'He was a gift sent by God for the good of Christendom, and it seems best to bring the King to the West under the protection of the Grand Master and the knights of Rhodes.' Ten days later d'Aubusson and the council sent an envoy to Beyazit, informing him of their plan to sent Jem to France.

On 1 September 1482 Jem and his companions boarded a magnificent galley called the *Grand Nef de Tresor*, the flagship of the Rhodian fleet, commanded by the knight Guy de Blanchefort, nephew of Pierre d'Aubusson. The galley brought Jem and his party to Nice, from where they were eventually taken in turn by Blanchefort to a number of the Order's commanderies in France, ending at Bourgeneuf in the Auvergene.

King Matthias Corvinus was also interested in obtaining custody of Jem, whom he wanted to use as a figurehead in a war against the Turks. He raised the subject in discussions with an envoy of Pope Sixtus, but nothing came of the matter. Corvinus realised that Sixtus had no intention of helping him gain control of Jem, and thenceforth his relations with the Pope were embittered. This led Corvinus to agree to terms with Beyazit, and in the autumn of 1483 a five-year peace treaty was concluded between Hungary and the Ottoman Empire.

Beyazit's peace treaty with Corvinus left him free to invade Moldavia and Wallachia, and in the summer of 1484 he personally led his forces across the Danube, capturing Kilia and Akkerman on the Black Sea coast. Moldavia and Wallachia thus became trans-Danubian provinces of the Ottoman Empire, remaining under Turkish rule for nearly four centuries. Beyazit himself is said to have remarked that he had 'won the key of the door to all Moldavia and Hungary, the whole region of the Danube, Poland and Tartary, and the entire coast of the Black Sea'.

Pope Sixtus IV died on 12 August 1484 and was succeeded by Cardinal Giovanni Battista Cibo of Genoa, who became Pope Innocent VIII. Among the embassies that came to congratulate the new Pope on his accession was that of the Knights of St John on Rhodes, who were represented by Guillaume Caoursin and the English knight John Kendal. At the end of January 1485 Caoursin and Kendal were received by the Pope in a private audience to discuss the affairs of the Order. Innocent expressed his strong desire to have Jem brought from France and held in a fortress of the papacy, though remaining in the custody of the knights. The envoys demurred, saying that they had no authority to deal with this request, whereupon Innocent asked them to discuss the matter with d'Aubusson when they returned to Rhodes.

Innocent soon began secret negotiations with d'Aubusson to obtain custody of Jem, for he thought he could use the Turkish pretender as a symbolic leader in his crusade. They finally concluded an agreement on 13 February 1486, in the first part of which d'Aubusson agreed to allow Jem to be transferred to the custody of the Pope in Rome, where he would be guarded by knights of the Order of St John. The Grand Master would retain legal rights to Jem, along with 10,000 ducats of the yearly payment of 40,000 ducats from Beyazit. The second part of the agreement stated that the Pope would appoint d'Aubusson as a cardinal, while allowing him to continue serving as Grand Master of the Knights of St John. But it remained to be seen whether the transfer of Jem to the papacy could actually be carried out, since the French would have to agree. Charles VIII was only thirteen when he succeeded his father Louis XI on 30 August 1483; his older sister Anne de Beaujeu served as regent, and her approval was needed to take Jem to Rome.

The negotiations concerning Jem were complicated by the fact that several different powers were trying to obtain custody of him, some of them making extravagant offers to the French court to decide in their favour, including Pope Innocent, King Matthias Corvinus of Hungary, Sultan Beyazit and Sultan Kaitbey. The Venetians and the Knights of St John were also involved, with their envoys trying to persuade Madame de Beaujeu to allow Jem to be taken to Rome. The French finally agreed to give custody of Jem to the Pope, on condition that Innocent give a cardinal's hat to the Archbishop of Bordeaux, André d'Epinay.

The agreement was signed on 5 October 1488, whereupon the knights immediately began making arrangements to have Jem taken to Rome, where he arrived on 13 March 1489. Jem was confined to a luxurious suite in the Apostolic Palace in the Vatican, while the Pope began thinking of how he could use him in furthering his plans for a crusade. On 8 May 1489 Innocent issued a brief requesting representatives of all the Christian powers to meet in Rome to make plans for united action against the Turks. His nuncios explained to the various Christian rulers that the Pope's possession of the Turkish pretender offered an extraordinary opportunity, for Jem had promised that if he regained his throne through their help he would withdraw all Ottoman forces from Europe and even give up Constantinople.

The congress called for by Innocent convened in Rome on 25 March 1490, its announced purpose being to organise an expedition '*contra Turcum*'. All the European powers sent representatives except Venice, which stayed away so as not to upset its peaceful relationship with Sultan Beyazit. The delegates had already prepared detailed plans for the military and naval forces required for the campaign, as well as the organisation of the various national contingents involved. But early in April the activities of the congress were brought to an abrupt halt by the news of the death of Matthias Corvinus, who had died of a stroke, aged forty-seven.

The death of Corvinus upset the delicate balance of power in central Europe, destroying the stability that Innocent needed to promote his crusade, and so the congress was adjourned until 3 June. When it reconvened, the delegates completed their detailed plans for the crusade, which they presented to the Pope and the College of Cardinals. They thanked Innocent for his exertions in obtaining custody of Jem, 'who was most valuable as a standing menace to the sultan, and as a means of breaking up his empire'. 'He should,' they said, 'be carefully guarded in Rome for the time being, and, later on, counsel should be taken on how he would be most advantageously employed in the campaign.' The congress was officially closed by Innocent on 30 July 1490, to be reconvened when the delegates had received the requisite full powers to make binding agreements on the part of their governments.

But the congress never reconvened, leaving Innocent's dream of a crusade against the Turks unfulfilled. Sigismondo de'Conti was of the opinion that the crusade would have been carried through had it not been for the untimely death of Matthias Corvinus. The Hungarian king had endured years of land warfare against the Ottomans, experience that would have been invaluable in Innocent's crusade. His death cost eastern Europe its strongest leader, and, with the accession of the weak Ladislas II of Bohemia to the Hungarian throne, the Magyar nobles took control and the kingdom reverted to medieval anarchy, destroying the principal bulwark that had protected central Europe from the Turks.

Innocent died on 25 July 1492, and on 26 August he was succeeded by the Catalan Cardinal Roderigo Borgia, who became Pope Alexander VI. Among the messages of congratulation that the new Pope received upon his coronation was one from Pierre d'Aubusson, who hoped that under the wise leadership of Alexander Christendom might see the East freed from Turkish tyranny. He added that Alexander was fortunate 'in having next to him the illustrious Jem Sultan, the terror, the exterminator of the Turks'.

By the time of Alexander's election he had fathered six children, and he was credited with siring two or three more during the years of his papacy, despite the fact that he was over sixty when he became Pope. His first son, Pedro Luis, became Duke of Gandia, and when he died in 1488 the title passed to his younger brother, Juan. The year after Alexander became Pope he gave cardinal's hats to his son Cesare as well as to Alessandro Farnese, brother of Giulia Farnese, the Pope's youngest mistress. Alexander's favourite among his children was his daughter Lucrezia, who, unlike her notorious brother Cesare, did not deserve her lurid reputation. Prince Jem was well known to Lucrezia and the Pope's other children, particularly his sons Cesare and Juan.

During the first months of his reign Alexander worked on creating a triple alliance of the Holy See with Milan and Venice, which, by excluding King Ferrante of Naples, would tilt the balance of power in favour of the papacy and its allies. The new league, in which Siena, Ferrara and Mantua were also included, was announced in Rome on 25 April 1493. Two weeks earlier the Venetians had asked the Pope to include specific mention of Jem in the articles of the proposed alliance. Innocent concurred, and an article was included in the final treaty in which the Pope agreed to turn over Jem to the Venetians if they were attacked by the Turks, so that they could use the prince against Beyazit. The Turks learned of the new league and expelled the Venetian *bailo* in Istanbul 'when some of his letters in cypher' were intercepted. Fearing Beyazit's wrath, the Venetians sent Domenico Trevisan as an envoy to Istanbul, hoping that he could convince the sultan that the new league was not directed against him, but was for purely defensive purposes in Italy. But Beyazit was not convinced, and he let it be known that he was no longer willing to pay for Jem's custody, and that the formation of the new league had provoked him into building ships for a naval expedition against Italy.

Beyazit soon relented, sending an envoy named Kasım Bey, who arrived in Rome on 9 June 1493, bearing rich presents for the Pope as well as 80,000 ducats as payment for Jem's custody for the past two years. Alexander conveyed his thanks to Beyazit, and said that the sultan could show his friendship for Christendom by refraining from the attacks he had been making on Christians in the Balkans and the Aegean.

But Beyazit persisted in his attacks, launching an invasion of Croatia in the autumn of 1493. Alexander wrote a circular letter to the Christian states of Europe on 2 October, appealing to them to take common action for 'Italy and the Christian religion are in peril'. At the same time he sent an envoy to Beyazit, warning him to cease his invasion of Croatia, otherwise his brother Jem would be turned over to the Christian princes to lead a crusade against the Ottomans.

Before long, however, Alexander faced a new threat from a wholly unexpected quarter. The young King Charles VIII of France had become set upon the idea of pursuing an extravagant claim to the Neapolitan throne, which he envisaged as the first step in a crusade to recapture Constantinople and Jerusalem from the Muslims, using Prince Jem as a figurehead. Charles was greatly encouraged when he learned that King Ferrante of Naples had died on 25 January 1494. He sent two envoys to Rome to warn the Pope not to invest Ferrante's son Alfonso with the Kingdom of Naples, implying that if Alexander went ahead with this there would be serious trouble. Alexander took this as a threat that France would go to war if Alfonso were made King of Naples, and on 20 March 1494 he wrote to Charles pleading with him to desist for the good of Christianity.

On 29 August 1494 Charles took leave of his queen, departing to lead the expedition that he believed would immortalise his name. His army probably numbered some 40,000, 10,000 of whom were aboard the French fleet, commanded by the Duke of Orleans, while the rest marched across the French Alps.

The plan of defence against the French invasion had already been drawn up by the late King Ferrante, and his son King Alfonso now put it into operation in alliance with the Pope. To prevent the advance of the French, Alfonso sent his son Ferrantino with an army to the Romagna, whence he was to threaten Lombardy, while Piero de'Medici, the Florentine ruler, defended the frontiers of Tuscany. At the same time a Neapolitan fleet assembled at Leghorn under Don Federigo, Alfonso's brother. Federigo was to attack Genoa, since it was controlled by the Milanese, who were allied with the French. The Pope was to protect the papal states with troops stationed in Tuscany.

Pope Alexander and King Alfonso of Naples were joined in an anti-French league by Florence, Siena, Bologna, Pesaro, Urbino and Imola, while Venice declined to join because of its fear of violating its peace treaty with the Ottomans. Beyazit had sent an envoy to Naples to offer Alfonso military aid against the French, with the message that the sultan 'did not want them in Italy'.

Meanwhile, the French fleet commanded by the Duke of Orleans defeated the Neapolitan navy under Don Federigo at Rapello on 5 September. Two weeks later Fabrizio Colonna's troops, acting as allies of the French, captured the papal fortress of Ostia, which had been abandoned by Cardinal Giuliano della Rovere. Charles sent part of his fleet to the Tiber, and on 16 October a French garrison was set up in Ostia, thus controlling the maritime approach to Rome.

Charles led the French army into Pavia on 14 October and four days later he took Piacenza. The French troops crossed the Apennines, causing consternation in Rome, where the alarm was aggravated by the revolt of the Colonna and Savelli clans, instigated by Cardinal Ascanio Sforza. French galleys soon began to appear at the mouth of the Tiber, which made the enemy occupation of Ostia still more serious for Alexander.

The French occupied Tuscany and encountered little resistance. Piero de'Medici presented himself at the French camp on 26 October and surrendered all the cities under his control. Eight days later the people of Florence rose in revolt, forcing the Medicis to flee, leaving their palace to be looted by the rebel mob.

Charles entered Lucca on 8 November, and on the following day he was welcomed in Pisa by the townspeople, who hailed him as their liberator from Florentine tyranny. Soon afterwards Viterbo surrendered to the French, whose advance was so rapid that Giulia Farnese, the Pope's mistress, fell into their hands while travelling. She was soon released at the Pope's request, however, according to Giorgio Brognolo, the Mantuan envoy. Brognolo, in relating this incident, ends his report by saying: 'The French King will not meet with the slightest resistance in Rome.'

Rome was in a perilous situation, blockaded to seaward by the French-held fortress of Ostia and on land by the Colonna, and food was becoming scarce. The gates of Rome were chained and some were walled up. On 10 December Ferrantino, the Duke of Calabria, led the Neapolitan army into the city, with 5,000 infantry and 1,000 cavalry. Alexander prepared for the worst by moving into Castel Sant'Angelo, the papal fortress on the Tiber, taking Jem along with him.

The port of Civitavecchia was taken by Charles on 17 December, and on the same day the Orsini clan went over to the French and admitted them to their fortress of Bracciano, north-west of Rome, where the king set up his headquarters. French troops had already taken a number of castles along the roads leading into Rome, building wooden bridges over the Tiber. By 10 December they had even reached the walls of Rome, where they challenged the Neapolitan troops to come out and do battle with them. During the next three days French troops broke into the suburbs of Rome by Monte Mario and penetrated as far as the church of San Lazzaro and the fields close to Castel Sant'Angelo, where they seemed poised for an attack on the fortress.

By the end of December food supplies in Rome had just about run out, although Castel Sant'Angelo was still well stocked for a long siege. But the people of Rome had no intention of subjecting themselves to a protracted siege, and they made it known to the Pope that if he did not come to terms with Charles within two days they would themselves admit the king into the city.

Alexander now feared that he would lose the papacy along with Rome. He had hoped that the Holy Roman Emperor, Maximilian I, and Ferdinand of Spain would come to his aid, and even that the Venetians might help him. But all these possible allies were far away, and the French army was almost at the gates of Rome. Thus on Christmas morning Alexander finally decided to submit to Charles, who demanded that the Neapolitan army be withdrawn from Rome before the French entered the city. Ferrantino concurred and led his troops out of Rome under a promise of safe conduct from the French.

That evening three envoys sent by Charles entered Rome, and by the following day they had come to an agreement with Alexander on arrangement for the formal French entry into the city. On 30 December

Count Gilbert Montpensier, *marechal* of the French army in Italy, would enter Rome with his troops as military governor of the city. Charles himself would enter Rome on New Year's Eve and take up residence in the Palazzo San Marco.

Several points of contention remained, but these were put aside to be settled when the Pope and the king met in Rome. One of these was the question of Jem's custody. Charles demanded that Alexander unconditionally surrender Jem to him, while the Pope was uwilling to give him up until the king was actually ready to embark on his crusade, and even then only for a limited period of time. Charles agreed to respect all the Pope's rights, both temporal and spiritual. All of Rome on the left bank of the Tiber was to be occupied by the French army, while the Pope's troops, consisting only of 1,000 cavalry and a few foot soldiers, occupied the Borgo, the quarter between the Vatican and Castel Sant'Angelo.

On 27 December an advance force of 1,500 troops entered Rome with the permission of the Pope. The rest of the French army entered the city during the afternoon of New Year's Eve, along with King Charles, who took up residence in the Palazzo San Marco as agreed. During the days that followed a succession of cardinals and other dignitaries conferred with Charles and his advisers. Charles had three principal demands, the first of which was the right of free passage for his forces through the papal states, which would include the surrender to him of a number of fortresses, including Castel Sant'Angelo. Secondly, he wanted the Pope to acknowledge his right to the throne of Naples. Finally, he demanded custody of Jem, who, he said, was to be the centrepiece of his forthcoming crusade against the Turks.

Finally, on 15 January 1495, the Pope agreed to the king's demands, which had been modified during the course of the negotiations. By the terms of the agreement Cesare Borgia was to accompany the French army as 'cardinal legate' (though really as a hostage) for the next four months. Jem was to be handed over to Charles for the expedition against the Turks, though the Pope would continue to receive the 40,000 ducats that Beyazit sent each year for his brother's custody. The Pope was to keep Castel Sant'Angelo, and, on the king's departure, the keys to the city were to be returned to Alexander. Charles was to profess obedience to the Pope, to impose no restraint upon him either in matters temporal or spiritual, and to protect him against all attacks.

On 18 January Charles and Alexander met to settle one last point of disagreement, namely the guarantees to be given by the king for the restoration of Jem to the Pope after an interval of three months. Three days later, after the agreement had been signed, the king accompanied the Pope to Castel Sant'Angelo.

There Charles met Jem for the first time, speaking to him at length through an interpreter, Alexander acting as an intermediary. According to the Venetian diarist Marino Sanudo, the Pope said to Jem, 'Monseigneur, the King of France is to take you with him, what do you think about it?' Jem answered bitterly, 'I am only an unhappy slave, deprived of freedom, and I do not give any importance to whether the King of France takes me or if I remain in the hands of the pope.'

On 27 January Jem, accompanied by his companions, was formally handed over to Charles. The following day Charles bade farewell to the Pope and departed from Rome with the French army, heading for Naples, accompanied by Jem and Cesare Borgia. They spent the night at Marino, where Charles received word that King Alfonso had renounced his throne five days earlier and fled from Naples, leaving the throne to his son Ferrantino. They spent the next night at Velletri, where Cesare Borgia made his escape and disappeared, and when the Pope was questioned about this he said he knew nothing of his son's whereabouts. According to Marino Sanudo, Charles concluded from this that 'the Italians were a pack of rogues and the Holy Father the worst of all!'.

The French had been advancing south-eastward, capturing Montefortina on 31 January and San Germano on 3 February. When Charles entered San Germano he wrote to the Duke of Bourbon saying that he had conquered 'the first town and city of my Kingdom of Naples'.

After the surrender of several other towns King Ferrantino fled from Naples, and on 21 February the people of the city sent a deputation to lay their submission at the feet of King Charles. The following day Charles rode into Naples at the head of his army through the Porta Capuana, acclaimed by the townspeople as their liberator from Aragonese tyranny.

Jem had fallen ill on the march from Rome to Naples, where he was taken to the Castel Capuana, a fortified palace at the Porta Capuana. Charles was very concerned and sent his personal physicians to look after Jem, who lapsed into a coma on 24 February. He clung to life during the night, but then early the following morning he passed away, as his grieving Turkish companions repeated the Islamic prayer for the dead: 'Truly we belong to God and we will come back to Him, this is the fate of the world.' Jem was two months past his thirty-fifth birthday when he died, having spent a third of his life as an exile and prisoner of the Christians.

Charles ordered that Jem's death be kept a secret, but soon everyone in Naples knew that the Turkish prince had passed away. There were rumours that Jem had been poisoned by the Pope, but modern historians generally agree that he died of pneumonia or erysipelas, an acute streptococcal infection of the skin.

After the news reached Venice, Andrea Gritti was sent to Istanbul to inform Beyazit of his brother's death. Beyazit told Gritti that he wanted to secure Jem's body, and that he would send an envoy to discuss this matter with King Charles, who in the meanwhile had been crowned King of Naples.

After Jem's death Charles gave up his quixotic dream of a crusade, and the formation of an anti-French league forced him to abandon Naples on 20 May 1495 and take his army back to France. King Ferrantino reoccupied Naples on 6 July, but he died of malaria on 7 October of that same year. The former King Alfonso II died in exile on 10 November 1495, so that the succession passed to his brother Federigo d'Aragona, who thus became the fifth king to occupy the throne of Naples within three years, including Charles VIII.

Beyazit then entered into negotiations with King Federigo for the return of Jem's body, which was entombed in a coffin kept in the Castel dell' Ovo in Naples, guarded by the prince's faithful Turkish companions. The negotiations dragged on for nearly four years, until finally Beyazit's patience was exhausted to the point where he threatened war against Naples unless Jem's body was turned over to his representatives without further delay. Federigo was terrified, and on 29 January he submitted to Beyazit's demand, whereupon the remains of Jem, still guarded by his companions, were shipped back to Turkey.

Late in the summer of 1499 Beyazit interred Jem's remains in the Muradiye at Bursa, the imperial mosque complex that their grandfather Murat II had built in 1426, and where he was buried in 1451. The place chosen by Beyazit for Jem's burial was the tomb of their brother Mustafa, which had been built by Mehmet II after his second son had died in 1471. Beyazit could finally reign without the fear that his brother would be used against him in a crusade; he was now the last surviving son of Mehmet the Conqueror, ready to resume his father's march of conquest.

16 *The Tide of Conquest Turns*

Now that Beyazit no longer had to be concerned about Jem he was free to resume the campaigns of conquest that had been interrupted by the death of his father eighteen years before.

At a consistory held in Rome on 10 June 1499 Pope Alexander VI had a letter read to the College of Cardinals from Pierre d'Aubusson, dated 30 April. The Grand Master wrote that the Turk himself (Beyazit) was outfitting a huge fleet of 300 sail to lay siege to the city of Rhodes, where he was expected to arrive sometime in May. D'Aubusson expected the siege to be a long one, 'because the Turk was coming in person to the nearby province of Lycia, where vast preparations were being made of all things essential to a siege'.

But it soon became clear that the target of the Ottoman expedition was not Rhodes but Lepanto, the Venetian fortress town at the north-west end of the Gulf of Corinth. Beyazit had prepared a fleet of some 240 warships, which set sail from the Sea of Marmara in June 1499, just about the time that Jem's coffin was on the last stage of its journey back from Italy to Turkey. The sultan had also mustered two armies, one under his own command and the other led by Mustafa Pasha, both of which were to move in coordination with the fleet. On 14 August 1499 the Ottoman forces attacked Lepanto, and fifteen days later the garrison of the fortress surrendered, a severe blow to Venetian prestige.

The Venetians tried to make peace with Beyazit, sending Alvise Manenti to the Ottoman court at Edirne, where he was received by several of the sultan's pashas on 17 February 1500. Manenti spoke of Venetian love for the 'Signor Turco' and reminded the pashas of the Serenissima's long-standing good relations with the Ottomans. He emphasised that during all the years that Jem had been in exile Venice 'had never tried to make a move against His Excellency [Beyazit], and had always wanted friendship and peace with him more than with any other ruler in the world'.

One of the pashas responded by saying that Venice was responsible for the war, because its citizens in the Morea and Albania had been attacking Ottoman subjects, 'and we have written to the Signoria to punish them, but it has never done so'. Manenti was then told that the pashas had all urged the sultan to make peace with Venice, 'which they all knew to have been a good and faithful friend of their lord, in the time of Jem Sultan as at other times'. The price of peace would be the cession to the Ottomans of the remaining Venetian fortresses in the Morea – Navarino, Koroni, Methoni, Monemvasia and Nauplia – as well as an annual tribute to the sultan of 10,000 ducats, 'as was given in the time of his father'. It was then clear to Manenti that the sultan had 'decided to have the sea as his boundary with the Signoria', meaning that Beyazit wanted Venice to abandon all her possessions within the Ottoman Empire. Manenti replied that such heavy demands could not possibly be met, and the pashas replied that there was no further point in continuing the discussions.

The Ottoman attacks on the Venetian fortresses in Greece continued relentlessly. The Turkish forces took Methoni in August 1500 after a six-week siege led by Beyazit himself, the first time that he had commanded his troops in battle as sultan. The fall of Methoni soon led the garrisons at Koroni and Navarino to surrender as well, defeats from which Venetian power in the Morea never recovered. The Venetians were forced to sue for peace, on terms dictated by Beyazit, in mid-December 1502, a date long remembered in Venice as the beginning of the decline of the Serenissima's maritime empire.

The fall of Lepanto and the Venetian fortresses in the Morea led Pope Alexander to make a desperate plea for a renewed crusade against the Turks. But the internal conflicts in Christian Europe once again made this impossible. The Pope himself became involved in one of these disputes, when he gave approval to the Kings of France and Spain to depose King Federigo and divide the Kingdom of Naples between themselves. The French and Spanish then quarrelled over their Neapolitan possessions and went to war with one another in the summer of 1502, a severe setback for Alexander's hopes for a crusade against the Turks.

Pierre d'Aubusson had been elected by the European powers to command the Pope's crusade, for he had been a champion in the Christian struggle against the Turks all his life. But d'Aubusson died on 30 June 1503, aged eighty, after having been Grand Master of the Knights of St John for twenty-seven years, leaving the crusade without a commander. Later that summer the Christian world lost another leader when Pope Alexander died suddenly on 12 August, aged seventy-three, whereupon his crusade ended before it had even begun.

On 22 September 1503 Cardinal Francesco Piccolomini was elected to succeed Alexander, taking the name of Pius III in honour of his late uncle Aeneas Sylvius Piccolomini, Pope Pius II. The new Pope was in failing health at the time of his election, and he passed away less than a month later. A new conclave, the shortest in the history of the papacy to that time, began on 31 October 1503 and ended the next day with the almost unanimous election of Cardinal Giuliano della Rovere, who became Pope Julius II.

The decade-long reign of Julius II was an extremely turbulent period, in which the Pope tried to revive the temporal power of the papacy and to establish the independence of the Holy See, at a time when Italy was riven by internal wars and under attack by other European powers, most notably France and Spain. The Turks, at least, were less of a threat to Europe during that period, for in the years 1500–11 the Ottoman Empire was involved in a war with Persia.

While the war with Persia was still raging Beyazit became seriously ill in 1508, and for the next three years he was bedridden. By that time a three-sided war of succession had developed between his three surviving sons, Ahmet, Selim and Korkut, all of whom were serving as provincial governors in Anatolia. Selim knew that Beyazit planned to abdicate and leave the throne to Ahmet, the eldest, and to forestall that he took his army across to Europe in the summer of 1511 and camped near Edirne, raising the pay of his soldiers so that he drew recruits from his father's forces.

The following spring Beyazit was forced to submit to Selim, who entered Istanbul with his army on 23 April 1512 and took control of the city. The same day Selim met with his father, whom he had not seen in twenty-six years, and he forced Beyazit to abdicate. The next day Selim was girded with the sword of Osman and became the ninth sultan in the Osmanlı dynasty, the third to rule in Istanbul.

Selim allowed Beyazit to retire to Demotika in Thrace, his birthplace. But the deposed sultan died halfway there, passing away in great agony on 26 May 1512. A number of those in his entourage believed that Beyazit had been poisoned by his Jewish physician Hamon on the orders of Sultan Selim.

Selim was forty-two when he became sultan, having served for eighteen years as provincial governor in Trabzon, the Greek Trebizond. His fierce mein and cruel manner led the Turks to call him Yavuz, or the Grim. Shortly after his accession Selim set out to deal with his rivals to the throne. During the next year he defeated and killed his brothers Ahmet and Korkut, after which he executed six of his nephews. His campaign to eliminate all possible rivals to the throne did not stop there, and on 20 December 1512 he executed three of his own sons, whom he suspected of plotting against him. This left Selim with only a single male heir to the throne, his son Süleyman, whom he was grooming as his successor.

The Christian powers of Europe enjoyed a respite from Ottoman aggression during Selim's reign, which was distinguished by two victorious campaigns in Asia. In the first of these campaigns Selim defeated Shah Ismail of Iran at the Battle of Çaldıran on 23 August 1514, adding all of eastern Anatolia and western Persia to the Ottoman domains. In the second campaign Selim conquered the Mamluks of Egypt, capturing Cairo on 20 January 1517, thus extending the boundaries of the Ottoman Empire around the eastern Mediterranean. Tradition has it that at this time Caliph al-Mutawakkil transferred the rights of the caliphate to Selim, whose successors proudly added this to their title of 'sultan' right down to the end of the Ottoman Empire.

Selim prepared for a campaign into Europe in the summer of 1520, probably intending to invade Hungary, though he had not divulged his plans to his pashas. The sultan led his army out from Istanbul in early August, but a day's journey short of Edirne he became so seriously ill that the march had to be halted. Selim never recovered, and after suffering for six weeks he finally passed away on 22 September 1520. The cause of his death is suggested by the remark of an anonymous European chronicler, who noted that 'Selim the Grim died of an infected boil and thereby Hungary was spared'.

The news of Selim's death occasioned services of thanksgiving throughout Europe. As Paolo Giovio wrote of the reaction of Pope Leo X, who had succeeded Julius II in 1513: 'When he heard for a surety that

Selimus was dead, he commanded that the litany of common prayers be sung throughout all Rome, in which men should go barefoot.'

Ferhat Pasha, the commanding Ottoman general, kept Selim's death a secret so that Süleyman, the deceased sultan's only surviving son, who was serving as provincial governor in Manisa, could rush to Istanbul to take control of the government and ensure his succession to the throne.

Süleyman was nearly twenty-six when he came to the throne. Foreign observers found him to be more pleasant than his grim father, and they were hopeful that his reign would bring better relations between the Ottomans and Christians. As the Venetian Bartolomeo Contarini wrote just before Süleyman's accession: 'He is said to be a wise lord, and all men hope for good from his reign.'

Soon after his accession Süleyman and his grand vezir Piri Pasha began making preparations for a campaign into Europe. Süleyman's objective was Belgrade, the gateway to all the lands along the middle Danube, which he captured on 29 August 1521. When word of the fall of Belgrade reached Venice, the doge, Antonio Grimani, wrote to his envoy in England, 'This news is lamentable, and of importance to all Christians.'

The following year Süleyman launched an expedition against Rhodes, which his great-grandfather Mehmet had failed to take in 1480. Süleyman began the siege of Rhodes on 28 June 1522, when his fleet of 700 ships crossed the strait from Marmaris carrying a force of some 100,000 troops, vastly outnumbering the knights and their allies. The defenders fought on valiantly for nearly six months, but then on 22 December the Grand Master, Philip Villiers de L'Isle Adam, finally agreed to surrender, on condition that he and his men would be allowed to leave the island unharmed, along with all the Rhodians who chose to accompany them.

Süleyman honoured the terms of the surrender, and on 1 January the Grand Master and his 180 surviving knights sailed away from Rhodes, along with 4,000 Rhodians. The Knights of St John had held Rhodes for 223 years, blocking Turkish expansion in the eastern Mediterranean, which was now open to Süleyman. The knights retired first to Crete, and then in 1530 they moved to Malta, where they constructed a mighty fortress that became a bulwark against Turkish expansion into the western Mediterranean.

Meanwhile, the balance of power had shifted with the rise of the Habsburgs. Charles V, grandson of Maximilian I, had through his inheritances become the most powerful ruler in western Europe, his possessions in Spain, the Netherlands and Germany hemming in France.

The French king, Francis I, believed that his territories were threatened and that Charles wanted 'to be master everywhere'. Francis was captured after his army was defeated by the forces of Charles V at Pavia in 1525. While in captivity Francis wrote secretly to Süleyman, suggesting that the sultan attack Hungary.

Süleyman agreed to the proposal and invaded Hungary the following year, with the Ottoman army under the command of the grand vezir Ibrahim Pasha. The campaign climaxed on 29 August 1526 at the Battle of Mohacs, when the Ottomans utterly defeated the Hungarians in a battle that lasted less than two hours. King Lewis II and most of the Hungarian soldiers died in the battle, and the few who survived were executed immediately afterwards by Süleyman, who had ordered that no prisoners be taken.

After his victory at Mohacs, Süleyman led his army back to Istanbul, where he remained for six months before starting off on his next campaign into Europe, with Ibrahim Pasha once again in command. The goal of the expedition was Vienna, which the Ottoman forces besieged unsuccessfully. After suffering heavy losses Süleyman was forced to raise the siege on 15 October 1529, so as to march his army back to Istanbul before the winter began. Early in 1532 Süleyman mounted another expedition against Vienna under Ibrahim Pasha, but his army penetrated only as far as the Austrian frontier.

Süleyman's failure to capture Vienna was the only major setback he suffered in more than four decades of campaigning in Europe, while at the same time his buccaneering fleets were the terror of the Mediterranean, capturing most of the Venetian-held islands in the Aegean. Süleyman mounted a powerful expedition against Malta in 1565, but the Knights of St John defended the island with their usual valour, and the Ottoman forces were compelled to withdraw, having lost some 35,000 men, including their commander Dragut Pasha. The defeat at Malta marked the limit of Ottoman expansion in the Mediterranean, just as their failure at Vienna was the high-water mark of their penetration into Europe, both occurring during the reign of Süleyman the Magnificent, as he was known in Europe.

Süleyman died a year after the failure of his forces to capture Malta, passing away on the night of 5/6 September 1566 while leading his army in another invasion of Hungary. The Ottoman Empire had reached its peak during his reign, the longest and most illustrious in the history of the Ottoman Empire.

Süleyman was succeeded by his son Selim II, nicknamed 'the Sot', the first in a succession of weak and inactive sultans, some of them insane, who ruled during the long decline of the Ottoman Empire that began in the late sixteenth century. During Selim's reign (1566–74) the sultan left the direction of the government largely to his capable grand vezir, Sokollu Mehmet Pasha, who had been the last to hold that post under Süleyman. After the Ottomans were defeated by a Christian fleet at the Battle of Lepanto in October 1571 Sokollu Mehmet rebuilt the Turkish navy during the following winter, and used it to conquer Cyprus in 1573 and to take Tunis from the Spaniards the following year.

Despite the evident decline in the empire the Ottoman forces still won occasional victories, most notably Murat IV's capture of Erivan in 1635 and Baghdad in 1638, as well as the final conquest of Crete in 1669, during the reign of Mehmet IV (1648–87). Mehmet IV mounted an expedition against Vienna in the spring of 1683 under the grand vezir Kara Mustafa Pasha, who had persuaded the sultan that when he took the city 'all the Christians would obey the Ottomans'. But after besieging the city for two months the Ottoman army was routed by a Christian force and fled in disorder, a defeat that cost Mustafa Pasha his head and Sultan Mehmet his throne, for he was deposed in 1687 as a result of the disorder that followed the disastrous attempt to take Vienna.

The Ottoman defeat at Vienna encouraged the Christian powers of Europe to form a Holy League for another crusade against the Turks. Emissaries from Austria, Poland and Venice met in March 1684, with the support of Pope Innocent XI, and the following year they invaded the Ottoman dominions on several fronts, beginning a war that would last for thirty years.

The crusade mounted by the Holy League was the first in a series of wars between the European powers and the Turks that would continue up to the end of the Ottoman Empire, which lost successive chunks of territory in the peace treaties that followed each of these conflicts. The Treaty of Karlowitz, signed on 26 January 1699, ended the war with the Holy League, in which the Christian powers were victorious on both land and sea against the Ottomans, who ceded Hungary to the Austrians and Athens and the Morea to the Venetians. The Ottomans recovered their lost territory in Greece within fifteen years, but most of Hungary was lost to the empire for ever.

The Treaty of Passarowitz, which ended another war with the Christian powers on 21 July 1718, cost the Ottomans all their remaining territory in

Hungary, along with much of Serbia, Bosnia and Wallachia. The Treaty of Küçük Kaynarca, signed on 21 July 1774, ended a war in which Russia conquered Moldavia, Wallachia and the Crimea. By that time the decay of the Ottoman Empire was such that the Western powers began to refer to Turkey as the 'Sick Man of Europe', as they prepared to divide up its remaining territory. In the Treaty of London, signed in 1827, Britain, France and Russia agreed to intervene in the Greek War of Independence from the Ottoman Empire, leading to the foundation of the modern Greek Kingdom six years later.

Meanwhile, Mehmet Ali, the Turkish viceroy of Egypt, set out to establish his independence from Sultan Mahmut II, sending an army under his son Ibrahim Pasha to invade Ottoman territory in the summer of 1831. Within a year Ibrahim conquered Palestine, Lebanon and Syria, taking Damascus on 18 June 1832. Ibrahim then led his troops across the Anatolian plateau, defeating two Ottoman armies, and on 12 February 1833 he took Kütahya, only 150 miles from Istanbul. Sultan Mahmut was so frightened by this that he called on the Russians for help. Tsar Nicholas I sent a fleet to Istanbul, and on 20 February they landed troops on the Asian shore of the upper Bosphorus at Hünkâr Iskelesi. This led Ibrahim to come to terms with Sultan Mahmut, and he signed a peace treaty in Kütahya that gave Mehmet Ali control of Egypt, Syria, Arabia and Crete. Ibrahim thereupon evacuated his troops from Anatolia.

Representatives of Tsar Nicholas and Sultan Mahmut signed a treaty at Hünkâr Iskelesi on 8 July 1833 in which Russia and the Ottoman Empire agreed to an eight-year non-aggression pact, wherein the sultan agreed to close the Bosphorus and the Dardanelles to the ships of any countries that were in conflict with the two signatories. This agreement alarmed the British and French, who saw the prospect of the tsar taking control of the straits, and thenceforth they were determined to protect the Ottoman Empire and defend it against Russian encroachment.

A crisis arose in 1840 when the Ottoman admiral Ahmet Fevzi Pasha sailed the Ottoman fleet to Alexandria and surrendered it to Mehmet Ali, for fear that the grand vezir Mehmet Husrev Pasha would turn it over to the Russians. The foreign minister, Mustafa Reşit Pasha, negotiated with the European powers – Britain, France, Russia, Austria and Prussia – to intervene, promising that Sultan Abdül Mecit would institute far-reaching reforms in the Ottoman Empire. The five powers intervened and forced Mehmet Ali to allow the Ottoman fleet to be returned to Istanbul, on the promise that Abdül Mecit would make him the governor of an autonomous Egypt.

Mustafa Reşit then worked with Abdül Mecit on the reforms he had promised the Western powers. These were embodied in a Hatti Şerif, or imperial decree, proclaimed by Abdül Mecit at a pavilion in the lower gardens of Topkapı Sarayı known as Gülhane, the Rose Chamber. The Gülhane decree announced that Abdül Mecit thenceforth would rule as an enlightened monarch, protecting the lives and property of all his subjects – Muslims, Christians and Jews alike – and that he would create a government in which there would be equitable taxation, regular legislative councils, and a fair system of conscription to obtain manpower for a modern army and navy. This was the beginning of the *Tanzimat*, or Reform Movement, which would continue under Abdül Mecit's immediate successors.

The British mounted an expedition against Ibrahim Pasha in 1840 and forced him to withdraw from Syria early the following year. A British fleet then bombarded Alexandria and prepared to land troops, which led Mehmet Ali to evacuate Crete and the Arabian peninsula. Sultan Abdül Mecit then issued a decree on 13 February 1841 confirming Mehmet Ali and his heirs as the hereditary Ottoman governors of Egypt, settling the so-called Eastern Crisis for the time being.

Another crisis arose in October 1853, when Russia refused to evacuate Moldavia and Wallachia, the trans-Danubian principalities that had been taken from the Turks in 1774. This gave rise to the Crimean War, which began on 28 March 1854, when the British and French joined the Turks in fighting against the Russians on the Crimean peninsula. The Crimean War ended with the Treaty of Paris, signed on 30 March 1856. The terms of the treaty left the map much as it had been before the war. Turkey was admitted to the Concert of Europe, the harmonious family of civilised European nations, and the other signatories undertook 'to respect the independence and the territorial integrity of the Ottoman Empire'.

Abdül Hamit II succeeded as sultan on 7 September 1876, and three months later, under pressure from the great powers of Europe and the Turkish reform movement, he agreed to the adoption of a constitution. The constitution provided for the creation of an Ottoman parliament, which met for the first time on 19 March 1877.

Russia declared war on the Ottoman Empire on 16 April 1877, its soldiers invading Turkish territory in both eastern Anatolia and the Balkans, capturing Edirne and penetrating to the suburbs of Istanbul before they were stopped by pressure from the great powers. The war was officially ended by the Treaty of Berlin, signed on 13 July 1878, in which part of Bulgaria became independent of the Ottoman Empire along with all of Montenegro, Serbia and Romania, while a large part of north-eastern Anatolia was ceded to Russia, to which Sultan Abdül Hamit II agreed to pay a huge indemnity. Aside from the financial losses, the Treaty of Berlin cost the Ottoman Empire 40 per cent of its territory and 20 per cent of its population, of whom almost a half were Muslims. Another casualty of the war was the Ottoman parliament, which Abdül Hamit dissolved on 14 February 1878, suspending the constitution as well.

That same year the Ottoman Empire entered into a defensive alliance with the United Kingdom. As part of the agreement Britain took over the administration of Cyprus as a British protectorate, seeking to safeguard its sea lanes to Egypt.

The movement of reform in the Ottoman Empire was led by a group known as the Young Turks, who formed a number of loosely knit coalitions, among which the Committee of Union and Progress (CUP) eventually came to the fore. On 23 July 1908 the leaders of the CUP gave an ultimatum to Abdül Hamit, warning him that unless the constitution was restored within twenty-four hours the army in Macedonia would march on Istanbul. The sultan was terrified, and on the following day he restored the constitution and declared that the parliament would be reconvened. After elections the second Turkish parliament opened on 17 December 1908, with Abdül Hamit now reduced to the status of a constitutional monarch.

Meanwhile, the neighbours of the Ottoman Empire had taken advantage of its weakness to grab whatever Turkish territory they could. On 6 October 1908 Austria annexed Bosnia and Hercegovina from the Ottoman Empire. On that same day all of Bulgaria declared its independence, including the part that had remained Ottoman territory in 1878. Then on the following day Greece announced its annexation of Crete, which had been under the control of the great powers since the Ottomans had been forced to remove their troops from the island in 1898.

Abdül Hamit was deposed by an army coup on 23 April 1909 and replaced as sultan by his brother Mehmet V Reşat, who was merely a puppet of the Young Turks, a group of officers led by Talat Pasha, Cemal and Enver Pasha, who controlled the Ottoman government for the next decade.

Italy's designs on north Africa led it to declare war on the Ottoman Empire on 29 September 1911, putting Tripoli under blockade. The Italians opened another front by occupying the Ottoman-held island of Rhodes and bombarding the forts at the entrance to the Dardanelles.

The Balkan states now sought to take advantage of the Tripolitan War by forming alliances against the Ottomans in the summer and early autumn of 1912, their coalition comprising Greece, Bulgaria, Serbia and Montenegro. The First Balkan War began when Montenegro invaded Ottoman territory in northern Albania on 8 October 1912, with the other allies beginning offensives against the Turks shortly afterwards. The war continued until an armistice was arranged on 30 May 1913, by which time the Bulgars were at Çatalca, less than twenty-five miles from Istanbul, having captured Edirne, while the rest of the Ottoman possessions in Europe were occupied by the other Balkan allies. Ten days later the Treaty of London was signed, establishing the boundaries of the Ottoman Empire in Europe as close as sixty miles from Istanbul.

The Second Balkan War began on 29 June 1913, when the Bulgars launched surprise attacks on the Greeks and Serbs, who were soon aided by Romania and Montenegro. The four allies proved too much for the Bulgars and soon forced them to surrender. Enver Pasha seized the opportunity and led an army to recapture Edirne on 21 July. The war was officially ended by the Treaty of Bucharest, signed on 10 August 1913, in which Greece took most of Epirus and western Thrace from the Ottoman Empire.

Enver Pasha had been busy behind the scenes preparing the way for a pact with Germany, for he knew that Russia was now entering an alliance with Britain and France known as the Triple Entente. A treaty of alliance between the Ottoman Empire and Germany was signed secretly on 2 August 1914, just as the Triple Entente and the Central Powers were declaring war on one another. Three months later the Ottoman Empire entered the First World War as an ally of Germany. Then on 2 October 1914 Britain annexed Cyprus, declaring it a crown colony of the British Empire.

During the First World War the Ottoman forces were engaged on several fronts: the Caucusus, eastern Anatolia, the Persian Gulf, Iraq, Syria and Palestine, Thrace, and the Dardanelles, where in 1915 the Turks under Mustafa Kemal Pasha drove back the Allies in an eight-month battle on the Gallipoli peninsula in which more than 100,000 men lost their lives on both sides. The Young Turks were in complete control of the government throughout most of the war, with Talat Pasha appointed grand vezir on 3 February 1917, forming a triumvirate with Cemal and Enver. Mehmet V Reşat died on 2 July 1918 and was succeeded the following day by his brother Mehmet VI Vahidettin, fated to be the last sultan of the Ottoman Empire.

Meanwhile, the Ottoman forces had suffered a series of defeats in both Iraq and Syria, where Mustafa Kemal Pasha commanded the Seventh Army. Damascus fell to the British on 1 October 1918 and the French took Beirut the following day, as the Ottoman army retreated to make a last stand in Anatolia. As they did so Mustafa Kemal sent a cable to the sultan urging him to form a new government and sue for peace.

Talat Pasha resigned as grand vezir on 8 October, and soon afterwards he, Enver and Cemal fled from Turkey on a German warship. Six days later the sultan appointed Ahmet Izzet Pasha as grand vezir, and he immediately began making overtures to the British for peace. An armistice was signed at Mudros to come into effect on 31 October 1918, eleven days before fighting between Germany and the Allies stopped on the western front. The Mudros Armistice called for the total and unconditional surrender of the Ottoman army, with all strategic positions in Turkey to be occupied by Allied forces. A large Allied fleet sailed through the straits and reached Istanbul on 13 November, landing troops to begin the occupation of the city.

At the Paris Peace Conference, which began in January 1919, the Allies considered various plans for dividing up what was left of the Ottoman Empire. Greece, which had come in on the Allied side late in the war, put in a claim for Izmir and its hinterland in western Asia Minor. The Greek prime minister Eleutherios Venizelos received support from Lloyd George and Clemenceau, the British and French prime ministers, to send an expeditionary force to Asia Minor, and on 14 May 1919 an Allied armada landed a Greek division at Izmir. The Greek army quickly headed inland, and by 22 June they had captured Bursa. Another Greek army invaded Thrace in July, and within a week they were within striking distance of Istanbul, from which they were held back only by Allied pressure.

The Ottoman government continued to function under the aegis of the Allied High Commissioners. Meanwhile, a national resistance movement was developing in Anatolia under the leadership of Mustafa Kemal Pasha. On 19 March 1920 Kemal announced that the Turkish nation was establishing its own parliament in Ankara, the Grand National Assembly. The new assembly met for the first time on 23 April 1920, choosing Kemal as its first president.

The Allies agreed on the post-war boundaries of the Ottoman Empire at the Treaty of Sèvres, signed on 10 August 1920. The treaty greatly diminished the extent of the empire, putting the straits under international control, while leaving Istanbul nominally under the sultan's rule.

The Greeks began another offensive in late October 1920, leading Kemal to put Ismet Pasha in charge of the western front. The Greeks were halted early the following year in two battles on the river Inönü, which Ismet Pasha later took as his last name.

The final stage of the war began on 26 August 1922, when Kemal led the Nationalist forces in a counter-offensive that utterly routed the Greeks, who fled in disorder towards Izmir. The Turkish cavalry entered Izmir on 9 September, by which time the Greek army had been evacuated from Asia Minor. A fire broke out in Izmir four days later, destroying half the city with great loss of life, just as the war ended.

An armistice was signed at Mudanya on 11 October, in which it was agreed that the Nationalists would occupy all of Thrace east of the river Maritza except for Istanbul and a zone along the straits, which would continue to be held by the British until a final peace treaty was signed.

On 1 November 1922 the Grand National Assembly in Ankara passed legislation separating the sultanate and the caliphate, with the former being abolished and the latter reduced to a purely religious role subservient to the state. The Allied High Commissioners were informed that henceforth Istanbul would be under the administration of the assembly and that Vahidettin was no longer sultan, though he retained the title of caliph. On 17 November 1922 Vahidettin left Istanbul aboard the British warship *HMS Malaya*, never to return. His brother Abdül Mecit II succeeded him as caliph on 24 November 1922.

The final articles of the Treaty of Lausanne, signed on 24 July 1923, established the present boundaries of the Turkish Republic, except for the province of Hatay in south-eastern Anatolia, which was acquired after a plebiscite in 1939. A separate agreement between Greece and Turkey provided for a compulsory exchange of their minorities, in which some 1.3 million Greeks and about half a million Turks were uprooted. The only exceptions to the exchange were the Turks of western Thrace and the Greeks of Istanbul and the islands of Imbros and Tenedos.

The Allied occupation of Istanbul came to an end on 2 October 1923, when the last detachment of British troops embarked from the city. Four days later a division of the Turkish Nationalist army marched into Istanbul.

On 13 October the Grand National Assembly passed a law making Ankara the capital of Turkey.

Then on 29 October the assembly adopted a constitution that created the Republic of Turkey, and on that same day Kemal was elected as its first president, whereupon he chose Ismet Inönü as prime minister. Kemal subsequently took the name Atatürk, meaning 'Father of the Turks', symbolising his leadership in creating the new Turkish Republic that rose out of the ashes of the Ottoman Empire.

On 3 March 1924 the Grand National Assembly passed a law abolishing the caliphate, thus severing the last tenuous bond that linked Turkey with the Ottoman Empire. This same law deposed Abdül Mecit as caliph, and he and all his family and descendants were forbidden to reside within the boundaries of the Turkish Republic. The following day Abdül Mecit left Istanbul, never to return.

And thus the Ottoman Empire finally came to an end, with the departure of the last member of the Osmanlı dynasty that had ruled in Turkey for more than 700 years. The House of Osman had fallen, and the dynasty that he had founded was sent off into exile, most of them into western Europe, which for centuries had lived in fear of the Grand Turk.

17 *The Conqueror's City*

Istanbul is a much larger and more populous city than it was in the time of the Conqueror, though some aspects of it are essentially unchanged, for most of the monuments erected by Mehmet II and members of his court remain standing, many still performing the same function for which they were first built.

The first census of Ottoman Istanbul, including Galata, was ordered by Mehmet II in 1477, twenty-four years after his conquest of Byzantine Constantinople. The census, which counted only civilian households and did not include the military class or those residing in the two imperial palaces, Topkapı Sarayı and Eski Saray, registered the number of families in the various religious, ethnic and national categories. It recorded 9,486 Muslim Turkish, 4,127 Greek, 1,687 Jewish, 434 Armenian, 267 Genoese and 332 European families from places other than Genoa. The total population of Istanbul is estimated from this census as being between 80,000 and 100,000, about double what it had been in Byzantine Constantinople just before the Conquest. Seventy per cent of those living within the walled city of Istanbul were Muslim Turks, with the rest non-Muslims, mostly Greeks and Armenians and some Jews, with just the reverse being true in Galata. The Jewish population greatly increased in the early 1490s, when the Conqueror's son and successor Beyazit II gave refuge to the Jews who had been evicted from Spain by Ferdinand and Isabella.

The population of the city increased to some half a million by the mid-sixteenth century, during the reign of Süleyman the Magnificent. It then remained constant until the last half-century of Ottoman rule, when Muslim Turkish refugees from the lost territories of the empire in the Balkans poured into Istanbul, increasing its population to over a million.

The first census under the Turkish Republic, taken in June 1924, showed that Istanbul had a population of 1,165,866, 61 per cent of whom were Muslim Turks, 25 per cent Greeks, 7 per cent Armenians and 6 per cent Jews. The population began increasing in the late 1950s, when people from the rural areas of Anatolia began moving to Istanbul and the other large cities of Turkey in search of a better life. The population of Istanbul has been increasing at an accelerated rate since then, reaching approximately 1,466 million in 1960, 2,132 million in 1970, 4,433 million in 1980, 7.5 million in 1990, and just under 10 million in 2000, with the number today estimated at between 12 million and 15 million. The size of the city expanded as well, beginning in 1980, when its area increased by a factor of four, so that Istanbul now stretches up both shores of the Bosphorus to within sight of the Black Sea, extending far along the European and Asian shores of the Marmara. The ethnic composition of Istanbul has changed as well, for about 99 per cent of the present population is Muslim Turkish, with about 50,000 Armenians, 40,000 Jews and 3,000 Greeks, the latter three minorities being those that were recognised as separate *millets*, or nations, by Mehmet the Conqueror.

Two bridges now span the Bosphorus. The first of them opened on 29 October 1973, on the fiftieth anniversary of the Turkish Republic, crossing the strait about 6 kilometres from its southern end at the Sea of Marmara. The second bridge, which opened in the summer of 1988, crosses the strait some 12 kilometres upstream from the Marmara. The upper span is called Fatih Mehmet Köprüsü, the Bridge of Mehmet the Conqueror, honouring the first Ottoman sultan to rule in Istanbul, whose conquest of Constantinople is commemorated each year on 29 May.

Fatih Mehmet Köprüsü spans the Bosphorus just upstream from Anadolu Hisarı and Rumeli Hisarı, long known in English as the Castles of Asia and Europe, respectively. As may be recalled, Anadolu Hisarı was built in 1395 by Beyazit I when he began the first Turkish siege of Constantinople, which was aborted when he was defeated and killed by Tamerlane in 1402, while Rumeli Hisarı was constructed by Mehmet II in the summer of 1452 in preparation for his attack on the Byzantine capital the following year.

Rumeli Hisarı is a splendid late medieval fortification, the largest fortress ever built by the Ottoman Turks. The fortress spans a steep valley with two tall towers on opposite hills and a third at the bottom of the valley at the water's edge, where stands the sea gate protected by a barbican. A curtain wall, defended by thirteen smaller towers, joins the three main bastions, forming an irregular triangle some 250 metres long by 125 broad at its maximum. Sultan Mehmet himself selected the site, drew the general plan of the fortress and spent much time in supervising the work of the 1,000 skilled and 2,000 unskilled workmen he had collected from the various provinces of his empire. He entrusted the construction of each of the three main towers to one of his vezirs, whose names are still associated with them. The north tower was assigned to Saruca Pasha, the south one to Zaganos Pasha and the sea tower to Halil Pasha, his grand vezir, all three of whom competed with one another to complete the work with speed and efficiency. Over the door to the south tower an Arabic inscription records the completion of the fortress in the month of Recep 856 (July–August 1452), just four months after it was begun.

The fortress was restored in 1953 to commemorate the 500th anniversary of Sultan Mehmet's conquest of Constantinople. At that time the picturesque little village of wooden houses inside the walls of the fortress was demolished, and its residents, some of whom claimed descent from men of the Conqueror's army and workforce, were resettled in the village of Rumeli Hisarı. The area inside the fortress has been made into a charming park, and the circular cistern on which once stood a small mosque (part of its minaret has been left to mark its position) has been converted into the acting area of a Greek-type theatre. Here in the summer productions of Shakespeare's and other plays are given against the stunning background of the castle walls and towers, the Bosphorus and the gleaming lights of the villages of Asia.

Immediately after the Conquest, Sultan Mehmet built another fortress in the south-eastern corner of the old city, near the Marmara end of the Byzantine land walls at the famous Golden Gate. As Kritoboulos writes, after recording Mehmet's efforts in rebuilding the city and starting work on the Eski Saray: 'He further ordered the construction of a strong fortress near the Golden Gate where there had formerly been an imperial castle, and he commanded that all these things should be done with all haste.'

The fortress at the Golden Gate is known as Yedikule, the Castle of the Seven Towers, a curious structure partly Byzantine, partly Turkish. The western side is formed by that part of the ancient Theodosian city walls that includes the Golden Gate, part of a triumphal arch built c. 390 by Emperor Theodosius I. Along this side are four of the seven towers: the two square marble pylons flanking the Golden Gate and two polygonal towers belonging to the Theodosian wall itself. Eastward of these, inside the city, Sultan Mehmet constructed three large towers connected with each other and with the Theodosian walls by tall and massive curtain walls. The area thus enclosed forms a rather irregular hexagon. The structure was never used as a castle in the usual sense, but two of the towers saw service in Ottoman times as prisons; the others were used as storage places for part of the state treasure.

Yedikule has been restored and is now open as a museum, with its entrance in the middle of the inner wall of the enclosure. The bastion to the left of the entrance is called the Tower of Inscriptions, because some of the many unfortunates who were imprisoned there have carved messages on the walls, in Greek, Latin, French and German. The southern pylon of the Golden Gate was used in Ottoman times as a prison and a place of execution, one of the exhibits being the 'well of blood', a pit down which the executioner threw the heads of those he had executed. Osman II was executed here on 19 May 1622, although not by being beheaded, according to Evliya Çelebi, who writes that the young sultan, who was only nineteen, 'was deposed by a rebellion of the Janissaries and put to death in the Castle of the Seven Towers, by the compression of his testicles, a mode of execution reserved by custom for the Ottoman emperors'.

Istanbul's largest and most famous marketplace is still the Kapalı Çarşı, or Covered Bazaar, which Sultan Mehmet founded on the Third Hill in 1456, three years after the Conquest. The Turkish architectural historian Ayverdi claims that more than half the shops in the bazaar go back to the time of the Conqueror, though they have certainly been restored on several occasions, most recently after the earthquake of 1894 and the fire that ravaged the marketplace in 1954.

The Kapalı Çarşı is probably the largest market of its kind in the world. At first it seems a veritable labyrinth, but its central area forms a regular grid, with shops selling the same kind of merchandise congregated in their own streets, the names of which come from the various market guilds that originally had their establishments in these places in the time of the Conqueror. Thus there are streets of jewellers, goldsmiths, silversmiths and rug dealers, though others named for sword makers, turban merchants and armourers now deal in more modern merchandise. The streets are roofed with vaults and domes, the wide ones often flanked with columned arcades, side alleys leading into ancient *hans*, or inner-city caravanserais.

The grid is centred on the Old Bedesten, one of the original structures erected by the Conqueror, used then and now for the storage and sale of the most precious objects. Sultan Mehmet built an almost identical *bedesten* across the Golden Horn in Galata, where it now serves as a market hall for heavy machinery, identified by a sign as the Fatih Çarşısı, the Marketplace of the Conqueror.

The first mosque complex that Sultan Mehmet erected in Istanbul was Eyüp Camii, outside the city walls on the upper reaches of the Golden Horn. Eyüp Camii was built by Mehmet in 1458, and its original *külliye*, or building complex, included the great mosque itself, the tomb (*türbe*) of Eba Eyüp Ensari, Companion of the Prophet, a *medrese*, a refectory (*imaret*) and a public bath (*hamam*). The original mosque was destroyed, perhaps by the great earthquake of 1766, and the present structure was erected in 1800 by Sultan Selim III. The *medrese* has vanished, the *imaret* is in ruins and only part of the *hamam* survives (a very fine panel of twenty-four Iznik tiles from this bath is now in the Victoria and Albert Museum). But the *türbe* of Eba Eyüp Ensari survives intact, and its superb decorations make it one of the masterpieces of Ottoman art.

The mosque is approached through a picturesque outer courtyard with two great baroque gateways. Another gateway leads into the inner court, bordered by an unusually tall and stately colonnade along three sides. The inner court is shaded by venerable plane trees, in which grey herons and storks nest in the spring, a few of the latter remaining behind in a hollow of one of the trees when they can no longer fly. The flocks of pigeons are as numerous and pampered as those of the Piazza San Marco in Venice, and the courtyard is always thronged with pilgrims and with young boys celebrating their rites of circumcision. The tomb of Eyüp is opposite the central door of the mosque. Although the tomb was restored and redecorated in later times, its interior still appears to retain the form that it had in the days of the Conqueror.

From the time of Beyazit II onwards it was the custom for new sultans to be girded with the sword of their ancestor Osman Gazi at Eyüp's tomb, a ceremony equivalent to coronation. The newly girded sultan would then lead a procession to Fatih Camii, the Mosque of the Conqueror, where he would pay obeisance to Sultan Mehmet II. The first to do so was Beyazit II, who had buried his father there earlier that day, 21 May 1482, beginning a practice that continued down to the end of the empire.

Fatih Camii is on the Fourth Hill of the city, built on the site of the famous church of the Holy Apostles, which the Conqueror demolished to make way for his *külliye*, the first imperial mosque complex to be erected in Istanbul. The complex was built in the years 1463–70, dates given in the calligraphic inscription over the main gateway to the outer courtyard. The architect was Atik (Old) Sinan, tentatively identified as a Greek named Christodoulos, who was apparently executed by Sultan Mehmet in 1471, supposedly because the dome of the Conqueror's mosque was smaller than that of Haghia Sophia, although that story is most probably apocryphal.

The original mosque was completely destroyed by an earthquake on 22 May 1766, and the other buildings in the complex were damaged in varying degrees. Sultan Mustafa III immediately undertook the reconstruction of the complex, and the present baroque mosque, completed in 1771, was designed on a wholly different plan from the original. The caravanserai, hospital and library have disappeared, but all of the other structures in the *külliye* survive from their restoration by Mustafa III, presumably in their original form.

Fatih Camii was the largest and most extensive mosque complex ever built in the Ottoman Empire, laid out on a vast, nearly square area – about 325 metres on a side – with almost rigid symmetry. This and other *külliyes* became the civic centres of the new Ottoman city of Istanbul, with the mosque itself surrounded by other religious and philanthropic institutions serving the Muslims of the surrounding quarter, which in this case is still known as Fatih. The original Fatih Camii *külliye* consisted of the mosque, eight *medreses*, a refectory, a hospice, a caravanserai, a hospital (*darüşşifa*), a library (*kütüphane*), a primary school (*mektep*), a market (*çarşı*) and two tombs (*türbe*), one for Sultan Mehmet and the other for his wife Gülbahar, mother of his son and successor Beyazit II.

The graveyard behind the mosque contains the tombs of Sultan Mehmet and his wife Gülbahar, both of which were reconstructed after the 1766 earthquake though on the old foundations. Mehmet's tomb is very baroque and its interior decorations extremely sumptuous in the Empire style. Gülbahar's is simple and classical and must reproduce the original fairly closely.

Old prints show that Mehmet's tomb was filled with captured weapons and other trophies, placed there by sultans after victorious campaigns. When newly girded sultans visited Mehmet's tomb they are said to have prayed to him to endow them with the courage he exhibited in his many conquests, particularly in his capture of Constantinople. Anatolian peasants still offer their prayers to the Conqueror when they visit his tomb, continuing a practice that dates back to the time of his death.

Gülbahar's tomb has never been open to the public, which legend says is due to the fact that she was a Christian who never converted to Islam, a tradition first recorded by Evliya Çelebi in his *Narrative of Travels*:

> I myself have often observed, at morning prayer, that the readers appointed to chant lessons from the Kuran all turned their backs upon the coffin of this lady, of whom it is so doubtful whether she had departed in the faith of Islam. I have often seen Franks [Europeans] come by stealth and give a few aspers to the tomb-keeper to open her *türbe* for them, as the gate is always kept locked.

The same story is told by the Italian traveller Cornelio Magni, in a work published at Parma in 1679, in which he says that the custodian of Gülbahar's tomb told him that it remained closed and shuttered because the deceased was a Christian princess who lived and died in her faith. 'The *türbe*,' he says, 'remains always shut, even the windows.' He asked the reason for this and was told by the custodian: 'The sepulchre of her whose soul lives among the shades deserves not a ray of light!' After much entreaty and the intervention of an emir who was passing by, the custodian finally let him in. 'I entered with veneration and awe,' he writes in conclusion, 'and silently recited a *De Profundis* for the soul of this unfortunate princess.'

The oldest extant mosque in Istanbul that retains its original form is Mahmut Pasha Camii, erected in 1462 on the Second Hill. The market quarter in which it stands is still named after Mahmut Pasha, the greatest of the Conqueror's grand vezirs.

Besides the great mosque, Mahmut Pasha's original *külliye* included a *medrese*, an *imaret*, a primary school, a *türbe*, a *hamam*, a *han* and a *mahkeme*, or Court of Justice. All that remains of the medrese are its lecture hall and one or two ruined cells in a corner of the garden. The *imaret*, *mektep* and *mahkeme* have vanished, but the *türbe*, *hamam* and *han* survive. Mahmut Pasha's magnificent and unique *türbe* stands a short way to the south-west of his mosque, dated by its inscription to AH 878 (AD 1474), the year in which he was executed by the Conqueror.

The other two surviving structures of the *külliye* are some distance to the west of the mosque, both of them on or near a street named Mahmut Pasha Yokuşu, which leads past the Kapalı Çarşı on its way down to the Golden Horn.

A short way down Mahmut Pasha Yokuşu after leaving the Kapalı Çarşı one comes on the left to a turning that leads to an imposing domed building. This is what remains of Mahmut Pasha's *hamam*, which is now used as a market hall. The building, dated by an inscription to the year AH 871 (AD 1476), was completed by his heirs two years after his death.

A short way further down Mahmut Pasha Yokuşu one comes on the left to an archway that leads to the Kürkçü Hanı, the Han of the Furriers. This is the *han* of Mahmut Pasha's *külliye*, the oldest building of its kind in Istanbul. The furriers for whom it is named have been doing business here since at least 1638, when Evliya Çelebi describes them in his *Narrative of Travels*. Evliya mentions more than twenty-five *hans* by name that still stand in Istanbul, most of them in the area in and around the Kapalı Çarşı, some going back to the time of the Conqueror, many of them built on Byzantine foundations. They were designed as inns for merchants, with storage space for the goods that they brought to Istanbul on camel caravans, later replaced by lorries. Typically they are buildings of two or three storeys around a central courtyard, or even two courtyards, as in the case of the Kürkçü Hanı and one or two others.

A number of mosques and other structures founded by the Conqueror's vezirs are still standing. The earliest of these are Murat Pasha Camii and Rum Mehmet Pasha Camii, which rank just after Mahmut Pasha Camii as the second and third oldest mosques in the city that retain their original form. Like Mahmut Pasha, Murat Pasha and Rum Mehmet Pasha were of Greek origin and converted to Islam when they joined the service of Mehmet the Conqueror.

Murat Pasha Camii was built on the Seventh Hill in 1469, a date recorded in an inscription over its main doorway. The founder, Murat Pasha (also known as Hass Murat), was from the Byzantine imperial family of the Palaeologues, and attained the rank of first vezir under the Conqueror, who numbered him among his special favourites. He died as a relatively young man in 1473 during Sultan Mehmet's campaign against Uzun Hasan, commanded by Mahmut Pasha, whom the sultan blamed for the death of his favourite.

Rum Mehmet Pasha Camii is on the Asian side of the city in Üsküdar, standing on a hill above the point where the Bosphorus flows into the Marmara. According to an Arabic inscription over the door of the mosque, it was founded in 1471 by Rum Mehmet Pasha, the year that he became grand vezir, only to be executed the following year by the Conqueror. The founder is buried in an octagonal *türbe* in the garden behind his mosque. Josef von Hammer, the nineteenth-century Austrian historian, wrote of Rum Mehmet Pasha that 'he left in Ottoman history no other memories than those of his crimes'.

The oldest functioning Turkish bath in the city is the Gedik Pasha Hamamı on the Third Hill, built c. 1475. Its founder was Gedik Ahmet Pasha, who served as grand vezir in the years 1473–4 and again in 1476, commanding victorious armies for both Mehmet II and Beyazit II, who executed him in 1482. The whole bath glistens with bright new marble; it is much patronised by the inhabitants of the surrounding district, as indeed it has been since the days of the Conqueror.

Another ancient *hamam,* now unfortunately disused, forms part of a little *külliye* just outside the walls of Topkapı Sarayı on the Marmara slope of the First Hill. The *külliye* consists of just the *hamam,* a monumental structure now partially in ruins, and a much-restored little mosque. Both were built in 1476 by Ishak Pasha, who served as the Conqueror's grand vezir in the years 1468–71 and held the office again under Beyazit II. His contemporary Kritoboulos describes Ishak as 'a man of the wisest sort, experienced in many spheres, but especially a military leader and a man of courage'. The mosque is of the simplest sort, a square room covered by a dome, the same style as the earliest extant Ottoman mosques of the 1330s. The mosque has been restored several times, not very well, and it has lost its porch in a street widening.

Ishak Pasha Camii is one of eight small mosques in Istanbul dating from the time of the Conqueror that have been rebuilt so that they no longer have their original form. Only two of these mosques are definitely dated, though the others are almost certainly from the first quarter-century after the Conquest, when Sultan Mehmet was rebuilding and repopulating his new capital.

Yarhisar Camii is on the slope of the Fourth Hill leading down to the Golden Horn. According to the Register of Pious Foundations, it was built in 1461, thus antedating Mahmut Pasha Camii by a year or so. Its founder, Musliheddin Mustafa Efendi, was chief judge of Istanbul under the Conqueror. It was once a handsome edifice, but it was badly damaged in the great fire of 1917 that consumed most of this district, and then in 1954–6 it was restored so badly that it lost all its original character.

Another ancient mosque ruined by an appalling restoration is Kumrulu Mescit, which stands on the Fifth Hill. This mosque is of interest because its founder and builder, Atik Sinan, was chief architect to Sultan Mehmet II and built the original mosque of Fatih Camii. Kumrulu Mescit, the Mosque of the Turtle Dove, takes its name from a fragment of Byzantine sculpture used in the adjoining fountain. Atik Sinan's grave is in the garden of the mosque; the inscription records that he was executed in 1471, the year after Fatih Camii was completed, but the reason for his execution is not given.

The other five ancient mosques from the Conqueror's time are all on the slope of the Third Hill leading down to the Golden Horn, a district that has been the city's principal market area since Byzantine times and which, under Mehmet II, became the city's first Turkish quarter.

Yavaşça Şahin Camii is a small mosque on Uzun Çarşı Caddesi, the Avenue of the Long Market, which follows the course of an ancient Byzantine colonnaded way that led down from the summit of the Third Hill to the Golden Horn. The mosque was founded soon after the Conquest by Yavaşça Şahin Pasha, who was captain of the Ottoman fleet in the Conqueror's siege of Constantinople. It is one of a small group of early mosques that form a distinct type. The mosque was badly damaged by fire in 1908 but well restored in 1950.

Just opposite Yavaşça Şahin Camii a street leads steeply uphill, and at the first corner on the left it comes to Samanveren Camii, the Mosque of the Inspector of Straw. This ancient and dilapidated structure was built in the time of the Conqueror by a certain Sinan Ağa, who was the sultan's *samanveren*, or inspector of straw – hence the name of the mosque. Though in a very advanced state of decay it is a quaint and interesting building of brick and stone construction; what is left of the minaret has some curious leaf-like decorations in brick.

Across from Samanveren Camii a street with the picturesque name of Devoğlu (Son of the Giant) rambles downhill to the north until it debouches opposite another ancient mosque, Timurtaş Camii, which was completely restored in the 1960s. The Turkish architectural historian Ayverdi has established that the mosque was built in the time of the Conqueror by a certain Timurtaş Ağa, who may have been an associate of Sinan Ağa, the founder of Samanveren Camii, since their two mosques are (or were) almost identical.

Two other old mosques from the time of the Conqueror stand on the shore road that runs along the Golden Horn between the Galata Bridge and the Atatürk Bridge. One of them, Kazancılar Camii, the Mosque of the Cauldron Makers, is midway between the two bridges in the district of

Küçük Pazar (the Little Market) while the other, Sağrıcılar Camii, the Mosque of the Leather Merchants, is beside the Atatürk Bridge in the quarter known as Unkapanı (the Flour Store), the names of the mosques and the areas in which they stand going back to the time of the Conqueror, when Turks first settled in this part of the city.

Kazancılar Camii is also known as Üç Mihrablı Camii, the Mosque of the Three Mirhaps. Founded, according to a document known as the *Hadika*, by a certain Hoca (Teacher) Hayrettin Efendi in 1475, it was enlarged first by the Conqueror himself, then by Hayrettin's daughter-in-law, who added her own house to the mosque, which thus came to have three *mihrabs* – whence its name. The main body of the building seems to be original in form though heavily restored. South of the main building is a rectangular annex with a flat ceiling and two *mihrabs*; it is through this room that one enters the mosque nowadays. According to Ayverdi, this section is 'wholly new', which may be true, but so far as form goes it might well be the house added by Hayrettin's daughter-in-law, in which case this is the only ordinary dwelling place left in the city from the time of the Conqueror.

Sağrıcılar Camii was founded c. 1455 by Yavuz Ersinan, who was standard-bearer in Mehmet's army at the time of the Conquest and an ancestor of Evliya Çelebi, who was born in a house beside the mosque. The founder is buried in a little graveyard that was laid out between the mosque and his house, now vanished. Buried beside Yavuzer Sinan is his old comrade-in-arms Horoz Dede, Grandfather Rooster, one of the most famous Muslim folk saints of Istanbul. Horoz Dede received his name during the siege of Constantinople, when he made his rounds at dawn each day and roused Mehmet's troops with his loud rooster call. He was killed in the final assault on the city, and then after the conquest Yavuz Ersinan buried him beside his mosque, with Sultan Mehmet among the mourners at his grave. The mosque is of the simplest type, a square room covered by a dome. It was restored in 1960 with only moderate success.

Mehmet's example was followed by his successors as sultan as well as by the great men and women of their courts, who built mosque complexes and other structures throughout the city. The most notable of the imperial mosque complexes crown the six hills above the Golden Horn: Sultan Ahmet I Camii on the First Hill, Nuruosmaniye Camii on the Second Hill, Beyazit II Camii (the Beyazidiye) and Süleyman I Camii (the Süleymaniye) on the Third Hill, the new Fatih Camii of Mustafa III on the Fourth Hill, Selim I Camii on the Fifth Hill and Mihrimah Camii on the Sixth Hill, not to mention the scores of other Ottoman mosques, *medreses*, schools, libraries, hospitals, refectories, *hans*, baths, markets, palaces and fountains that adorn not only the old city but its present extension along both shores of the Bosphorus.

Some of the other structures in the city remaining from the Conqueror's time are in Topkapı Sarayı, most notably Çinili Köşk and two complexes in the Third Court, namely the Privy Chamber and the Conqueror's Pavilion. Çinili Köşk now serves as a museum of Turkish tiles; the Privy Chamber is the Pavilion of the Holy Mantle, containing sacred objects associated with the Prophet Mohammed; while the Conqueror's Pavilion houses the Treasury of Topkapı Sarayı, an extraordinary collection of precious objects once owned by the Ottoman sultans, including a number that belonged to the Conqueror.

The Conqueror's Pavilion also houses the Imperial Wardrobe, a collection of robes and other clothing belonging to all the sultans from the Conqueror down to the end of the Osmanlı dynasty. The Conqueror's robe exhibited in this collection is similar to the kaftan he wears in the portrait that Gentile Bellini painted of him in 1480. Mehmet would have sat for that portrait in Topkapı Sarayı, for his poor health kept him in the palace through the whole of that year. The room in which he sat for his portrait would have been the marble loggia in the north-east corner of the Third Court, for the light is best there, opening as it does through great archways to the north-east and south-east.

After Mehmet's death his son and successor Beyazit II seems to have got rid of his father's portrait along with other Western paintings, as Giovanni-Maria Angiolello writes in his account of Bellini's visit to Istanbul.

Muhammed caused him [Bellini] to make many paintings and portraits of subjects of a lascivious character (*massime di cose di lussuria*), and some of these were so beautiful that he caused a great number of them to be hung in the palace. When Beyazit succeeded his father, he immediately caused these paintings to be sold in the bazaars, and many of them were bought by our [Venetian] merchants.

Bellini's portrait of Mehmet was not seen again until 1865, when it was purchased from a collector in Venice by Augustin Layard, the famous archaeologist, who had been the British ambassador in Istanbul during the reign of Abdül Hamit II. After Layard died his widow presented the painting to the National Portrait Gallery in London, where it remains today.

The Conqueror's portrait briefly returned to Istanbul in December 1999, when it was exhibited at the gallery of the Yapı Kredi Cultural Centre. I had not seen the painting in nearly forty years, and then only briefly, but now I looked upon it long and intently, trying to see the man behind the enigmatic face. He seemed to be peering absently into the distance, which from the place where he sat for Bellini would have been towards the confluence of the Bosphorus and the Golden Horn, where their waters meet and flow together into the Sea of Marmara around the city that he had conquered twenty-eight years earlier, changing the world for ever.

Mehmet was not yet forty-nine at the time he sat for his portrait, looking like a vigorous man at the prime of his life, with no indication that he had only a few months to live. Although he was mortally ill during those months he dragged himself from his bed to lead one more campaign, marshalling his forces on the Asian side of the Bosphorus, only to meet death one day's march out of Istanbul, the city he conquered four and a half centuries ago and which still bears his imprint today.

An inscription above the Imperial Gate of Topkapı Sarayı, dated two years before his death, could well serve as the epitaph of Mehmet the Conqueror, the Grand Turk, dominating the entrance to the principal monument that he erected in the city that became his capital.

By the grace of God and by His approval, the foundations of this auspicious castle were laid, and its parts were solidly joined together to strengthen peace and tranquility by the command of the Sultan of the two Continents and the Emperor of the two Seas, the Shadow of God in this world and the next, the Favourite of God on the Two Horizons, the Monarch of the Terraqueous Orb, the Conqueror of the Castle of Constantinople, the Father of Conquest, Sultan Mehmed Khan, son of Sultan Murad Khan, son of Sultan Mehmed Khan, may God make eternal his empire, and exalt his residence among the most lucid stars of the firmament, in the blessed month of Ramadan of the year 883 [November and December 1478].

Notes

All references to authors relate to their works listed in the bibliography. Notes refer to page numbers in the text.

PROLOGUE: PORTRAIT OF A SULTAN

xv	'the Glorious Empire ...', Knolles, vol. I, p. 1
xv	'a venomous dragon', Pastor, vol. III, p. 24
xvi	'Modern history begins ...', Coles, p. 7
xvi–xvii	'Partly because of empire ...', Said, *Culture and Imperialism*, p. xxv
xvii	'son of Satan ...', Setton, vol. II, p. 150

1. THE SONS OF OSMAN

2–3	Thus is Ertogrul ..., Knolles, vol. I, p. 134
4	'and the two amused ...', Imber, *The Ottoman Empire, 1300–1481*, p. 23
4	'received a great army...', ibid., p. 25
10	'the Lady, daughter of Abdullah', Babinger, p. 11
10	'offered his daughter...', Doukas, p. 175
10	'longed more for this ...', ibid., p. 176
10	'knew that Belgrade ...', Imber, *The Ottoman Empire, 1300–1481*, p. 119
10	'many men and lords ...', ibid.
11	'Your father has sent ...', Babinger, p. 24
12	'Mehmet must certainly...', Raby, 'Mehmet the Conqueror's Greek Scriptorium', p. 23
13	'in regal splendor...', Babinger, p. 30
14	'I have given ...', Imber, *The Ottoman Empire, 1300–1481*, p. 129

2. THE BOY SULTAN

15	'march with a powerful army...' Setton, vol. II, p. 78
15	'notwithstanding any treaties ...', ibid., p. 83
16	'fled like sheep ...', Imber, *The Ottoman Empire, 1300–1481*, p. 134
16	'after making prisoner...', ibid., p. 27
18	'for his deceased ...', Babinger, p. 59
19	'from the oppression ...', Setton, vol. II, p. 103
19–20	'Proceeding for about ...', Doukas, p. 188
20	'When he became heir...', Kritoboulos, pp. 13–14
20	'His physical powers ...', ibid., p. 14
20	'insolence, savagery and violence', Doukas, p. 192
20	'Bury me in ...', Freely, *Turkey around the Marmara*, p. 186
21	'And to whomsoever...', Gibb and Bowen, p. 36
21–22	'This man, who just ...', Sphrantzes, p. 59
22	'Your potential bride ...', ibid., p. 61
22	'with delight and ...', ibid.
22	'had made a vow...', ibid.
22	'he gave himself ...', Kritoboulos, p. 14
22	'depose some of the governors ...', ibid.
22	'the registers and ...', ibid., p. 15
22	'In addition to this ...', ibid.
23	'much of the public ...', ibid.
23	'He greatly increased ...', ibid.
23	'agreed to give up ...', Tursun Beg, p. 33
24	'stupid and foolish Romans', Doukas, p. 193
24	'a sincere friend', ibid.
24	'resolved to carry...', Kritoboulos, p. 22
24	'to build a strong ...', ibid., pp. 15–16
24	'ordered all the materials ...', ibid., p. 16
25	'I take nothing ...', Doukas, p. 195
25	'he filled thirty...', Kritoboulos, p. 13
25	'marked out with stakes ...', ibid., p. 19
25	'as they were removing ...', Doukas, p. 197
25	'This was the beginning ...', ibid., p. 198
26	'I would rather see ...', Pastor, vol. II, p. 260
26	'Wretched Romans, how...', Doukas, p. 204
26	'Night and day...', ibid., p. 201
27	'Go in peace', ibid., p. 202
27	'a recital of previous ...', Kritoboulos, p. 23

27   'Let us not then ...', ibid., p. 33
27   'practically all of those ...', ibid.
27   'wanted to advise ...', ibid.
27   'However, seeing the ...', ibid.

3. THE CONQUEST OF CONSTANTINOPLE

31   'informing them furthermore ...', Setton, vol. II, p. 109
31   'prepared the fleet ...', Kritoboulos, p. 37
31   'the total number...', ibid., pp. 37–8
31   'They set sail ...', ibid., p. 38
32   'in the greatest possible ...', Sphrantzes, p. 70
32   'a city of ruins ...', Inalcık, 'The Policy of Mehmed II toward the Greek
             Population ...', p. 231
34   'killed some of them ...', Kritoboulos, p. 40
34   'But after encountering ...', ibid.
34   'came before Constantinople ...', Barbaro, p. 27
34–35   'moved with a great ...', ibid.
35   'that if they were ...', Kritoboulos, p. 40
35   'were willing to make ...', ibid., p. 41
37   'were astounded at ...', ibid., p. 57
37   'The city was ...', Barbaro, p. 43
38   'at the fourth hour...', ibid., p. 46
39   'the Turks made frenzied ...', ibid., p. 57
40   'not to be frightened ...' Melville Jones, p. 33
41   'Spare us, O Lord, ...', Doukas, p. 221
41   'Finally, my fellow...', Melville Jones, p. 35
41   'asked to be forgiven ...', Sphrantzes, pp. 124–5
42   'Friends, we have ...', Kritoboulos, p. 71
43   After this the Sultan ..., Kritoboulos, pp. 76–7

4. ISTANBUL, CAPITAL OF THE OTTOMAN EMPIRE

45   'The sultan then having ...', Evliya Çelebi, vol. I, part I, pp. 43–4
46   On the following Friday..., ibid., p. 45
46   'The spider is the ...', Freely, *Istanbul, the Imperial City*, p. 177
47   'Among these was Notaras ...', Kritoboulos, p. 83
47   'Twenty-nine nobles ...', Barbaro, p. 72

48   'on the grounds that...', Sphrantzes, p. 74
48   'my beautiful daughter...', ibid., p. 75
48   'appointed some of...', Kritoboulos, pp. 85–6
49   'that no *doghandji*...', Inalcık, *Essays in Ottoman History*, p. 277
49   'In sum, he has...', Melville Jones, p. 134
49   'Nothing worse than this...', Schwoebel, p. 1
49   'of the horrible...', Setton, vol. I, p. 139
49   'shame of Christendom', ibid., p. 140
50   'Also in this yere...', Schwoebel, p. 4
50   'On the day when...', ibid.
50   'to his vezirs...', Inalcık, 'The Policy of Mehmed II toward the Greek
            Population...', p. 233
50   'a most intelligent...', Kritoboulos, p. 85
50   'put him in charge...', ibid.
50   'had often sent letters...', Melville Jones, p. 39
50   'he ordered that Halil...', ibid., p. 40
51   'He sent an order...', Kritoboulos, pp. 93, 105
51   'along the shores...', ibid., p. 83
51   'commanded also that...', ibid.
51   'This was in a way...', ibid., p. 93
52   'He issued orders...', Sphrantzes, p. 134
52   'that no one should...', Babinger, p. 104
52–53   'The Franciscan brothers...', ibid., p. 419
53   'his father was domineering...', ibid., p. 411
53   I saw the ruler..., ibid., p. 418
54   'the finest and best location...', Kritoboulos, p. 93
54   'ordered the construction...', ibid.
54–55   Mehmet II having..., Evliya Çelebi, vol. I, part II, p. 35
55   'command... to all...', Kritoboulos, p. 140
55   'also commanded them...', ibid.
55   'to construct many...', ibid., pp. 140–1
55   'This man had so fine...', ibid., pp. 88–9

5. EUROPE IN TERROR

57   'A city which was...', Freely, *Jem Sultan*, p. 2
57–58   Here we have horrible news..., Setton, vol. II, p. 150
58   'son of Satan...', ibid.
58   'even to the shedding...', ibid., p. 164

58	'How very much indeed ...', ibid., p.165
59	'they shall be safe ...', ibid., p. 141
59	The sovereign, the Grand Turk ..., Melville Jones, p. 126
59	He is a man continually..., ibid., p. 12
60	All those among the men ..., Mihailović, p. 99
60	'Mehmet spent many nights ...', Babinger, p. 428
63	'The Sultan invaded ...', Sphrantzes, p. 176
63–64	He saw it and was amazed ...', Kritoboulos, p. 136
64	'Proceeding according to plan ...', ibid., p. 137
66	'marched straight into ...', Sphrantzes, p. 80
66	'The Christian Empires ...', Medlin, pp. 78ff
68	'it was common knowledge ...', Runciman, *The Fall of Constantinople 1453*, p. 173
68	'Why tire yourself, my son ...', ibid., p. 174
68	And we marched in ..., Mihailović, p. 117
68	'The Emperor stayed there ...', ibid., p. 119
68–69	'if you do not give ear...', Babinger, p. 195
69	'Sultan of the two ...', Necipoğlu, p. 34

6. WAR WITH VENICE

71	'We have done nothing ...', Setton, vol. II, p. 233
71–72	Once you have ..., Babinger, p. 200
73	'inquired about the tombs ...', Kritoboulos, p. 181
73	He is reported to have said ..., ibid.
73	'build a great navy...', ibid., p. 185
73–74	Then he gave orders ..., ibid.
74	If Mehmet only demanded ..., Babinger, p. 216
75	'The killing of such ...', Stavrides, p. 149
75	Impelled by his lusts ..., Babinger, pp. 224–5
75–76	'setting forth the power...', Setton, vol. II, p. 371
76	'We shall do battle ...', ibid., p. 261
76	You Germans who do not ..., Babinger, p. 235
78	'who alone keep watch ...', Freely, *Jem Sultan*, p. 17
79	'And King Matyas, having ...', Mihailović, p. 141
79	'indicate that, if he ...', Setton, vol. II, p. 270
79	'common enemy and calamity...', ibid., p. 275
79	'many and grave difficulties ...', ibid., p. 276
80	'and as to the money...', ibid., p. 278
80	The Sultan himself ..., Kritoboulos, p. 208

7. THE HOUSE OF FELICITY

81   Both as to view..., Kritoboulos, p. 207
82   The Emperor Mehmet..., Freely, *Inside the Seraglio*, p. 26
82   'three courts each...', Necipoğlu, p. 32
82–83   And here in this..., ibid., p. 202
87   'I entered into the...', ibid., p.62
88   'Which of you worthies...', Freely, *Inside the Seraglio*, p. 38
89   'second seraglio for damsels', Necipoğlu, p. 160
90   'When you go to...', Freely, *Istanbul, the Imperial City*, p. 206
90   'magnificent and excellent portico...', Necipoğlu, p. 89
91   'At the other end...', ibid., p. 96
91   'From both sides...', Sumner-Boyd, pp. 300–1
92   There has been formed..., Miller, *The Palace School of Muhammad the Conqueror*, p. 40
92   On the left side..., Necipoğlu, pp. 141–2
92–93   This bath is always..., ibid., p. 124
93   'Never hath a more delightful...', Evliya Çelebi, vol. I, part I, p. 49

8. A RENAISSANCE COURT IN ISTANBUL

95   He himself spent..., Kritoboulos, p. 209
96   He [Mehmet] also ran..., ibid.
96   'how the Sultan...', ibid., p. 177
96   Among the companions..., ibid.
96–97   So he called for..., ibid., pp. 209–10
97   'developments in the West...', Babinger, p. 248
98   Let no one doubt..., ibid., p. 249
99   'To the Supreme Emperor...', Kritoboulos, p. 3
100   'Rum and Frankish', Raby, p. 19
100   'How the Sultan...', Kritoboulos, p. 181
100   'must have been colored...', Raby, p. 21
101   'held philosophical discussions...', Kritoboulos, p. 209
101   'about the principles...', ibid.
101   'seems to have been...', Raby, p. 19
101   'a Hebrew commentary...', ibid., p. 17
101–102   'Mordechai Comtino...', ibid.
102   'the most original...', Runciman, *The Last Byzantine Renaissance*, p. 2
102   'Neither, it will not...', Wilson, p. 56

128–129 Mahmut Pasha asked ..., Tursun Beg, p. 60

129 'At this time ...', Stavrides, p. 177

129 'It is said that ...', ibid.

130 'he made the envy...', Stavrides, p. 180

130 'The Turkish *Signor*...', ibid., p. 339

130 'that the Christians attack ...', Setton, vol. II, p. 320

130 'And would that we ...', ibid.

130 'so that we may...', ibid.

130 'ride against the Ottomans ...', Babinger, p. 321

131 'The king is of ...', Barbaro and Contarini, pp. 37ff

131 'His eldest son ...', ibid.

11. CONQUEST OF THE CRIMEA AND ALBANIA

134 The carpets which were spread ..., Stavrides, p. 344

134 [Her funeral oration] lasted more ..., Miller, *The Palace School of Muhammad the Conqueror*, p. 31

135 'My last request ...', Stavrides, p. 350

135 'The spy that ...', ibid., p. 182

135 'It is impossible ...', ibid., p. 181

135 'From the time ...', Kritoboulos, p. 89

137 'that the world ...', Babinger, p. 338

138 'that the Turks had ...', Imber, *The Ottoman Empire, 1300–1481*, pp. 224–5

140 'and put Süleyman Pasha's ...', ibid., p. 231

140 'We put Count Stephen to flight ...', ibid.

140 'The Prince [Stephen] fled ...', Tursun Beg, p. 62

141 'disregarding the fact ...', Imber, *The Ottoman Empire, 1300–1481*, p. 232

141 'Out of consideration ...', Tursun Beg, p. 62

142 There was great fear..., Imber, *The Ottoman Empire, 1300–1481*, p. 235

142 'The enemy is at ...', Babinger, p. 358

144 'the Doge and the ...', Imber, *The Ottoman Empire, 1300–1481*, p. 279

145 'By the God of Heaven ...', Babinger, pp. 369–70

145 Thus after sixteen years ..., Brown, p. 318

12. THE SIEGE OF RHODES

147 'of the arrest of ...', Setton, vol. II, p. 337

147–148 By letters of Bernardo ..., ibid.

148 'with some of our...', ibid., p. 341

149 He [Gedik Ahmet Pasha] ..., ibid.

149 'He also laid waste ...', Imber, *The Ottoman Empire, 1300–1481*, p. 243

151 'of fine person ...', Freely, *Jem Sultan*, p. 74

151 'a good painter', Babinger, p. 378

152 '*Maometto Secondo i suo...*', ibid., p. 379

153 '*les plaisairs du monde*', ibid., p. 377

153 '*grande gourmandise*', ibid.

153 'Lest people notice ...', Freely, *Jem Sultan*, p. 30

154 'there was nothing ...', ibid., p. 73

156 'The city is well provided ...', Brockman, p. 65

156 'The sea was covered ...', ibid., p. 66

156 'three great bronze ...', ibid., p. 67

156–157 'the ground trembled ...', ibid., pp. 67–8

157 We resist with all our power..., ibid., p. 71

158 'for three whole days ...', ibid., p. 79

158–159 Neither did the Grand ..., ibid., p. 75

159 'My place is ...', ibid., p. 78

159 'The city will be devastated ...', ibid., p. 81

159 'Take your armies home ...', ibid., p. 81

161 'There were corpses ...', ibid., pp. 88–9

161 'many of our Knights ...', ibid., p. 89

161 'including the Bailiff ...', ibid.

162 'not sounding instruments...', Imber, *The Ottoman Empire, 1300–1481*, p. 249

162 'for praise of God ...', Freely, *Jem Sultan*, p. 31

13. THE CAPTURE OF OTRANTO

163 'for it is of course ...', Setton, vol. II, p. 361

164 We think of nothing else ..., ibid., p. 343

165 'fire, flame, ruin ...', Babinger, p. 391

165 This morning four horsemen ..., Setton, vol. II, p. 343

165 'the number of ships ...', ibid., pp. 343–4

165 'who says that ...', ibid., p. 344

166 'by a great miracle ...', Schwoebel, p. 144

166 'Venetian merchants had suffered ...', Setton, vol. II, p. 340

167 In Rome the alarm ..., Pastor, vol. IV, p. 334

168 Sixtus IV would have ..., ibid., p. 335

168	'How perilous it has become ...', Setton, vol. II, p. 364
168	'if the faithful, and ...', ibid.
168	'for we confess ...', ibid., p. 366
168	'seventeen successive years ...', Setton, vol. II, p. 365
169	'preferred being associated ...', Schwoebel, p. 134
169	'owing to the great perils ...', ibid., p. 139
169	'because we are prepared ...', Setton, vol. II, p. 367
169	'We do not believe ...', ibid.
169	'he would add another...', ibid., p. 370
170	'all the Spains', ibid.
170	'and the king of England ...', ibid.
170	'that the Venetians are ...', ibid.
170	'of which mention is ...', ibid.
170	'and in making the ...', ibid.
170	'as good a friend ...', ibid.
170	'western Europe go the way...', ibid., p. 371
170	'before the Eternal City...', Freely, *Jem Sultan*, p. 35

14. DEATH OF THE CONQUEROR

172	'the twenty-second hour', Imber, *The Ottoman Empire, 1300–1481*, p. 252
172	'Besides the gracious gift ...', ibid.
172	'the wind whistling ...', Freely, *Jem Sultan*, p. 39
173	'Long live Beyazit!', ibid., p. 41
176	'There are no ties ...', Babinger, p. 405
177	'Victory or Death!', Freely, *Jem Sultan*, p. 48
177	'The Karaman crows ...', ibid.
180	'*La Grande Aquila è morta!*', Babinger, p. 408
180	'It is fortunate for Christendom ...', Freely, *Jem Sultan*, p. 37
180	'this second Lucifer...', ibid.
180–181	If a pen could describe ..., Setton, vol. II, pp. 362–3
181	For about the time ..., ibid., p. 363
181–182	'showing us a light ...', ibid., p. 371
182	'We have our fleet ready...', ibid.
182	'with the Turkish tyrant's death ...', ibid.
182	'gave him his legate's ...', Pastor, vol. IV, p. 343
182	'weapons were brandished ...', ibid.
183	'which we have been waiting for...', Setton, vol. II, p. 373
183	'This is the time of deliverance ...', ibid.

183   'lest we prove unequal ...', ibid.

184   'would, like Eugenius IV...', Pastor, vol. IV, p. 347

184   'the present terror of the world', Knolles, vol. I, p. 1

184–185 The death of this mighty man ...', ibid., p. 483

15. THE SONS OF THE CONQUEROR

188   'the good and sincere ...', Freely, *Jem Sultan*, p. 67

188   'glorious victory', ibid.

188   'rid the world of ...', ibid., p. 83

189   'He was a gift ...', ibid., p. 85

190   'won the key of ...', ibid., p. 127

191   '*contra Turcum*', ibid., p. 185

191   'who was most valuable ...', ibid., p. 188

192   'in having next to ...', ibid., p. 218

192   'when some of his ...', ibid., p. 222

193   'Italy and the Christian ...', ibid., p. 230

194   'did not want them in Italy', Setton, vol. II, p. 454

195   'The French King will ...', ibid., p. 247

197   'Monseigneur, the King of ...', ibid., p. 263

197   'I am only an unhappy...', ibid., p. 263

197   'the Italians were a pack ...', ibid., p. 269

197   'the first town and ...', ibid., p. 270

197   'Truly we belong to ...', ibid., p. 273

16. THE TIDE OF CONQUEST TURNS

199   'because the Turk ...', Freely, *Jem Sultan*, p. 294

200   'Signor Turco', ibid., p. 295

200   'had never tried ...', ibid.

200   'and we have written ...', ibid.

200   'which they all knew...', ibid.

200   'as was given in ...', ibid.

200   'decided to have the sea ...', ibid., pp. 295–6

202   'Selim the Grim died ...', ibid., p. 304

202–203 'When he heard ...', ibid.

203   'He is said to be ...', Freely, *Istanbul, the Imperial City*, p. 194

203   'This news is lamentable ...', Freely, *Jem Sultan*, p. 305

204	'to be master...', ibid., p. 306
206	'Sick Man of Europe', Freely, *Istanbul, the Imperial City*, p. 257

17. THE CONQUEROR'S CITY

215	'He further ordered...', Kritoboulos, p. 93
216	'was deposed by...', Freely, *Istanbul, the Imperial City*, p. 219
219	I myself have often..., ibid., p. 189
219	'The *türbe*', ibid.
219	'The sepulchre of her...', ibid.
219	'I entered with veneration...', ibid.
221	'he left in Ottoman...', Sumner-Boyd, *The Seven Hills of Istanbul*, p. 950
221	'a man of the wisest...', Kritoboulos, p. 88
223	'wholly new', Sumner-Boyd, *The Seven Hills of Istanbul*, p. 573
224	Muhammed caused him..., Miller, *The Palace School of Muhammad the Conqueror*, p. 42
225	By the grace of God..., Necipoğlu, pp. 335–6

Glossary

The following are some Turkish words and technical terms in architecture that are used in the text. Turkish words enclosed in parenthesis are the form that they take when they are modified by a preceding noun; e.g. Yeni Cami = the New Mosque, whereas Sultan Ahmet Camii = the Mosque of Sultan Ahmet.

Ağa: title given to the chief black and white eunuchs and the commander of the janissaries
bayram: religious holiday
bedesten: multi-domed building, usually in the centre of a Turkish market, where valuable goods are stored and sold
beylerbey: governor general
beylik: Türkmen principality
büyük: big
cadde (*caddesi*): avenue
cami (*camii*): mosque
caravanserai: Turkish inn for travellers
çarşı (*çarşısı*): market
çeşme (*çeşmesi*): Turkish fountain
darüşşifa: Ottoman hospital
dershane: lecture hall of an Islamic school of theology
devşirme: periodic levy of Christian youths inducted into the Ottoman army
divan: a type of Turkish and Persian poetry
Divan: the Imperial Council
eski: old
gazi: warrior for the Islamic faith
grand vezir: the sultan's chief minister
hamam (*hamamı*): Turkish bath
han (*hanı*): Turkish commercial building; an inner-city caravanserai
harem: women's quarters in an Ottoman home or palace
hisar (*hisarı*): Turkish fortress or castle

imam: cleric who presides over public prayers in a mosque

imaret: refectory or public kitchen of a mosque

janissary: member of the elite corps of the Ottoman army

kapı (*kapısı*): gate or door

kadı: judge

kapıcı: gatekeeper or guard

köşk (*köşkü*): kiosk

küçük: little

kule: tower

külliye (*külliyesi*): Ottoman religious complex, usually consisting of a mosque and its associated pious and philanthropic foundations

kütüphane (*kütüphanesi*): library

medrese (*medresesi*): Islamic school of theology

mektep (*mektebi*): primary school

mescit (*mescidi*): small mosque

mihrab: niche in a mosque indicating the direction of Mecca

mimber: pulpit in a mosque:

müezzin: cleric who chants the responses to the prayers of the imam in a mosque and who makes the call to prayer from the minaret

minaret: tower from which the imam makes the call to prayer

oda (*odası*): room or chamber

pasha: a title given to generals, vezirs and governors general

pazar (*pazarı*): bazaar

şadırvan: ablution fountain in a mosque courtyard

sancak: subdivision of a province

sancakbey: governor of a *sancak*

saray (*sarayı*): Turkish palace

selamlık: men's quarters in an Ottoman home or palace

sipahi: member of the feudal cavalry

şeyhülislam: head of the Islamic religious hierarchy in the Ottoman Empire

sokak (*sokağı*): street

tabhane: hospice, often for itinerant dervishes

tekke (*tekkesi*): dervish lodge

timarhane: insane asylum

türbe (*türbesi*): tomb

ulema: member of the learned class, educated in Islamic law

vezir: one of the sultan's ministers

yeni: new

The Ottoman Dynasty

Osman Gazi (c. 1282–1326)
Orhan Gazi (1326–62)
Murat I (1362–89)
Beyazit I (1389–1402)
Interregnum
Mehmet I (1413–21)
Murat II (1421–44, 1446–51)
Mehmet II (1444–6, 1451–81)
Beyazit II (1481–1512)
Selim I (1512–20)
Süleyman I, the Magnificent (1520–66)
Selim II (1566–74)
Murat III (1574–95)
Mehmet III (1595–1603)
Ahmet I (1603–17)
Mustafa I (1st reign) (1617–18)
Osman II (1618–22)
Mustafa I (2nd reign) (1622–3)
Murat IV (1623–40)
Ibrahim (1640–8)
Mehmet IV (1648–87)
Süleyman II (1687–91)
Ahmet II (1691–5)
Mustafa II (1695–1703)
Ahmet III (1703–30)
Mahmut I (1730–54)
Osman III (1754–7)
Mustafa III (1757–74)
Abdül Hamit I (1774–89)

Selim III (1789–1807)

Mustafa IV (1807–8)

Mahmut II (1808–39)

Abdül Mecit I (1839–61)

Abdül Aziz (1861–76)

Murat V (1876)

Abdül Hamit II (1876–1909)

Mehmet V Reşat (1909–18)

Mehmet VI Vahidettin (1918–22)

Abdül Mecit (II) (caliph only) (1922–4)

Bibliography

Alderson, A. D., *The Structure of the Ottoman Dynasty*, Oxford, 1956

Angiolello, Giovanni-Maria, *Breve narrazione della Vita e fatti del sig. Ussun-Cassano ré di Persia*, in G.B. Ramusio, *Navagationi et Viaggi*, vol. II, English trans. in *A Narrative of Italian Travels in Persia*, London, 1873

_____, *Historia Turchesa* (1300–1514), ed. I. Ursu., Bucharest, 1909

Babinger, Franz, *Mehmed the Conqueror and His Time*, trans. Ralph Manheim, ed. William C. Hickman, Princeton, NJ, 1978

Barbaro, Josafa and Ambrogio Contarini, *Travels to Tana and Persia*, trans. W. Thomas and S. A. Roy, ed. Lord Stanley of Alderly, London, 1873, reprint New York, 1963

Barbaro, Nicolo, *Diary of the Siege of Constantinople*, trans. J. R. Jones, New York, 1969

Bearman, P.J., T. Bianquis, C. E. Bosworth, E. van Donzel and W. P. Heinrichs (eds), *The Encyclopedia of Islam*, 2nd edn, 12 vols, Leiden, 1960–2005

Bisaha, Nancy, *Creating East and West: Remaissance Humanists and the Ottoman Turks*, Philadelphia, 2004

Brockman, Eric, *The Two Sieges of Rhodes, 1480–1512*, London, 1969

Brotton, Jerry, *Trading Territories: Mapping the Early Modern World*, Ithaca, NY, 2002

_____, *The Renaissance Bazaar: From the Silk Road to Michelangelo*, Oxford, 2002

Brown, Horatio F., *Venice: An Historical Sketch of the Republic*, London, 1893

Browning, R., 'A Note on the Capture of Constantinople in 1453', *Byzantion*, 22 (1952), pp. 379–87

Bryer, A. and H. Lowry (eds), *Continuity and Change in Late Byzantine and Early Ottoman Society: Papers Given at a Symposium at Dumbarton Oaks in May 1982*, Birmingham, AL, 1986, pp. 123–38

Cahen, Claude, *Pre-Ottoman Turkey*, London, 1968

_____, *The Formation of Turkey: The Seljukid Sultanate of Rum, Eleventh to Fourteenth Century*, trans. and ed. P. M. Holt, Harlow, 2001

Cantemir, Dimitrie, *The History of the Growth and Decay of the Othman Empire*, trans. M. Tindal, London, 1734–5

Caoursin, Guillaume, *Obsidionia Rhodiae Urbis Descriptio*, Venice, 1480; trans. John Kaye, London, 1496, under the title *The Delectable newess & Tithyngs of the Gloryoos Victorye of the Rhodyns Agaynst the Turke*

Chew, Samuel C., *The Crescent and the Rose: Islam and England during the Renaissance*, New York, 1937

Çırakman, Aslı, *From the 'Terror of the World' to the 'Sick Man of Europe': European Images of Ottoman Society from the Sixteenth to the Nineteenth Centuries*, New York, 2002

Coles, Paul, *The Ottoman Impact on Europe*, London, 1968

Commynes, Philippe de, *The Memoirs of Philippe de Commynes (1445–1509)*, trans. Isabelle Cazeaux, ed. Samuel Kinser, 2 vols, Columbia, SC, 1969, 1973

Cook, Michael (ed.), *A History of the Ottoman Empire to 1730*, Cambridge, 1976

Crampton, R. J., *A Concise History of Bulgaria*, Cambridge, 1997

Crowley, Roger, 1453, *The Holy War for Constantinople and the Clash of Islam and the West*, New York, 2005

Davis, Fanny, *The Palace of Topkapi in Istanbul*, New York, 1970

Domenic of Jerusalem, *Domenico's Istanbul*, trans. and commentary Michael J. L. Austin, Warminster, 2001

Doukas, *Decline and Fall of Byzantium to the Ottoman Turks*, trans. Harry J. Magoulias, Detroit, 1975

Evliya Çelebi, *Narrative of Travels in Europe, Asia and Africa [the Seyahatname]*, trans. Josef von Hammer, London, 1834

Faroqhi, Suraiya, *The Ottoman Empire and the World around It*, London, 2004

Fine, John V. A., Jr., *The Late Medieval Balkans: A Critical Survey from the Late Twelfth Century to the Ottoman Conquest*, Ann Arbor, MI, 1994

Finkel, Caroline, *Osman's Dream: The Story of the Ottoman Empire 1300–1923*, London, 2005

Fisher, Sydney Nettleton, *The Foreign Relations of Turkey, 1481–1513*, Urbana, IL, 1948

Freely, John, *The Companion Guide to Turkey*, 2nd edn, London, 1993

————, *Istanbul, the Imperial City*, London, 1996

————, *Turkey around the Marmara*, Istanbul, 1998

————, *Inside the Seraglio: Private Lives of the Sultans in Istanbul*, London, 1999

————, *Blue Guide Istanbul*, 5th edn, London, 2000

————, *Jem Sultan: The Adventures of a Captive Turkish Prince in Renaissance Europe*, London, 2004

————, *Storm on Horseback: The Seljuk Warriors of Anatolia*, London, 2008

Gibb, E. J. W., *A History of Ottoman Poetry*, 6 vols, London, 1900–7

Gibb, Hamilton and Harold Bowen, *Islamic Society and the West: A Study of the Impact of Western Civilization on Moslem Culture in the Near East*, Oxford, 1950

Gibbons, Herbert Adams, *The Foundation of the Ottoman Empire: A History of the Osmanlis up to the Death of Bayezid I (1300–1403)*, Oxford, 1916

Goffman, Daniel, *The Ottoman Empire and Early Modern Europe*, Cambridge, 2002

Goodwin, Godfrey, *A History of Ottoman Architecture*, London, 1971

————, *The Janissaries*, London, 1994

Halecki, Oskar, *The Crusade of Varna: A Discussion of Controversial Problems*, New York, 1943

Hankins, James, 'Humanist Crusade Literature in the Age of Mehmet II', *Dumbarton Oaks Papers*, 49 (1995), pp. 11–147

Hay, Denys, *Europe in the Fourteenth and Fifteenth Centuries*, 2nd edn, London and New York, 1989

Hodgkinson, Harry, *Skanderbeg*, eds Bejtullah Destani and Westrow Cooper, London, 1999

Holt, P.M., Ann K.S. Lambton and Bernard Lewis (eds), *The Cambridge History of Islam*, 2 vols, Cambridge, 1970

Hopwood, Keith R., 'The Byzantine-Turkish Frontier, c. 1250–1300', in Markus Kohbach, Gisela Prochaska-Eisl and Claudia Romer (eds), *Acta Viennensia Ottomanica*, Vienna, 1999, pp. 153–61

Housley, Norman, *The Later Crusades: From Lyons to Alcazar 1274–1580*, Oxford, 1992

Ibn Battuta, *The Travels of Ibn Battuta, A. D. 1325–54*, 4 vols, trans. H. A. R. Gibb, London, 1995

Ihsanoğlu, Ekmelledin (ed.), *History of the Ottoman State, Society and Civilization*, Istanbul, 2001

Imber, Colin, *The Ottoman Empire, 1300–1481*, Istanbul, 1990

———, *The Ottoman Empire, 1300–1650*, New York, 2002

Inalcık, Halil, *The Ottoman Empire: The Classical Age, 1300–1600*, trans. Norman Itzkowitz and Colin Imber, New York, 1959

———, 'The Policy of Mehmed II toward the Greek Population of Istanbul and the Byzantine Buildings of the City', *Dumbarton Oaks Papers*, 23–24 (1969–70), pp. 231–49

———, 'The Emergence of the Ottomans', in Holt, P.M., Ann K.S. Lambton and Bernard Lewis (eds), *The Cambridge History of Islam*, vol. I, Cambridge, 1970, pp. 231–62

———, *The Middle East and the Balkans under Ottoman Rule*, Bloomington, IN, 1993

———, 'The Ottoman State: Economy and Society, 1300–1600', in H. Inalcik with D. Quataert (eds), *An Economic and Social History of the Ottoman Empire, 1300–1914*, Cambridge, 1994, pp. 9–409

———, *Essays in Ottoman History*, Istanbul, 1998

———, *The Ottoman Empire: Conquest, Organization and Economy*, London, 1998

Inalcık, Halil and Günsel Renda (eds), *Ottoman Civilization*, 2 vols, Istanbul, 2003

Iorga, Nicolae, *Byzantium after Byzantium*, Iasi, Romania, 2000

Itzkowitz, Norman, *Ottoman Empire and Ottoman Tradition*, New York, 1972

Jones, J. R. Melville (ed.), *The Siege of Constantinople, 1453: Seven Contemporary Accounts*, Amsterdam, 1972

Kafadar, Cemal, *Between Two Worlds: The Construction of the Ottoman State*, Berkeley, CA, 1995

Kafescioğlu, Çiğdem, 'Heavenly and Unblessed, Splendid and Artless: Mehmet II's Mosque Complex in Istanbul in the Eyes of its Contemporaries', in Çiğdem Kafescioğlu and L. Thys-Senocak (eds), *Essays in Honor of Aptullah Kuran*, Istanbul, 1999, pp. 211–22

Kiel, Machiel, *Ottoman Architecture in Albania, 1385–1912*, Istanbul, 1990

Kinross, Lord, *The Ottoman Centuries: The Rise and Fall of the Ottoman Empire*, London, 1977

Knolles, Richard, *The Generall Historie of the Turkes from the first beginning of That Nation to the rising of the Othoman Familie, with all the notable expeditions of the Christian Princes against them, Together with the Lives and Conquests of the Othoman Kings and Emperours unto the yeare 1610*, 2 vols, 2nd edn, London, 1609–10

Köprülü, M. F., *The Origins of the Ottoman Empire*, trans. G. Leiser, Albany, NY, 1992

Kortepeter, C. Max, *The Ottoman Turks: Nomad Kingdom to World Empire*, Istanbul, 1991

Kritoboulos of Imbros, *History of Mehmed the Conqueror*, trans. Charles T. Riggs, Princeton, NJ, 1954

Kuban, Doğan, *Istanbul: An Urban History*, Istanbul, 1996

Lane, Frederic C., *Venice: A Maritime Republic*, London and Baltimore, 1973

Layard, Sir Austen Henry, *Autobiography and Letters*, 2 vols, London, 1903

Levy, A., *The Jews of the Ottoman Empire*, Princeton, NJ, 1994

_____, *Jews, Turks and Ottomans: A Shared History, Fifteenth through the Twentieth Century*, Syracuse, NY, 2002

Lewis, Bernard, *Istanbul and the Civilization of the Ottoman Empire*, Norman, OK, 1994

Lovrenović, Ivan, *Bosnia: A Cultural History*, London, 2001

Lowry, Heath W., *The Nature of the Early Ottoman State*, Albany, NY, 2003

_____, 'Pushing the Stone Uphill: The Impact of Bubonic Plague on Ottoman Urban Society in the Fifteenth and Sixteenth Centuries', *Osmanlı Araştırmaları*, 23 (2003), pp. 93–132

_____, 'Ottoman Renaissance, The Conqueror's Dream', *Cornucopia*, 32 (2004), pp. 26–9

Malcolm, *Bosnia: A Short History*, New York, 1995

Manners, Ian R., 'Reconstructing the Image of a City: The Representation of Constantinople in Christopher Buondelmonti's *Liber Insularum Archipelagi*', *Annals of the Association of American Geographers*, 87 (1997), pp. 72–102

Manz, Beatrice, *The Rise and Rule of Tamerlane*, Cambridge, 1989

Medlin, William K., *Moscow and East Rome*, Geneva, 1952

Ménage, Victor L., *Neşri's History of the Ottomans: The Sources and the Development of the Text*, London, 1964

_____, 'Seven Ottoman documents from the reign of Memmed II', in S.M. Stein and R. Welzer (eds), *Documents from Islamic Chanceries*, Oxford, 1965, 112–18

_____, 'Devshirme', in P.J. Bearman, T. Bianquir, C.E. Bosworth, E. van Donzel and W.P. Heinrichs (eds), *The Encyclopedia of Islam*, 2nd edn, vol. II, Leiden, 1965, 210–13

Mihailović, Konstantine, *Memoirs of a Janissary*, trans. B. Stolz, commentary S. Soucek, Ann Arbor, MI, 1975

Miller, Barnette, *Beyond the Sublime Porte: The Grand Seraglio of Muhammad the Conqueror*, Cambridge, 1941

_____, *The Palace School of Muhammad the Conqueror*, Cambridge, MA, 1941

Miller, William, *Essays on the Latin Orient*, Cambridge, 1921

_____, *Trebizond: The Last Greek Empire*, London, 1926

Minorsky, V. C. and C. E. Bosworth, 'Uzun Hasan', in *Encyclopedia of Islam*, new edn, vol. X, 1960, pp. 936–7

Morris, Jan, *The Venetian Empire: A Sea Voyage*, London, 1990

Necipoğlu, Gülrü, *Architecture, Ceremonial and Power: The Topkapı Palace in the Fifteenth and Sixteenth Centuries*, Cambridge, MA, 1991

Nicol, Donald M., *The Last Centuries of Byzantium: 1261–1453*, 2nd edn, Cambridge, 1993

_____, *The Immortal Emperor: The Life and Legend of Constantine Palaiologios, Last Emperor of the Romans*, Cambridge, 1994

Nicolle, David, *Constantinople 1453: The End of Byzantium*, Oxford, 2000

_____, *Nicopolis, 1396: The Last Crusade*, Westport, CT, 2005

Papadakis, A., 'Gennadius II and Mehmet the Conqueror', *Byzantion*, 42, 1972, pp. 88–106

Pastor, Ludwig, *The History of the Popes, from the Close of the Middle Ages, drawn from the secret archives of the Vatican and other original sources*, trans. from German, 5th edn, 10 vols, London, 1950

Pears, Edwin, *The Destruction of the Greek Empire and the Story of the Capture of Constantinople by the Turks*, New York, 1967

Peirce, Leslie, *The Imperial Harem: Women and Sovereignty in the Ottoman Empire*, New York and Oxford, 1993

Penzer, N. M., *The Harem*, London, 1974

Philippides, Mario (trans. and ed.), *Byzantium, Europe and the Early Ottoman Sultans, 1373–1513: An Anonymous Greek Chronicle of the Seventeenth Century (Codex Barberinus Graecus III)*, New Rochelle, NY, 1990

_____, (trans. and ed.), *Emperors, Patriarchs and Sultans of Constantinople, 1373–1513: An Anonymous Greek Chronicle of the Sixteenth Century*, Brookline, MA, 1990

Pitcher, Donald Edgar, *An Historical Geography of the Ottoman Empire, from Earliest Times to the End of the Sixteenth Century*, Leiden, 1972

Raby, Julian, 'Cyriacus of Ancona and the Ottoman Sultan Mehmet II', *Journal of the Warburg and Courtwald Institute*, 43 (1980), pp. 242–6

———, 'Mehmet the Conqueror's Greek Scriptorium', *Dumbarton Oaks Papers*, 37 (1983), pp. 15–34

Renda, Günsel, 'Mehmed the Conqueror and the Arts', in *The Artist, the Sultan and His Portrait: Mehmed the Conqueror according to Gentile Bellini*, catalogue of exhibition by Yapı Kredi Cultural Center, Istanbul, 7 December 1999–7 January 2000

Rice, Eugene F. Jr. and Anthony Grafton, *The Foundations of Early Modern Europe, 1460–1559*, New York, 1970

Rice, Tamara Talbot, *The Seljuks in Asia Minor*, London, 1961

Rossi, Ettore, 'The Hospitallers at Rhodes, 1421–1523', in Kenneth M. Setton, *A History of the Crusades*, vol. III, Madison, WI, 1975, pp. 314–39

Rozen, Mina, *A History of the Jewish Community in Istanbul: The Formative Years, 1453–1566*, Leiden and Boston, 2002

Runciman, Steven, *The Fall of Constantinople 1453*, Cambridge, 1965

———, *The Great Church in Captivity: A Study of the Patriarchate of Constantinople from the Eve of the Turkish Conquest to the Greek War of Independence*, London, 1968

———, *The Last Byzantine Renaissance*, Cambridge, 1970

Said, Edward W., *Orientalism*, London, 1978

———, *Culture and Imperialism*, New York, 1993

Sayılı, Adnan, *The Observatory in Islam*, Ankara, 1960

Schwoebel, R., *The Shadow of the Crescent: The Renaissance Image of the Turk, 1453–1517*, New York, 1967

Setton, Kenneth M., *The Papacy and the Levant (1204–1571)*, 4 vols, Philadelphia, 1976

Shaw, Stanford, *History of the Ottoman Empire and Modern Turkey*, Vol I, *Empire of the Gazis: The Rise and Decline of the Ottoman Empire*, Cambridge, MA, 1976

Somel, Selçuk Akşin, *Historical Dictionary of the Ottoman Empire*, Lanham, MD and Oxford, 2003

Spandounes, Theodore, *On the Origin of the Ottoman Emperors*, trans. and ed. Donald M. Nicol, Cambridge, 1997

Sphrantzes, George, *The Fall of the Byzantine Empire*, trans. Mario Philippides, Amherst, 1980

Stavrianos, Leften Stavros, *The Balkans since 1453*, London, 2000

Stavrides, Theoharis, *The Sultan of Vezirs: The Life and Times of the Ottoman Grand Vezir Mahmud Pasha Angelović (1453–64)*, Leiden, 2001

Sugar, Peter F., *Southeastern Europe under Ottoman Rule, 1354–1804*, Seattle and London, 1977

———, (ed.), *A History of Hungary*, Bloomington, IN, 1990

Sumner-Boyd, Hilary, *The Seven Hills of Istanbul*, Istanbul, 2008

Sumner-Boyd, Hilary and John Freely, *Strolling through Istanbul*, Istanbul, 1972

Treadgold, Warren, *A History of the Byzantine State and Society*, Stanford, CA, 1997

Trow, M. J., *Vlad the Impaler: In Search of the Real Dracula*, Stroud, 2003

Turan, Osman, 'Anatolia in the Period of the Seljuks and the Beyliks', in P. M. Holt, Ann K. S. Lambton and Bernard Lewis (eds), *The Cambridge History of Islam*, vol. I, Cambridge, 1970, pp. 263–323

Tursun Beg, *The History of Mehmed the Conqueror*, trans. Halil Inalcik and Rhoads Murphey, Minneapolis, 1978

Vacalopoulos, Apostolos, E., *The Greek Nation, 1453–1669: The Cultural and Economic Background of Modern Greek Society*, trans. Ian Moles and Phania Moles, New Brunswick, NJ, 1976

Van Millingen, Alexander, *Byzantine Constantinople: The Walls of the City and Adjoining Historical Sites*, London, 1899

————, *Byzantine Churches in Constaninople*, London, 1910

Vickers, Miranda, *The Albanians, A Modern History*, London, 1995

Vryonis, Speros, *The Decline of Medieval Hellenism in Asia Minor and the Process of Islamization from the Eleventh through the Fifteenth Century*, Los Angeles, 1971

Wilson, Nigel, *From Byzantium to Italy: Greek Studies in the Italian Renaissance*, London, 1992

Wittek, Paul, *The Rise of the Ottoman Empire*, London, 1938

Woods, J., *The Aqquyunlu: Clan, Confederation, Empire*, Minneapolis, 1976

Zachariadou, Elizabeth A. (ed.), *The Ottoman Emirate, 1300–1389*, Rethymnon, Greece, 1993

Zakynthos, Dionysos A., *The Making of Modern Greece: From Byzantium to Independence*, trans. and introd. K. Johnstone, Totowa, NJ, 1976

Index

Murad Bey 124
Murat I, sultan 5, 6, 150
Murat II, sultan 7, 8, 9, 10, 11, 12,
    13, 14, 15, 16, 18, 52, 58, 62, 113,
    134, 178
Murat III, sultan 83, 89, 90
Murat IV, sultan 205
Murphey, Rhoads 107
Musa, son of Beyazit I 7
Mustafa III, sultan 218
Mustafa, son of Mehmet II 19, 62,
    67, 122, 126, 127, 128, 133, 134,
    135
Mustafa Ali, Turkish historian 60
Mustafa Kemal Pasha (Atatürk) 209,
    210, 211, 212
Mustafa Pasha 199
Mustafa Reşit Pasha 206, 207

Naples 19, 31, 62, 104, 111, 120, 123,
    125, 126, 137, 149, 160, 161, 163,
    164, 165, 167, 168, 169, 170, 182,
    183, 193, 194, 195, 196, 197, 198,
    200
Nasuh Bey 177
Nauplion (Nauplia) 66, 115, 200
Nea Phokaia 60
Negroponte (Chalkis) 64, 65, 115,
    116, 117, 118, 119, 122
Nergiszade, daughter of Prince
    Mustafa 134
Nesri, Turkish historian 172
Nicholas I, tsar 206
Nicholas V, pope xvii, 17, 26, 31, 38,
    49, 57
Nicopolis, battle of 6, 150
Notaras, Loukas, duke 26, 35, 38,
    47, 48, 50
Ömer Bey 63, 64, 75, 112
Orhan Gazi, sultan 3, 4
Orhan, grandson of Beyazit I 21, 23,
    24, 30, 47

Osman II, sultan 216
Osman III, sultan 83
Osman Gazi xv, 2, 3
Otranto 165, 166, 167, 170, 173, 175,
    179, 182, 183, 184

Pachymeres, George 3
Palaeo Phokaia 60
Palestine 206, 209
Paris, treaty of 207
    peace conference 210
Passarowitz, treaty of 205
Patras 63, 66, 76, 112
Paul II, pope 79, 97, 98, 110, 111,
    116, 122, 123, 125, 183
Pendinelli, Stefano, archbishop
    166
Persia (Iran) 201, 202
Pesaro, Lorenzo 111
Philip the Good, duke 19, 110
Philip Villiers de L'Isle Adam 203
Philippe de Commines 153
Piero de'Medici 194
Pierre d'Aubusson 151, 152, 153–62,
    163, 180, 188, 189, 190, 199, 201
Pir Ahmet, Karamanid emir 113,
    114, 121, 126, 179, 201
Piri Pasha 203
Pius II, pope xv, 57, 66, 67, 71, 72,
    74, 76, 78, 79, 104, 154
Pius III, pope 201
Plethon, George Gemisthus 102
Poland 6, 11, 123, 138, 205
Poo, Juan 161
Portugal, Portuguese 183
Prussia 206
Pugiese, Fra Giacomo 117, 118

Querini, Lazzaro 124

Raby, Julian 12, 99, 101, 102
Radu cel Frumos, prince 8, 72, 137

WEST END